STUDIES IN US RELIGION, POLITICS, AND LAW

Leslie C. Griffin

Laura R. Olson

Tisa Wenger

Series Editors

Land Is Kin

Sovereignty, Religious Freedom, and Indigenous Sacred Sites

Dana Lloyd

University Press of Kansas

© 2024 by the University Press of Kansas
All rights reserved

Published by the University Press of Kansas (Lawrence, Kansas 66045), which
was organized by the Kansas Board of Regents and is operated and funded by
Emporia State University, Fort Hays State University, Kansas State University,
Pittsburg State University, the University of Kansas, and Wichita State University.

Library of Congress Cataloging-in-Publication Data

Names: Lloyd, Dana, author.
Title: Land is kin : sovereignty, religious freedom, and Indigenous sacred
    sites / Dana Lloyd.
Description: Lawrence : University Press of Kansas, 2023. | Series: Studies
    in US religion, politics, and law | Includes bibliographical references and index.
Identifiers: LCCN 2023016738 (print) | LCCN 2023016739 (ebook)
    ISBN 9780700635894 (cloth)
    ISBN 9780700635900 (ebook)
Subjects: LCSH: Indians of North America—Legal status, laws, etc. |
    Indians of North America—Land tenure—Law and legislation. | Indians of
    North America—Rites and ceremonies. | Indians of North America—
    Religious life. | Indians of North America—Government relations. | Indigenous
    peoples—Legal status, laws, etc.—United States. | Freedom of religion—
    United States. | Self-determination, National—United States. | BISAC:
    RELIGION / Religion, Politics & State | LAW / Legal History
Classification: LCC KF8205 .L56 2023 (print) | LCC KF8205 (ebook) | DDC
    342.7308/72—dc23/eng/20230614
LC record available at https://lccn.loc.gov/2023016738.
LC ebook record available at https://lccn.loc.gov/2023016739.

British Library Cataloguing-in-Publication Data is available.

Printed in the United States of America

10 9 8 7 6 5 4 3 2 1

The paper used in this publication is acid free and meets the minimum
requirements of the American National Standard for Permanence of Paper
for Printed Library Materials Z39.48-1992.

For Anya

Contents

Acknowledgments

At the center of this book is Yurok, Karuk, Tolowa, and Hupa land, but it was written on Onondaga, Osage, and Lenape lands.

This book would not have existed if it weren't for Phil Arnold. Phil believed in this project, and that I was the person to carry it out, from the start. His support as dissertation advisor and as chair of the Department of Religion at Syracuse University was both intellectual and material, but one of the best things he has done for me was to bring Winni Sullivan on board. Winni's work has always inspired me, and her mentorship remains invaluable. The other members of my dissertation committee were thoughtful, challenging, and encouraging all at once: I thank Ken Baynes, Ann Gold, Scott Manning Stevens, and Jim Watts.

At University Press of Kansas, Tisa Wenger and David Congdon have been the best editors I could have hoped for. Their smart and generous reading (and rereading) of the manuscript made its writing (and rewriting) possible. I thank them for their enthusiasm about this book at an early stage and for their guidance in bringing it into the world.

Special thanks are due to Cutcha Risling Baldy and to Jace Weaver for reading the whole manuscript and providing feedback without which the book could not have been what it is. I am grateful for their time, for their careful reading, for the knowledge they shared with me, and for pushing me to think better and to write better. I am also grateful for a professional development grant from Villanova University's College of Liberal Arts and Sciences that enabled my time and work with Cutcha and Jace.

Michael McNally is the most generous reader I've had, and he remains the audience I have in mind when I write. My NART writing group has been essential to completing this manuscript and everything else I have written in the past few years. I thank Natalie Avalos, Sarah Dees, and Abel Gómez for many excellent conversations and for their friendship. Orna Coussin has taught me lots of things, but most importantly, she showed me how to find my voice.

I wrote the first draft of this book as a postdoctoral fellow at the John C. Danforth Center on Religion and Politics at Washington University in St. Louis. I thank the Danforth community, captained by Marie Griffith, for formal and informal daily conversations that helped shape my thinking about the questions at the heart of this book.

A research fellowship at the Indigenous Values Initiative allowed for conversations with Phil Arnold, Sandy Bigtree, Adam DJ Brett, Gail Bundy, Jake Haiwhagai'i Edwards, and Betty Lyons that pushed my thinking on Indigenous sovereignty forward.

I finished writing this book as the Department of Global Interdisciplinary Studies at Villanova University was becoming my academic home and the faculty and staff there were becoming my academic family. I feel very fortunate to have them all in my life.

Many colleagues read and commented on various parts of the manuscript. Ben Berger, Evan Berry, Kevin Bruyneel, Jen Graber, Himanee Gupta, Beth Hurd, Pamela Klassen, Winni Sullivan, and Robert Yelle, thank you for your time, support, and insight.

I presented this project at various venues, and I am grateful for those who invited me to present it and to audiences who engaged with it: the Maimonides Center for Advanced Studies at the University of Hamburg, the Center for Peace and Justice Education at Villanova University, Osgoode Hall Law School, the Faculty of the Study of Religion at Ludwig-Maximilians University in Munich, the SSRC Religion and the Public Sphere Summer Institute, the Department of Religious Studies at University of Pennsylvania, and the Department of Religious Studies at the University of Alabama. I also presented various aspects of this project at several conferences: American Academy of Religion; American Studies Association; International Society for the Study of Religion, Nature, and Culture; Association for the Study of Law, Culture, and the Humanities; National Women's Studies Association; Native American and Indigenous Studies Association; and the Political Theology Network. I am grateful to have all these intellectual communities.

Attorney Stephen Quesenberry, Mark Royman, law clerk at the United States District Court for the District of Northern California, Laura Svoboda at the California Indian Legal Services, and archivist Aaron Seltzer at the National Archives at San Francisco have been most helpful in locating materials related to the *Lyng* case.

At University Press of Kansas, working with Derek Helms, Kelly Chrisman Jacques, and Penelope Cray was an absolute joy.

At the Yurok Tribal Court, Chief Judge Abby Abinanti, Associate Judge Bill Bowers, Laura White Woods, Alanna Lee Nulph, Maggie Poffenbarger, Lori Nesbitt, and Elly Hoopes were welcoming and encouraging, and my conversations with them made writing this book possible. All proceeds from this book are directed to the Yurok Tribal Court. At the Seventh Generation Fund for Indigenous Peoples, conversations with Chris Peters and Tia Oros Peters were inspiring and energizing.

I thank Michael Thom for permission to use the gorgeous photo of the High Country, taken by his father, Charlie Thom, as a cover for this book.

An early version of chapter 1 was published as "Storytelling and the High Country: Reading *Lyng v. Northwest Indian Cemetery Protective Association*," in *Journal of Law and Religion* 36, no. 2 (2021): 181–201. Parts of chapter 2 and parts of chapter 3 were published as "Indigenous Sovereignty in *Lyng*," in *American Examples: A New Conversation About Religion*, volume 2, ed. Michael J. Altman, Samah Choudhury, and Prea Persaud (Tuscaloosa: University of Alabama Press, 2022).

Finally, I could not have done any of the thinking and writing for this book without the love and care of my family. Roza Wishkovsky, Rachel Barnea, Liat Ginzburg, Gilad and Anat Shneor-Barnea, Debbie and Ric Lloyd: I love you. Vincent and Anya, thank you for being there with me all along, and thanks to Leroy, who came just in time.

FOREWORD

Dana Lloyd—an immigrant from a troubled land, a lawyer, and a humanist scholar—came and saw what others have not; she saw the truth and has spoken the truth in *Land Is Kin*. For this truth speaking we shall ever be grateful. She has also given us all a pathway toward systemic change in terms of what should be the law regarding Indigenous people's relationship to place, and the life that occupies place, thus putting aside what she rightly has described as the Supreme Court's "colonial framework," which told Indigenous plaintiffs "we need you gone."

That sentiment has been the foundation of "Indian Law" in this country. What she has added to the discussion is context, saying directly that the existing "government needs Indigenous peoples to disappear, either through removal, death, or assimilation, not only so that it can take their lands but also so that its (our) metaphysics, epistemology, and ethics are never challenged." That context exposes the self-serving logic that guides the invaders and the genocidal practices used in the acquisition of our lands; it is a context grounded in the truth of this country and its residents.

Dana rightly points out that without this truth being considered in the rationale for the establishment of "the laws" of this country, we have a precedential framework that is grounded in lies. The court has allowed itself to become a tool supporting genocidal practices that benefit the invaders as they continue their mission of acquisition. Dana's work examines the way the court has put the Indigenous party's religious freedom in tension with the property rights of others. She describes and dissects each argument, showing that this is *not* the correct or truthful framing of the issue. Rather, this framing is designed to yield the answer desired by those who see themselves as the "discovering, civilizing" saviors who perpetuate the foundational untruths of those who originally wished to acquire our homelands.

Dana examines these questions primarily in the context of a case named *Lyng v. Northwest Indian Cemetery Protective Association*, a 1988 US Supreme Court case known here at home as the G-O Road lawsuit. The lawsuit was named for the fact that the dispute was over whether or not a six-mile-long road would connect the towns of Gasquet and Orleans in Northern California to support a logging plan. The logging plan would have allowed the cutting of 733 million board feet of timber and ultimately destroyed the place Yurok, Karuk, and Tolowa nations call the High Country, a place of prayer and medicine.

Ultimately, the court and the people who established this court, and those of us who practice in this court, must ask the hard questions as to what we do when a foundational pillar has been demonstrated to be a blatant falsehood. The arguments that led to the findings in *Lyng* are not the factors that should have been considered to resolve these issues. These lies were chosen to get to a certain predetermined conclusion upholding the *power* of the invaders, rather than truly examining the issues presented. The Supreme Court has discussed the question of sovereignty often, including in *Lyng*, where it defined sovereignty as the supreme power or authority of a governing body—the power to decide the fate of a place. But who has the power to rule? Here again, we find ourselves in a cultural quandary because the Yurok's definition of sovereignty is very different from that of the court; for us, to live as sovereign means to live according to the values that must drive our practices, which requires that our Tribe and our peoples' responsibilities are interconnected with the land/kin.

Yuroks have always been a people driven by laws, but the laws must be founded in truth—that is a basic premise. We have not and will not become a people who will allow ourselves to formulate law based upon untruth, particularly after we have seen the harm caused to the people and places that we know as our homelands. Having survived the invasion and the aftermath of chaos and continued destruction of our places and peoples, we understand ourselves as those who have the obligation to protect and preserve the gift we were originally given. We have seen the place we lived in harmony with for thousands of years become, in a couple hundred years of occupation, besieged and torn. Many of our relatives have suffered in this occupation period. All of our kin, our ancestors, and all of our children deserve better from us. Perpetuating policy driven by untruths will not satisfy the duties that arise from the gifts we have received.

We must all begin again, and Dana has given us a way to start that process: "What I have learned is that to protect what we have come to refer to as Indigenous sacred sites, it is necessary to understand that land is kin." We must start somewhere, and this is a good place—to reclaim the truth and our responsibility to live that truth in our lives. If we adopt a new rationale in the courts, in our public discussions, and in our law-making, we can build a new and lasting tomorrow, because land is kin and we as family members must acknowledge that fact and build our laws on truth if we wish to survive and thrive in a responsible fashion.

Thank you, Dana, for reaching across to us and for assisting and supporting us as we try to protect our homeland and relatives. Protecting this land will benefit all people, even those who came as invaders, because this continued destruction will ultimately harm everyone. Let us go forward together as kin.

Judge Abby Abinanti
Chief Justice of the Yurok Tribe

Land Is Kin

INTRODUCTION

·•·

THE HIGH COUNTRY

"The struggle by American Indians to protect their sacred sites and to have access to them for traditional ceremonies is a movement in which all peoples should become involved," wrote Lakota scholar Vine Deloria, Jr., in 1991.[1] The book you are holding in your hands, *Land Is Kin*, answers Deloria's call to join the movement. What is required is a rethinking of Indigenous sacred sites, indeed, a rethinking of land itself. Deloria called for incorporating and applying the "unique needs of Indian religions" into the religious freedom principle.[2] But a lot has changed in the thirty years that have passed since Deloria wrote this text: on the one hand, religious freedom has become the tool of conservative Christians; on the other, the United States has appointed a Laguna Pueblo member as its secretary of the interior. Religious freedom may not be the right tool to protect Indigenous sacred sites at all. Indeed, settler law does not offer the right tools for protecting them. This book explains why religious freedom in particular, and settler law more generally, is not the answer that those who want to protect Native American sacred sites are looking for, and it looks for alternatives. To do so, I ask what land means—and what it *could* mean—to the different parties involved in Indigenous sacred sites cases. Ultimately, it is those who are in kinship relationship with sacred lands who are leading the struggle to protect them. In writing this book, I, as a non-Indigenous immigrant to the United States, follow them as I respond to Deloria's call to join the movement. What I have learned is that to protect what we have come to refer to as Indigenous sacred sites, it is necessary to understand that land is kin.

Native American sacred sites cases present us with two competing rights—one party's religious freedom is in tension with another party's property rights. For example, a Native nation argues that a specific place is sacred to it, but this place is officially owned by someone else, usually the US government. If the nation asks to be able to use the place for religious purposes (to hold a ceremony, for example), one might think that what it is really asking is to suspend the government's property rights in order to protect Native religion. But if this is how the issue is framed—as a competition between property rights and religious rights—we can expect the Native claimants to lose, because in liberal political discourse, property is the paradigmatic right and land is the paradigmatic property. At the time of writing this book, a case of this kind is making its way through the federal court system. Various Apache peoples are asking the court to stop the US Forest Service from transferring to a mining company land that the Apache hold sacred. Chi'chil Bildagoteel, known in English as Oak Flat, is the place where Ga'an (guardians or messengers between Apache peoples and the Creator, Usen) reside. It is a 6.7-square-mile stretch of land within what is currently managed by the US federal government as Tonto National Forest, east of Phoenix, Arizona. Since 2014, a proposed copper mine has threatened to permanently alter the area through an underground mining technique that would cause the earth to sink, up to 1,115 feet deep and almost two miles across.[3] The Apache have argued that destroying their sacred sites would infringe on their free exercise of religion, but the Ninth Circuit Court of Appeals rejected their claim, allowing the federal government to use its property as it sees fit.[4] One might say that because of religion's special status in the US Constitution's First Amendment, religion actually transcends property relations, that it is the one thing that is excluded from property relations. However, in such cases, religion—understood as one right among many—does not challenge the logic of property; rather, it lies comfortably in the sphere to which this logic allocates it. Understanding sacred sites cases in this way sets two (ostensibly) mutually exclusive conceptions of land against each other: either land is sacred or it is property.

This book argues that this binary logic is false. Through an analysis of one sacred land case, which started its way through the federal court system some thirty years before the Oak Flat case, the book demonstrates that land can play different roles simultaneously and that a multilayered understanding of land is possible and leads to a more just treatment of this land and its inhabitants. These arguments respond to the very questions that animate the field of North American religions, about how the state, and specifically legal systems, shapes religion while managing the land. While religious studies scholar Kerry Mitchell examines these questions through the example of national parks,[5] and law and religion scholar Winnifred Sullivan offers the example of cemeteries,[6] *Land Is Kin* looks at one controversy around the intended development of a sacred area in a national forest.

The sacred land that is offered as an example in this book is the High Country, a forest of Douglas firs taller than three hundred feet, where prehuman entities called *woge* reside, Indigenous doctors across tribal nations and borders train, and medicine to heal the sick and bring peace to earth is gathered and made. The High Country is managed by the US Forest Service as the Six Rivers National Forest, among the Siskiyou Mountains in Northern California, and it is the sacred homeland of the Yurok, Karuk, and Tolowa Indigenous nations. The area includes Peak Eight, Doctor Rock, Golden Stairs, Chimney Rock, Elk Valley, and Sawtooth Mountains, but it is called the High Country because of its spiritual power rather than its elevation. Yurok, Karuk, and Tolowa men and women who are called by the Creator or the Great Spirit to attend the High Country go there to gather and make medicine and to attain the power, or maximize their potential, to act in a desired way. Making medicine may involve rituals and prayer, but it is essentially an inward experience, and following all prescribed rituals does not guarantee that one would succeed in making medicine. By the mid-1920s, because of white invasion of the area, only one sweathouse remained in the High Country, but natural prayer seats still abound there. Reading the 1988 US Supreme Court case *Lyng v. Northwest Indian Cemetery Protective Association* would not tell you all of this. In a case where the Supreme Court allowed the Forest Service to construct a road and to harvest timber in the High Country, despite the Yurok, Karuk, and Tolowa nations' argument that these actions would severely harm their ability to practice their religion in the area, including gathering medicine, training medicine people, and communicating with the *woge*, the High Country is referred to simply as "federal land." The road construction and timber harvest were constitutional, according to the court, because, sacred or not, the High Country was government property.

The Yurok, Karuk, and Tolowa nations argued in court against cutting

733 million board feet of the trees in the High Country over eighty years and against the construction of the final, six-mile-long section of a road, known as the G-O Road because it was supposed to connect the towns Gasquet and Orleans in Northern California and thus support the logging plan. They argued that the construction of the road and the logging would irreparably damage their ability to practice their religion in the High Country and that their right to practice their religion freely is granted to them by the Free Exercise Clause of the US Constitution's First Amendment and by the American Indian Religious Freedom Act of 1978.[7] While the case has been argued, decided, and studied as one about the free exercise of religion, I argue that *Lyng* is a case about sovereignty. This is so because the question at its heart is the following: who is the sovereign who can (and should) decide the fate of the High Country? If we do not think of *Lyng* through the lens of sovereignty, it would be difficult to explain how it came to be that a dispute over a six-mile segment of a road reached all the way to the Supreme Court. It would be even more difficult to explain why the Indigenous plaintiffs lost the case.

The court is charged with the task of interpreting land, and the interpretation it chooses would determine the fate of the High Country: on the one hand, Yurok, Karuk, and Tolowa traditional lands, a sacred area vitally important to ongoing cultural and social practices and, on the other, public property. But what does "public property" mean? Who is the "public" whose opinion about the fate of this land should be considered? This question is complicated by the fact that this is Karuk aboriginal territory, but one does not learn that from reading the Supreme Court decision in *Lyng*.

Despite the binary sacred/property presented in the Supreme Court decision, at least five ways to understand land are offered to us in the *Lyng* case and its aftermath. The Yurok and Karuk witnesses in the *Lyng* trial relate to the High Country as their home and their kin, but they are heard by the Forest Service and by the courts as relating to this area as sacred; the Forest Service and the Supreme Court also tell a story about land as property—something that can be owned and whose resources may be used by the owner. Environmentalists who were involved in the case as plaintiffs see the High Country as wilderness, and eventually Congress protected it from development as such. I used to think this was only strategic, but the more I read, the more I learned how essential the idea of wilderness is to American identity, and especially to American environmentalists' identities. All these discourses on land coexist in *Lyng*. While they sometimes appear to contradict each other, this book sets out to show that they can complement and complicate each other in productive ways. Bringing together these discourses on land sheds light on the multifaceted nature of sacred sites cases that the *Lyng* decision conceals.

This book explores the different discourses on land and the roles they played in the *Lyng* case and its aftermath, as the Yurok Tribe organized according to the Indian Reorganization Act[8] in 1993 and established a tribal court that has become a model for other tribal courts around the United States. The Yuroks' recent acquisition of more than fifty thousand acres of ancestral lands and their resolution to recognize the Klamath River, which is sacred to them and central to their vitality, as a rights-bearing entity are only some examples of bringing together notions of land as property, as kin, and as home to inspire action and to assert their sovereignty in the area without seeking the recognition of the US Supreme Court. Through close readings of legal documents, as well as accounts by Yurok and Karuk elders, I tell the story of the High Country and the different roles it has played—as property and commodity, as home and kin, and as sacred wilderness—in the Yurok and Karuk struggles for sovereignty and for religious freedom.

The High Country and the G-O Road Case

Located in the aboriginal territory of the Karuk people, the High Country is about three hundred miles northeast of San Francisco. A rural region surrounded by national forest, it is in the Klamath River basin. A series of peaks in the Siskiyou Mountains ranging from 4,500 to 5,700 feet in elevation, it is about twenty miles east of the Pacific Ocean and thirty miles south of the Oregon-California border. The area is thickly forested by a mix of Douglas, white, and Shasta fir, sugar, western white, and Jeffrey pine, and incense cedar. Dense brush makes it hard, sometimes impossible, to access the area by car or even on foot. Chimney Rock, Doctor Rock, and Turtle Rock are some of the boulders and hills where medicine people can go to ask for powers that would allow them to perform ceremonial dances, such as the Brush Dance, the White Deerskin Dance, and the Jump Dance, in order to restore balance to the universe. I have never been to the High Country because it is not intended for me to visit, and I am not describing the religious practice that takes place there because this knowledge is not mine to share. However, Charlie Thom's (Karuk) description of the High

Country may give you a sense of the place and its significance to the Yurok, Karuk, Tolowa, and Hupa peoples:

> How do we maintain our natural resources? Take the fisheries or any of the living things—trees, rocks, streams, animals, human beings of all races— all of those things are prayed over from the highest medicine mountains. From Chimney Rock you can see a lot of different high peaks; the top of Mt. Shasta, the tip of Preston Peak, a very dim view of Mt. Whitney. You can see all the way to the ocean around the Crescent City area when there is no overcast. Heavy prayers are put on all those places. All the medicine mountains for the people around here are visible from that spot. Medicine Mountain in the Marble Mountain Wilderness, the Trinity Alps, Salmon River country. You can see all that, all the tips of the Siskiyou Mountains can be seen, and they're all prayed over. Everything's prayed over, Doctor Rock is right in view of Chimney Rock. Everything that we go through. Fasting—not eating for several days, very little liquid, maybe some acorn soup. Sweating to become purified before you go in there, so that you're very clean. Those things are very true. You take a prayer that's very strong that an Indian believes in, and you'll find that it's followed with stronger belief than any other religion.[9]

Other Native people similarly describe the High Country as bearing exceptional religious power. The brief filed in the Supreme Court by the Yurok, Karuk, and Tolowa compares the High Country with a church and with Mecca. Yurok Tribal Council attorney Amy Cordalis and legal scholar Kristen Carpenter (of Cherokee descent) add that the land is considered so sacred that it cannot be used for any other purpose than gathering medicine, preparing for ceremonies, and training Indian doctors. Indeed, Indigenous people do not even talk about the High Country for nonreligious purposes. The spirits who reside in the area, along with the plants, give the High Country its medicine that only medicine people can find there.[10] Because the area is so sacred, only doctors or those who undergo training to become doctors can go there, and they must cleanse themselves through days of fasting and abstinence beforehand.

Yurok Chief Judge Abby Abinanti writes in an open letter to Justice Sandra Day O'Connor:

> Have you ever been to this country? It is beautiful. It is more than beautiful. Words are not the medium to describe the home of the Yuroks. Words do

not breathe; they are not real. Words cannot create in your mind the picture of that place. Their [*sic*] our mountains, trees, dirt, rocks, animals and all those Yuroks from forever. This is where they lived and live. . . . Someone could write you of this place—how it looks, smells, feels, how it is. I wish I could. It is a place that never leaves you. It is in me. You can put me down anywhere in the world and I am a reflection of that place. It is there, in that place right behind my eyes. I do not know what you would see if you went there. It would not be the same for you, but maybe for a moment you would see. It is not just the place. The things you think are just "there," just "things," are not just things and not just a place. It is alive. Every part of it is alive. That is the wonder of it. And if you are a Yurok, you are connected to the beings of the place, all of the place.[11]

Journalist Sara Neustadtl describes Doctor Rock as "the place where a few select Yurok women can go questing for visions, after which they return to the villages to train with older women as doctors." At Chimney Rock, "men pray for wisdom and strength, and the medicine men pray for a power they can shoot down to the people on the river like a shaft of light." Her description is incomplete, just as the descriptions by white anthropologists such as Alfred Kroeber and Thomas Buckley are. All those descriptions focus on men's use of the High Country, and Native American studies scholar Cutcha Risling Baldy (Yurok, Karuk, Hupa) explains that this focus has two reasons: first, anthropologists such as Kroeber interpreted what they saw in Native California with their settler colonial, heteropatriarchal worldview and therefore were blind to the centrality of women to Native ceremony (women used the High Country not only for training but also for gathering medicine, teaching, and holding ceremonies such as the Flower Dance). Second, Indigenous informants were often reluctant to share information about women's roles and practices, to protect them from white sexual predators.[12] The result is that much of the writing about ceremonial practice in the High Country focuses on the Jump Dance and the White Deerskin Dance of World Renewal: "standing in a long line, they stamped their feet on the ground to balance the world."[13]

Medicine people guided the Yurok to pray for law. "When the law was broken, the universe blistered with sickness and storm, insanity and murder," and they still believe today that "the world is in turmoil because of individual wrongdoing. A lawbreaker is seized by a bad luck that shakes him into humility, for when the law is broken, the balance needs to be found again." Neustadtl concludes that "this Indian religion is no once-a-week genuflection; it is a voice of the universe, with the power to make itself heard."[14] When law is broken, only ceremony can fix it. And law—settler law—is indeed broken. It is so broken that it is willing to destroy the land where ceremony can take place to heal it. This book follows the Yurok, Karuk, and Tolowa peoples as they metaphorically, and literally, stamp their feet to restore balance to our universe. It ultimately follows the Yurok people as they turn away from settler law to establish Yurok law.

The Yurok, Karuk, and Tolowa Indigenous peoples of Northern California have resided along the nearby Klamath River since their creation. Unlike many other Indigenous communities, they have not been removed or relocated. Their aboriginal territory encompasses the sacred High Country, and they continue to use it for spiritual and medicinal purposes today. The *Lyng* decision does not tell us why the High Country is not part of any of the tribes' reservations. It does not tell us how the United States unilaterally converted (read: stole and absorbed) the territory into public land in the 1850s, after refusing to ratify eighteen treaties that they negotiated and signed with the tribes, which led to the loss of most Native lands in California, including the High Country. It does not tell us how the Yurok, Karuk, and Tolowa peoples fought to return to their homelands even when the US government tried to remove them once and again. And it does not tell us that it was Yurok, Karuk, and Tolowa continued activism that led to the founding of the Native American Heritage Commission by the State of California, and later to the founding of the Northwest Indian Cemetery Protective Association by Yurok leaders Milton Marks and Walt Lara, Sr., to address issues such as the frequent robberies of Indigenous graves in California by anthropologists and museum professionals.[15] These two organizations became the principal plaintiffs in *Lyng*.

In 1974, when Yurok and Karuk peoples found out about the Forest Service's plan for the High Country, they started organizing to protest it. The Forest Service's plan was to harvest 733 million board feet of timber over the course of eighty years and required construction of two hundred miles of logging roads in the areas adjacent to Chimney Rock. The part of the plan that gives the G-O Road case its name is a six-mile segment of this road, which was meant to be paved to connect the towns Gasquet and Orleans. This road would run through the High Country, separating Chimney Rock from Peak Eight and Doctor Rock. The Forest Service estimated that seventy-six logging and ninety-two other vehicles would travel through the Chimney Rock area every day. While some Yurok and Karuk members supported the plan initially, in hopes that it would lead to more jobs in the area, others objected to it from the start, worrying that it would destroy the High Country. An organized movement emerged to advocate against the Forest Service's plan, with the slogan "No-Go on the G-O road." "The Community used the movement to reclaim their turf, to tell their story, and to emerge as a political, social, and religious entity. They organized in the Indian way, by turning inward to rely upon the strength of the entire community to protect tribal rights," write Cordalis and Carpenter.[16]

At the same time, the Forest Service commissioned a study of Yurok, Karuk, and Tolowa cultural sites in the area. The resulting 423-page document came to be known as the Theodoratus Report, after its principal author, Dr. Dorothea Theodoratus.[17] It found the entire area to be "significant as an integral and indispensable part of Indian religious conceptualization and practice." The report went on to explain that "specific sites are used for certain rituals," and "successful use of the [area] is dependent upon and facilitated by certain qualities of the physical environment, the most important of which are privacy, silence, and an undisturbed natural setting." Because constructing a road along any of the available routes "would cause serious and irreparable damage to the sacred areas which are an integral and necessary part of the belief systems and lifeway of Northwest California Indian peoples," the report recommended that the G-O road not be completed.[18] The Forest Service rejected this recommendation, announcing in 1981 that the road would be built in the Chimney Rock section.

While the route selected by the Forest Service avoided some archeological and sacred sites, there were alternative routes that would have avoided the Chimney Rock area, but these were not selected because they would have required the purchase of private lands and had soil stability problems. The Forest Service called for one-half-mile protective zones around all the religious sites identified in the Theodoratus Report. But this was not responsive to the concerns of the Yurok and Karuk activists, who decided to sue the service.

The plaintiffs in the case included the Northwest Indian Cemetery Protective Association, four Yurok and Karuk members (Jimmie James, Sam Jones, Lowanna Brantner, and Christopher H. Peters), six environmental organizations (the Sierra Club, Wilderness Society, California Trout, Siskiyou Mountains Resources Council, Redwood Region Audubon Society, and Northcoast Environmental Center), and two individual members of the Sierra Club (Timothy McKay and John Amadio). A second lawsuit, filed by the State of California, acting through the Native American Heritage Commission, was consolidated for trial. The defendants were Secretary of Agriculture John R. Block, Forest Service Chief R. Max Peterson, and Regional Forester Zane H. Smith. (By the time the case reached the Supreme Court, Richard E. Lyng had become the secretary of agriculture and the case was known forever after as "*Lyng*.")

The Indigenous plaintiffs were represented by Marilyn Miles (Kickapoo) of the California Indian Legal Services, the environmental organizations were represented by attorney Michael Sherwood, and the State of California was represented by Deputy Attorney General Edna Walz. The Forest Service was represented by Rodney Hamblin, assistant US attorney. The plaintiffs brought eight claims, challenging the decisions by the US Forest Service (1) to complete construction of the last 6.02 miles (Chimney Rock Section) of a paved road from Gasquet, California, to Orleans, California (the "G-O road"), and (2) to adopt a forest management plan providing for the harvesting of timber for the Blue Creek Unit of Six Rivers National Forest. Plaintiffs argued that the Forest Service's decisions violated (1) the First Amendment of the Constitution of the United States, (2) the American Indian Religious Freedom Act, (3) the National Environmental Policy Act of 1969 (NEPA)[19] and the Wilderness Act,[20] (4) the Federal Water Pollution Control Act,[21] (5) water and fishing rights reserved to Native Americans on the Hoopa Valley Reservation, and defendants' trust responsibility toward those rights, (6) the Administrative Procedure Act,[22] (7) the Multiple-Use Sustained-Yield Act of 1960,[23] and (8) the National Forest Management Act of 1976.[24]

The case was assigned to Judge Stanley A. Weigel, a Jewish Republican who referred to himself as "agnostic" and was known for his toughness and independence. As Cordalis and Carpenter write, "It was a fortunate selection for the plaintiffs. A member of the national board of the American Civil Liberties Union at the time President John F. Kennedy appointed him to the bench, Weigel was unafraid to uphold unpopular causes, and had represented professors in a dispute over loyalty oaths with the University of California."[25] The two-week trial began on March 14, 1982. Twenty-three witnesses were examined over those two weeks: six individual Yurok and Karuk members testified alongside two expert witnesses (anthropologists Arnold Pilling and Dorothea Theodoratus) for the Indigenous plaintiffs. The State of California called and examined William James

Pink, the executive secretary of the California Native American Heritage Commission. The environmental organizations, together with the State of California, examined eight other expert witnesses.[26] The defendants called and examined eight Forest Service employees.[27] While the plaintiffs won the case in the district court and in the court of appeals, they lost in the Supreme Court, who acknowledged the religious significance of the High Country to the Yurok, Karuk, and Tolowa peoples but declared the federal government's ownership of the land as the decisive factor in the case. In other words, the land may be sacred to the Yurok, Karuk, and Tolowa peoples, but it is government property, and this is what really matters. If the government wants to destroy it, it is allowed to do so.

This story raises questions about what land means and what the implications of different conceptions of land might be, and in the introduction, I present these questions and set the stage for the following chapters to offer potential answers to them: What does it mean to treat a piece of land as someone's home? Can home be reduced to property? Should I treat a place differently if I think of it as belonging to someone else, or to myself, or to no one? What if I, or someone else, consider a place to be sacred? Can anyone own a sacred site? What if I discover a piece of land that is vacant? Should I cultivate it? Or preserve it? What if this land has something on it (or under it) that I can use to improve my life? Like trees or oil or gold? Is it okay to extract those resources from the land in order to use them? What if this land has something that I can use to advance some public good? Can dead bodies who are buried in the ground be excavated to enhance our knowledge of cultures, or genetics, or something else? What about other objects buried in the ground? The answers to these questions depend to a large extent on how we understand land in general and how we understand specific sites. And how we understand land also determines the question of sovereignty: who should decide what to do with the land? We can assume that those who have different relationships with a site are likely to answer the questions above in different ways—thinking of land in terms of kinship (as "Mother Earth") calls for a different treatment than thinking of it in terms of ownership or sacredness.

The Literature on *Lyng*

Among the vast literature on *Lyng*, legal scholarship is dominant, though some religious studies and Indigenous studies scholars have written about it as well. With the exception of one book chapter that tells the "law story" on *Lyng*,[28] one open letter to Justice O'Connor in response to the *Lyng* decision,[29] and an article that reads *Lyng* as an attack on bio-cultural sovereignty,[30] all of the materials I have read about this case analyze and/or criticize its interpretation and implications for religious freedom in general and for Native American religious freedom in particular. Numerous law review articles, notes, and comments have critiqued *Lyng* for its narrow understanding of religion, its narrow understanding of coercion, and its reliance on a Western conception of land as property.[31] Pawnee attorney Walter Echo-Hawk described it as one of the ten worst cases in US legal history.[32] Religious studies scholar Brian E. Brown calls it "a lamentable failure of First Amendment jurisprudence" and "a serious flaw in Constitutional analysis."[33] Shawnee legal scholar Robert J. Miller counts—and thinks of ways to correct—the many errors the Supreme Court made when deciding *Lyng*.[34] Legal scholar Allison Dussias writes that *Lyng* is "the Supreme Court case most clearly associated with the elevation of government property rights over Native American free exercise rights."[35] Yurok Chief Judge Abby Abinanti reads *Lyng* against the background of the Marshall Trilogy, as a case in federal Indian law: "Because it is the Yuroks that have a quarrel with the federal government, as opposed to any other religious group, the issue must be decided within the confines not just of our claims to religious freedom, but also within the structure of the federal-Indian relationship. The federal government has a different relationship with Indian tribes, different from any other citizen group. That relationship must be acknowledged."[36]

Legal scholar Howard Vogel asks to read the conflict over the G-O Road as a cultural conflict between communities, a clash between collective stories, rather than a simple conflict between individual rights and government power. He reads *Lyng* to demonstrate that "in those cases where cultural conflict involves the clash of master stories, conventional individual rights-based approaches are likely to perpetuate the conflict, rather than secure a resolution which can bring about social healing."[37] I agree with Vogel that an individual-rights approach to Indigenous sacred sites protection is inappropriate. But I do not think that federal courts can approach them otherwise—thinking about religious rights as communal, for example, as Michael D. McNally proposes[38]—and I therefore conclude that the answer must be looked for outside of the federal court system. For Vine Deloria, Jr., "most troubling about the Supreme Court decision was the insistence on analyzing tribal religions within the same conceptual framework as western organized religions."[39] According to Deloria, the court thinks of religion as no more than an individual aesthetic choice and therefore treats ceremonies and rituals that have been performed for thousands of years as if they were "popular fads or simply matters of personal preference."[40] Deloria thinks that in order for the West to understand "why it is so important that these ceremonies be held, that they be conducted only at certain locations, and that they be held in secrecy and privacy,"[41] it needs to view them within a much broader historical and geographical context. Again, I agree that this context is crucial to understanding Indigenous religions. My argument is that when the High Country is thought of within this broader context, it becomes clear that it is much more than a sacred site.

Elsewhere, Deloria says that the parties in *Lyng* should have sought a settlement for use of the High Country, as the Taos Pueblo did in the 1970s for the Blue Lake sacred area.[42] "In order to use the treaty relationship," he writes, "it would have been necessary for the Indians to approach Congress when the Forest Service first began its survey and seek special congressional action to set aside that part of the Six Rivers National Forest for their use." They could have cited the Taos Pueblo effort at Blue Lake as a precedent, "and even if no legislation had been passed immediately, raising the issue of the preservation of sacred sites while the Theodoratus Report was being written would have radically changed the emphasis in that document, giving the Indians considerably more leverage in articulating their point of view."[43]

Instead, the Yurok, Karuk, and Tolowa relied on the trust relationship, the existence of which the Forest Service admitted to in its first court appearance, but "the trust responsibility is far too abstract a notion to have impact on the decisions made by forest managers."[44] In other words, the government is incapable of thinking of this conflict in terms of responsibility instead of rights. Deloria concludes that for Native Americans, the message of the *Lyng* decision is clear:

> With the shunting aside of the trust responsibility in the *Lyng* case and the propensity of federal courts to interject the property doctrine when it is most convenient as a defense for the actions of government agencies, the most fruitful course of dealing with the U.S. government now seems to be in negotiated settlements. In other words, what is required is a modernization of the old diplomatic treaty relationship between Washington and the various Indian nations.[45]

What Deloria is saying is that if the United States insists on thinking about sacred lands in terms of rights rather than responsibility, then sacred sites protection should be negotiated as treaties were negotiated between the United States and Native peoples before 1871. In other words, as long as we are trapped in a discourse of rights, sacred sites cases should be treated as cases about Indigenous sovereignty, and cases about Indigenous sovereignty are not the business of federal courts.

Robert Miller looks at what happened when Indigenous peoples did go to Washington, as Deloria (and O'Connor) had suggested. He critiques *Lyng* for its definition of coercion. "The Court was plainly wrong when it said that the road building is not coercive or prohibitive of the Indians' religious practices. The Indians are coerced into violating their religion if they are not able to continue their religious practices."[46] To correct the outcome of *Lyng*, Miller tells us, Native groups have gone to the legislator, as O'Connor herself suggests in her majority opinion. He describes, in his 1990 law review article, efforts to amend AIRFA and to codify the *Sherbert* test into law.[47] While the *Sherbert* test has been codified into law since 1993 (in the Religious Freedom Restoration Act), it has not helped Native peoples in the courts.

Legal scholar Marcia Yablon argues against attempts to win judicial *or* legislative protection of Indigenous sacred sites. She favors reliance on the consultation process and Forest Service management of Indigenous sacred sites on public lands. "The *Lyng* Court made the right decision because it chose the method of protection that is optimal for society as a whole, even if it is less desirable from the view of individual tribes. . . . By encouraging agency protection, the Court attempted to increase sacred sites protection, but not to such an extent that it would have generated vast social inefficiencies over broad swaths of government-owned land."[48] It is not that Yablon takes for granted that the High Country should be necessarily conceived of as government property or that use is always better than nonuse. But she thinks that "the *Lyng* Court's Anglocentric reasoning is merely one in a number of striking illustrations of how agencies are better able to accommodate Indian values and beliefs than the courts or Congress."[49]

Legal scholars Stephanie Hall Barclay and Michalyn Steele (Seneca) write that "the *Lyng* conception of coercion treats tribal members as being on the same footing as other individuals exercising their religion in a predominantly private space, where government inhibitions on voluntary religious practice are the exception rather than the norm." However, Native

Americans seeking access to federally owned sacred sites are not exercising their religion under a "baseline of voluntary choice." Instead, because of the history of government dispossession of Native lands, Indigenous peoples are "at the mercy of government permission to access sacred sites."[50] They continue to argue that "the Court's reasoning in *Lyng* highlights (and is perhaps the origin of) the government's primary justification for denying protection of and access to sacred sites: the idea that no government coercion is involved in such denials."[51] The reason the court determines there is no government coercion in such denials is that there is no threat of penalties. However, Barclay and Steele argue, "Indigenous practitioners are subjected to a baseline of omnipresent government interference with their religious exercise," and therefore they "should be entitled to the same protections [as in prisons and the military], and the government should be required to offer similar affirmative accommodations."[52]

Sociologist Lori G. Beaman argues, "Aboriginal spirituality is legally constructed outside of the boundaries of religious freedom." Her explanation is similar to Barclay and Steele's: "Legal claims are framed in the rhetoric of individual rights that ignores the systemic disadvantages suffered by Aboriginal people."[53] She adds that in cases like *Lyng*, "it is the difference over the meaning of land that presents the most perplexing dilemmas in the confrontation between Native American religious communities and the dominant culture. The profound differences between colonizer and Native American understandings of land, and humans' relationship to it, are impossible to overstate, and result in the desecration of sacred Aboriginal sites for the convenience of the colonizer."[54] Those different meanings of land are at the heart of the present book. Religious studies scholar Robert S. Michaelsen describes this profound difference thus: "The overriding argument between Indians and European Americans involves dirt—soil, land. Whose is it? Who controls it? What does it signify? The dirt in the medicine man's pouch is analogous to the white man's deed or title. It is symbolic of and even embodies the claimant's right to the land."[55] Michaelsen's analysis takes us closer to the question of sovereignty, but this analysis remains in the realm of rights. And as long as the conflict is framed as a matter of rights, the white man's deed will be worth more than the dirt in the medicine man's pouch.

Religious studies scholar Michael D. McNally argues that when Native peoples use the language of religion in courts (in cases that are not necessarily about land), the courts "flatten" their claims to ones about spirituality.

This reduction of religiosity to spirituality has meant that some Native sacred claims have prevailed in courts and others consistently fail. The successful claims are those that fit well into the shape of religion that religious liberty law privileges—"private, individual, believed"—and McNally demonstrates this with legal cases about Native religious, or spiritual, practice in prison.[56] However, in cases about Native communities (rather than individuals) and about sacred lands (rather than practices), the reduction of religion to spirituality excludes Native claims from the protective umbrella of the First Amendment's Free Exercise Clause, because diminished spiritual fulfillment does not amount to a substantial burden on the exercise of religion. This reduction of religion to spirituality led to the loss of cases such as *Bowen v. Roy*,[57] *Lyng*, and *Navajo Nation v. U.S. Forest Service*.[58]

Reading McNally alongside Barclay and Steele is interesting because they all juxtapose sacred sites cases with cases about religious freedom in prison, and they all argue that Native religion is protected better in prisons than in sacred sites cases, but the explanations they provide are different. According to Barclay and Steele, the legal framework of the prison "creates an affirmative duty on the government to offer fairly robust accommodations to protect religious voluntarism."[59] They propose that courts think of Indigenous sacred sites as a framework similar to prisons, where the government has interfered so dramatically in people's ability to exercise their religion that it has a duty to offer them affirmative accommodations. McNally's reading is different. According to him, religious practice in prison is individual and therefore protected more easily than are sacred sites, where the religious claim is collective.[60]

Cordalis and Carpenter have challenged the narrative of conquest that dominates the literature on *Lyng*, emphasizing that through resistance to the G-O Road, the Yurok, Karuk, and Tolowa peoples maintained their relationship with the High Country, rebuilt their communities that had been gravely attacked throughout the Gold Rush and boarding schools eras, and revitalized their various ceremonies. Native American studies scholar Cutcha Risling Baldy (Hupa, Yurok, Karuk) powerfully argues that the continuation of gathering plants up the G-O Road is a demonstration of the continued bio-cultural sovereignty of her peoples even in the face of the *Lyng* decision: "The practice of gathering demonstrates the continued resistance against colonization, but also the continued management of land and space regardless of acknowledgement or support from government agencies," she writes, describing her own experience going "just up the G-O Road" with her aunt to gather bear grass.[61] Baldy adds: "Though the Court's language in this case attempted to solidify federal ownership of the land by divesting Native 'de facto' ownership, this ownership and sovereignty over the land were continually established by the Native peoples of the area through their interaction with and cultural preservation of the landscape."[62]

Walter Echo-Hawk, in his chapter on *Lyng* in *In the Court of the Conqueror*, presents the High Country thus: "We shall journey to the center of the spiritual world in Native North America. It is a beautiful, primordial place called the High Country. Located in the wilderness peaks and high meadows of the Siskiyou Mountains, it lies in the heart of the aboriginal homeland of several Indian tribes of northwest California—rare communities that still practice an ongoing indigenous religious system."[63] In this short paragraph, the High Country already appears as *wilderness*, *home*, and *sacred*.

On the next page, Echo-Hawk presents a *kinship* relationship between Yurok, Karuk, and Tolowa peoples and the High Country: "In this place, some of the prehuman 'beforetime' spirits departed to the heavens or turned into animals or rocks upon the coming of human beings; and this is where the souls of the great Indian doctors reside. It is possible in this place of many spirits to acquire power, fly through the hole in the sky into the heavens, catch a song, or learn esoteric knowledge. And, here is where we shall study how the laws of men and the laws of the Great Spirit intersect."[64] And on the following page, Echo-Hawk explains that "the settler state still views land in economic terms, as a resource to be exploited," adding the idea of land as *property* to the mix.[65] Thus, in a few short paragraphs, land appears in the several different roles assigned to it in the *Lyng* case: land as home, land as property, land as sacred, land as wild, and land as kin. The chapters of this book follow these conceptions of land and the ways these roles intersect in the High Country and in the *Lyng* case.

When I first read *Lyng* and became quite obsessed with it, the question that bothered me the most was how it came to be that such a seemingly insignificant matter—whether or not to finish pouring asphalt onto a six-mile stretch of land that connects two sections of a road in the middle of nowhere—was important enough for the Supreme Court to hear it. I understood that the place was not "the middle of nowhere" for the Yurok, Karuk, and Tolowa peoples. I understood that the question whether the road would be paved was far from insignificant for these peoples. But why the court was willing to hear it was beyond me. I thought that if I read materials from the original trial—the testimony and evidence available to the courts when deciding the case—I might learn something new. So I read them, and I did learn lots of new things that were not obvious to me from reading the Supreme Court decision. But it was not enough. It was a shift in my theoretical perspective on *Lyng* that helped me make sense of this case. It was only when I stopped trying to understand the religious freedom aspects of *Lyng* and started thinking of the case through the lens of setter colonial theory that I received an answer to the question about the significance of those six miles in the middle of nowhere.

Both the government and the court, in *Lyng*, as well as in the cases that informed it and were informed by it (most notably *Bowen v. Roy* and *Employment Division v. Smith*[66]), followed a "logic of elimination."[67] These cases are read as ones in which the court tells Indigenous plaintiffs that their free exercise right does not trump the government's right to conduct its internal affairs as it sees fit. We have seen a change in that attitude in recent cases, such as *Roman Catholic Diocese of Brooklyn, NY v. Cuomo*,[68] where the court has told the government that its need to conduct its internal affairs—to fight a global pandemic and protect the health and well-being of its citizens—was not good enough a reason to burden the religious freedom of those who want to attend church and synagogue services. But when I read *Roy*, *Lyng*, and *Smith* with a settler colonial framework in mind, I could see that what the government (backed up by the court) was telling Indigenous plaintiffs was "we need you gone." The government needs Indigenous peoples gone so that it can conduct its business with the logging industry and so that it doesn't have to question its social security system, or its unemployment benefits system, or its drug laws. The government needs Indigenous peoples to disappear, either through removal, death, or assimilation, not only so that it can take their lands but also so that its (our) metaphysics, epistemology, and ethics are never challenged.

Lyng remains significant today, thirty-five years after its devastating outcome in the US Supreme Court, because it continues to control court rulings on Indigenous sacred land claims despite statutory developments that in other contexts (such as *Burwell v. Hobby Lobby*[69]) change the basis for such claims away from *Lyng*'s interpretation of the First Amendment. *Lyng*'s logic—the understanding of land it handed down to us—has guided various courts in cases about the San Francisco Peaks,[70] Standing Rock,[71] Mauna Kea,[72] and Oak Flat.[73]

Political theorist Kevin Bruyneel writes about the false choice Indigenous peoples face—between being recognized as sovereign nations and being considered US citizens.[74] Here, too, the binary logic according to which land can either be sacred or property presents Indigenous peoples, in sacred sites cases, with a false choice, which the Yurok, Karuk, and Tolowa peoples have resisted, as I show throughout this book: to protect the High Country, they filed a religious freedom lawsuit but then proceeded to describe, in trial, the land as their home. They lobbied for protecting the High Country through a wilderness designation even as they continued to argue they have been managing it for centuries. They have purchased large parcels of ancestral land even as they declare the land their kin—a relationship that ostensibly excludes the possibility of ownership.

An Overview of the Book

Each of the following chapters has at its center one legal text, one concept of land that appears in that text, and a theoretical framework against which I understand the respective conceptions of land of the different chapters.

In chapter 1, I read the testimonies of Indigenous witnesses in the district court trial that led to the *Lyng* decision. In their testimony, the witnesses ask to protect the High Country from development (really, from destruction) because it is their home. This chapter explores the notion of land as home that arises from the testimonies. While most of the scholarship on *Lyng*—both the legal scholarship and the religious studies scholarship—focuses on the Supreme Court decision, this chapter centers on the trial. Listening to the Indigenous witnesses gives us a different outlook on the High Country and on land more generally. Focusing on the idea of home allows me to question the discourse on domesticity or domestication, which in the context of Native America means three things: (1) the discourse of domesticating or civilizing Indigenous peoples who were considered "savages"; (2) the attack on Indigenous sovereignty through the domestic sphere; and (3) the legal definition of Native Americans as "domestic dependent nations" in the Supreme Court in the nineteenth century. This chapter contextualizes the trial testimonies in *Lyng* within this notion of the domestic. A law and literature approach allows me to read the testimony as essential to understanding the *Lyng* case, and when I pay attention to the stories Indigenous witnesses tell in court, what I see is not only a concept of land as home but also Indigenous law, made of stories about the land and about the community, and Indigenous ceremony, in the form of telling these stories publicly, taking place in federal court.

In chapter 2, I read Justice O'Connor's majority opinion in the *Lyng* case and find in it a concept of land as property. Justice O'Connor famously writes in her majority opinion in *Lyng*, "Whatever rights the Indians may have to the use of the area . . . those rights do not divest the Government of its right to use what is, after all, *its* land." O'Connor's majority opinion follows the logic of discovery as it is expressed in *Johnson v. M'Intosh* (1823), where Chief Justice John Marshall created native title—a limited property right for Indigenous peoples that he called "occupancy right." Both O'Connor and Marshall allow Native peoples to use the lands they inhabit, but neither sees them as fully sovereign or as owning the lands they occupy.

This chapter explores what it means to think about land as property, arguing, together with Justice Brennan in his dissenting opinion in *Lyng*, that it was this notion of land as property, rather than an interpretation of free exercise of religion, that has led O'Connor to decide the case as she did. The notion of land as property has a history that most scholars trace back to John Locke's 1689 *Second Treatise on Government*. But while some have critiqued this notion as exclusively "Western," arguing that Indigenous peoples understand land differently—never in terms of something to be owned—others have noted that some Indigenous peoples indeed have systems of property and ownership that can, and should, be reinterpreted and taken into account in cases like *Lyng*. Reading O'Connor's majority opinion in *Lyng* alongside scholarship on land as property, as well as literature on Indigenous sovereignty, this chapter presents and analyzes the role of the discourse of land as property in the story of the High Country.

In chapter 3, I read Justice Brennan's dissenting opinion in *Lyng*: "Today's ruling sacrifices a religion at least as old as the Nation itself, along with the spiritual well-being of its approximately 5,000 adherents, so that the Forest Service can build a 6-mile segment of road that two lower courts found had only the most marginal and speculative utility, both to the Government itself and to the private lumber interests that might conceivably use it," he writes. For him, the sacredness of the High Country should control its fate. The court should protect the area from development because it is sacred to thousands of people. Prima facie, this is exactly what the Indigenous plaintiffs have asked the court to do. But Brennan's dissent, which is usually celebrated as legally correct and politically progressive, essentializes indigeneity through its understanding of Indigenous religions ("because of their perceptions of and relationship with the natural world, Native Americans consider all land sacred"), and for this, I criticize it in this chapter.

The legal discourse about Indigenous peoples that Brennan participates in producing characterizes Indigenous peoples as primitive and vanishing, existing in a mythic past and never evolving. This discourse erases the effects of settler colonialism on Indigenous peoples; it erases both the damage settler colonialism has done and Indigenous survivance. This chapter shows how Justice Brennan does it in his dissent in *Lyng*. The discourse and jurisprudence on religious freedom prior to *Lyng*, which is relied on as precedent, is part of the problem. While this jurisprudence understands religion as individual, believed, and free, the history of Indigenous religions and their suppression by the US government must be taken into account in Indigenous sacred sites cases and in other Native American religious freedom cases.

In 1984, while the *Lyng* case was still pending, Congress passed the California Wilderness Act, exempting much of the High Country from logging. In 1990, Congress passed the Smith River National Recreation Area Act, exempting the proposed site of the G-O Road from such construction. The High Country remains, to this day, undeveloped, and it is still used by local Indigenous communities for religious ceremonies and medicine-making purposes. Chapter 4 examines what it means to protect this area as wilderness. While wilderness is a central idea to American political theory, and one with spiritual significance, it also brings to mind the doctrine of terra nullius and the doctrine of Christian discovery, two doctrines that have justified the conquest of many lands in North America and elsewhere. This chapter tells the story of the protection of the High Country from development outside of the courts and through environmental lobbying, and then critiques the discursive implications of designating this area as wilderness, given the history of this idea and its role in dispossessing Indigenous peoples from their lands.

Anthropologists such as the infamous Alfred Kroeber have described Yurok religiosity through their kinship relations with the natural world in general and the High Country in particular. These accounts serve as central evidence in the *Lyng* case, and the Forest Service had relied on them when planning to develop the High Country. But Kroeber has been vastly criticized for his unethical ethnographic practices; and the reliance on ethnographic knowledge, produced by non-Indigenous experts, in making decisions regarding Indigenous lives, is in itself a colonial practice. Chapter 5, therefore, turns to what it means for Yurok leaders today, in the aftermath of the *Lyng* decision, to treat their environment as their kin. I focus on the Yurok's ongoing efforts to save the Klamath River from destruction and to bring back the salmon that are central to their religious ceremonies and essential to their survival. The struggle for Yurok sovereignty has always been entangled with the fate of the river. These struggles have taken different forms in different times in history: they range from the fish wars of the first half of the twentieth century, through administrative appeals to remove dams from the river in the early 2000s, to the 2019 resolution of the Yurok Tribal Council to recognize the Klamath River as a rights-bearing person. Sovereignty, to the Yurok, is tied to the ability of the Yurok Tribal Court to make decisions about tribal everyday life based on traditional values and with close attention to the river and its fish, which play a vital role in the economic, cultural, and spiritual identities of the Yuroks. Ultimately, treating their land as their kin implies a complex understanding of it, transcending the binary logic that allows land to be either property or sacred. With this rich and complex understanding of land, we finally leave the arena in which land is at the center of competing human rights (to religion, to property), thinking of land, instead, as itself bearing rights, indeed, as sovereign.

The *Lyng* case has set as oppositional conceptions of land as property and as sacred, and this binary understanding of land has since then framed every Native American sacred sites case, up to the Oak Flat case that is making its way through the federal court system at the time of this book's writing. Such a binary understanding of land obscures Indigenous frameworks of relationality and sovereignty. My reading of *Lyng* in this book aims to recover these Indigenous frameworks without giving up on the other conceptions of land—as property and as sacred. To do this, I read the case against different disciplinary backgrounds and with different audiences in mind. While I myself came to this case with legal background, I wrote this book as a humanities scholar who cares deeply about law. I also wrote this book as a non-Indigenous, white immigrant to the United States, because the burden of anti-colonial critique should be carried, or at least shared, by non-Indigenous people. As Vine Deloria, Jr., wrote shortly after the Supreme Court handed down the *Lyng* decision, all people should join the movement to protect Native American sacred sites. This book does not offer any legal strategies for winning Native American sacred sites cases, nor does it criticize those who choose the federal courts as their route to protecting sacred sites. Having read many law review articles on *Lyng* and other sacred sites cases, I find that a more humanistic approach is essential to imagining the G-O Road case as leading to a different outcome than it did. Even though this is mostly a work of humanities scholarship, I do hope that lawyers, environmental activists, and government officials who engage in cultural resource consultation will read it and find it useful. Let us now enter Judge Weigel's courtroom in San Francisco, on March 14, 1982.

I

—◆◆—

LAND AS HOME IN THE
G-O ROAD TRIAL

It is through oral history and ceremony that we as Auth understand
that our creation happened here in our respective homelands. The
mountains, rivers, and sacred rocks found within our homeland serve as
monuments that now stand in testimony to the mythological world and
corroborate the many components of our cosmology. Thus, nowhere else
in the world can such a profound emotional and spiritual relationship
exist other than within our homelands. We are spiritually connected to
this place in what is now called Northern California, what we call home.[1]

This is how Chris Peters (Yurok/Karuk), one of the named plaintiffs and
a central witness in the G-O Road trial, describes the High Country some
thirty-five years after the trial was over. Peters's description acknowledges
the religiosity, or spiritual importance, of the High Country to Yurok,
Karuk, and Tolowa peoples, but for him, the spiritual connection is to a
homeland. We cannot understand the religious centrality of this place to
Yurok, Karuk, and Tolowa people without thinking of it as their home. Peters and other Indigenous witnesses in the G-O Road trial talked about the
High Country as their home, but their testimonies, or the conception of
land as home advanced in these testimonies, have no trace in the Supreme
Court decision in the case that has come to be known as *Lyng*. Paying attention to these testimonies, however, reveals that the witnesses talk about
the High Country as their home.

In subsequent chapters, I tell the story of the High Country and the G-O Road case through the lenses of the Supreme Court decision, the legislative process, and the Yurok Tribal Court, where land is understood differently—as property, as sacred, as wild, and as kin—but I will approach these parts of the story with the understanding gained by listening to the witnesses, an understanding of this place as their home, as I explore in this first chapter. When we listen to the witnesses, we can hear a story that cannot be told in the court decision, because the case was about the free exercise of religion, and the legal framework of religious freedom imposes certain limitations on the stories the court can hear, and it shapes the story the court can tell in its decision. In this chapter, I let the witnesses in the G-O Road trial take the stage. The point is to show that what the plaintiffs seek to protect is their survivance, which is tightly connected with the Yurok's, Karuk's, and Tolowa's relationships with the High Country as their home. This relationship includes religion, so my argument is not that the G-O Road case is not about religion but that the religious-freedom framework conceals the political nature of both indigeneity and religion, as it imposes a "false binary," according to which land is either sacred or it is property.[2] The witnesses refuse to accept these limitations, and thus their testimony tells a more robust story than the one we learn if we read only the Supreme Court decision, as lawyers and law students, but also law and religion scholars, usually do.

When we read the Supreme Court decision in *Lyng*, we find no mention of any of the testimonies in the trial—neither the testimonies of the Yurok and Karuk witnesses nor the expert witnesses (ethnographers, engineers, and Forest Service employees). Justice Sandra Day O'Connor's opening words in her majority opinion in *Lyng* refer to the High Country not as Yurok, Karuk, and Tolowa homeland but as a portion of a national forest: "This case requires us to consider whether the First Amendment's Free Exercise Clause prohibits the Government from permitting timber harvesting in, or constructing a road through, a portion of a National Forest that has traditionally been used for religious purposes by members of three American Indian tribes in northwestern California. We conclude that it does not."[3] When the court's starting point is thinking of the land as a portion of a national forest—public land, belonging to the US public, managed by the US government—it is not surprising that the court's conclusion is that the government can do with this place as it wishes.

This land, which lies in a national forest, belonging to the American public and managed by the government, is not Yurok, Karuk, and Tolowa homeland, even if it "has traditionally been used for religious purposes." The "three American Indian tribes" are not named. But we who read this case do not have to accept O'Connor's starting point as given. We could think about this land as "the High Country," or as a "traditional home," or as "sacred grounds." We could think about the Yurok, Karuk, and Tolowa nations as specific peoples rather than some generic three tribes. Instead of saying that the land has traditionally been used by *members* of these nations, we could say that the land has been used by the *communities* or the *nations*. We don't even have to think of the Yurok, Karuk, and Tolowa peoples as *using* the High Country; maybe we should understand their relationship with the High Country otherwise. We could refer to the respondents as "Native Americans" instead of "American Indians," or better yet, name the specific tribal nations to which they belong. We can use the word "nations" rather than "tribes." The *Lyng* decision was written in the 1980s, and the terminology it uses is outdated, but as I am writing this chapter, I want to remember that I am not confined to its language and to the conceptions of land it advances.

O'Connor's point of departure is this: "In 1977, the Forest Service issued a draft environmental impact statement that discussed proposals for upgrading an existing unpaved road that runs through the Chimney Rock area."[4] Why open there, in 1977? Where else could O'Connor start? Surely the controversy over the G-O Road hadn't begun with the Environmental Impact Statement. When did this controversy start? Why not start there? Or, consider beginning with Yurok, Karuk, and Tolowa creation stories. The court has access to them as they were related by some of the witnesses in the trial and in the Theodoratus Report, which was commissioned by the Forest Service and submitted to the court as evidence.[5] And their creation stories should be essential to deciding a case about their right to freely exercise their religion in the High Country. Or, perhaps we should begin by questioning the inclusion of Indigenous sacred sites in a national forest rather than in one of the nations' reservations. Asking this question might require the court to go back a hundred and fifty years earlier, when the first American settlers arrived in Northwest California.

But O'Connor begins in 1977, when the Forest Service issued a Draft Environmental Impact Statement. This way of telling the G-O Road story gives agency to the US government and portrays the Yurok, Karuk, and

Tolowa nations as merely reactive. The way the court tells the story of the G-O Road, neither the High Country nor the peoples who have called it home for centuries have agency, and therefore their voices are missing from the Supreme Court decision. In this way, the *Lyng* Court participates in the erasure of Native peoples from the legal narrative about the American landscape. But in trial, the Indigenous witnesses write themselves back into this narrative. The truth is, they have never left. Māori scholar Linda Tuhiwai Smith has written about such rewriting as a decolonial research method;[6] Mishuana Goeman (Seneca) and Cutcha Risling Baldy (Hupa, Yurok, Karuk) propose (re)mapping and (re)writing, with (*re*) in parentheses, as a better phrasing, "to more fully demonstrate that Indigenous peoples are not just claiming and writing in the present, but they are participating in a (re)vivification that builds a future with the past, showing how these epistemological foundations speak to a lasting legacy that is both ancient and modern."[7]

In this chapter, I would like to imagine what it would look like to take the witnesses' stories, rather than settler law, geography, and history, as a starting point. The witnesses (re)write and (re)map—and, Baldy would add, (re)right and (re)rite—the High Country. And even if their stories do not resonate in the court's decision in *Lyng*, they were recorded into the trial transcript and became part of US settler law, disrupting its narrative in ways that I find productive. This chapter is "looking for law in all the wrong places," as the title of a recent book in the field of law and society encourages us to do.[8] Instead of looking for it in the *Lyng* Supreme Court decision, I listen to the stories that Yurok and Karuk witnesses tell about the High Country in the G-O Road trial. These stories reveal the High Country as their home, but they do more than that. They bring this home into the courtroom; the stories that ostensibly belong in the private, or domestic, sphere, nevertheless transgress and make an appearance in the most public place, the courtroom, where they would be transcribed and become part of the public record. They also do another thing: they bring Yurok, Karuk, and Tolowa law into a settler court, thus exposing all the absurdities that are created when the two bodies of law try to interact. I will highlight these absurdities throughout the chapter. The other thing I keep in mind as I read the testimonies is that Yurok, Karuk, and Tolowa people do not treat storytelling, law, and religion as separate. As Hupa historian Jack Norton explains:

[California Native societies'] daily lives began and ended with songs that were generally prayers. In the intervals between, they were urged, internally and externally, to "keep a good heart," "do not think badly of people," "be kind and respectful of the old." "Always," they said, "go up and talk with the elders, say hello, for when you walk away, the old person will say, 'ah, what a fine young man, I hope he lives to be as old as I.'" These urgings and blessings were reinforced by words, rituals, laws and customs during the important religious observances, and in hundreds of stories, gestures, and indirect statements that filled their lives.[9]

Religion and law come together, through words, through stories, to direct Indigenous youths' lives in Norton's description, and they similarly come together in the G-O Road courtroom. Perhaps what happens when these stories are told in settler court is that the wall that ostensibly separates the private or domestic from the public begins to collapse. As Turtle Mountain Ojibwe scholar Heidi Kiiwetinepinesiik Stark writes, "Stories are law. Once relegated to the field of folklore or mythology, little attention was paid to these rich sources. Recently, critical approaches to the study of Indigenous law have elucidated this point, noting stories lay out the central principles for how people order their world." Moreover, according to Stark, "understanding story as law not only unearths a rich body of thought containing alternate pathways for Indigenous-state relations, it also dispels the inviolability of law, demonstrating that law is, likewise, a set of stories."[10] According to Stark, laws and stories are intertwined, and this is true not only about Indigenous law but about settler law as well.[11] Therefore, when Indigenous stories are entangled with settler law, we can also say that it is Indigenous law that is entangled with settler stories, exposing the locality of the settler legal narrative that aspires to universality.[12]

"The truth about stories is that that's all we are," writes Cherokee author and scholar Thomas King.[13] What the witnesses do in trial is tell a story. The story they tell must follow a few rules. For example, they have to relate it in the form of answers to questions. The witness cannot tell what she was not asked to tell (she also has to tell the truth, the whole truth, and nothing but the truth, so help her God, but more on this later). Telling something you were not asked about requires courage; you may be scolded. There's a moment in the trial when Chris Peters, the central Yurok/Karuk witness, tells Judge Weigel that he is nervous. It is a powerful moment, especially because he then goes on to say that he is at his best when he is

nervous, and the judge's response—"That is true of some football play-
ers"—is both lighthearted and touching. Peters is given freedom to tell the
whole story as he understands it—"you are here to tell the truth," the judge
reminds him—and his speech sounds more like an opening statement than
a cross-examination.[14] Peters's story is about the religious practice that the
Yurok, Karuk, and Tolowa peoples are trying to protect, but he weaves
into the story the colonial context that has been threatening this practice.
As I show throughout this chapter, other Indigenous witnesses also bring
up, indirectly, colonial invasion, killing, burning, and kidnapping, but one
needs to listen carefully to hear in their testimony that which does not
perfectly fit into the religious freedom framework within which *Lyng* was
argued, heard, and decided.

Insisting on the complexity of his story (the truth, the whole truth, and
nothing but the truth), Peters is taking a risk when he stands before such
authority and shares details that do not conform to what the legal framework ostensibly requires. He risks being misunderstood or dismissed as
unreasonable, in a situation where what he needs to prove is, to a large extent, that what he is asking the court to do (protect his religious freedom)
is reasonable. Indeed, if he is dismissed as unreasonable, he is likely to lose
the case; even worse, his peoples are likely to lose the case. It is not surprising, therefore, that Peters is nervous and that he interprets Judge Weigel's
occasional questioning as scolding. Nevertheless, Peters tells this story in
court, and it is important that he does because, as King writes, "once a story
is told, it cannot be called back. Once told, it is loose in the world."[15] Peters,
it turns out, is not there to win a case; he is there to set his story of the High
Country loose in the world. As a result, the High Country is loose in the
world as Yurok, Karuk, and Tolowa home and kin, as sacred wilderness,
even as it remains government property.

Now, let us call our next witness to the stand.

Lowanna Brantner's Story

I was raised by my grandparents, so I was taught by the elders about our
tradition, about our church, about our people. I was fortunate. Today I'll
say "fortunate." Many times I thought it was not fortunate that I was born
to four of the biggest houses in the Yurok strip where the famous dances
had come up, the White Deerskin Dance, the Jump Dance and the Brush

Dance and many other games, and how the Indians had to use the High
Country to go and pray so that when they come back to the lowlands, we
can share with one another. My place has been that I have a lot of those
relics that I share with my neighbors, the Hoopas [*sic*], the Karok's [*sic*] and
my own people to uphold and to see that our religion go [*sic*] on as it has
for thousands of years past.[16]

Thus begins the testimony of Lowanna Brantner, a Yurok elder, who
was one of the witnesses for the plaintiffs in the G-O Road trial. Brantner
was "the quintessence of Yurok aristocracy from the death of the previous
traditional leader, Robert Spott, in 1953, until her own death, in 1984, over
30 years later."[17] Brantner was born in 1908, in Mettah, on the Klamath
River. When asked by the court clerk about her occupation, she says she
had been a housewife, but Brantner was also a medicine woman who came
from the great house responsible for the Yurok law dances, the ceremonies
held before the convening of the tribal court and those preceding tribal
executions. At the time of the G-O Road trial, Brantner still owned her
family's dance regalia and regarded them as living beings who kept her safe.
Asked what she means by "sharing" the relics, Brantner continues:

Well, down through the years, due to the fact that there were soldiers and
people who came through and destroyed, burned, killed, a lot of the relics
were burned or taken. So now, a few of us are left in the three tribes and we
take and share. So and so's got a Brush Dance. Their time come [*sic*], their
time to dance, we give them so many piece relics they need and the other
people do the same so that the dance can be performed the true way as it
has been for thousands of years.[18]

In her testimony, Brantner draws a connection between the importance
of her people's ceremonies and the violent conquest of the area by settlers.
Developing the national forest, according to Brantner's testimony, would
be a continuation of this violence and destruction. Constructing a road
through the sacred area and cutting down the trees there is not any different than destroying, burning, and killing, which had happened in earlier
generations. Brantner's testimony was powerful and seems to have had the
greatest impact on Judge Stanley Weigel—greater than that of any of the
other witnesses testifying in the two-week 1983 trial. But her perspective,
and the settler colonial aspects of the case, has no trace in the narrative
the Supreme Court constructs about the G-O Road, and as a result it is

missing from much of the scholarship on the *Lyng* case as well. This absence is not unique to the G-O Road case: Supreme Court justices do not hear witnesses, and even though they have access to trial transcripts, indeed, even if they read those transcripts, they do not have the firsthand impression of witnesses that district court judges have. Scholars who study landmark cases like *Lyng* often pay most, if not all, of their attention to Supreme Court decisions, thus missing the opportunity to engage with testimonies like Brantner's.

Part of the issue is that *Lyng* is a case about religious freedom, requiring the plaintiffs to prove that their religious practice in the High Country is based on a "sincerely held belief" and that it would be "substantially burdened" by the Forest Service's development plan. Therefore, the Supreme Court's job is to see if the plaintiffs have proven this. Any parts of the testimony that do not speak directly to this question can be ignored. Religion and Native American religious freedom are at the center of chapter 3. However, as Chris Peters tells us, to understand this case fully, "one must understand that for Indigenous peoples of Northwestern California, religious beliefs and everyday lifeways are one in the same."[19] Therefore, to fully understand the case, one must pay attention to parts of the testimony that may not sound as if they are about religion.

A law and literature approach to the G-O Road case allows me to center witnesses' voices without imposing the religious freedom question upon the stories that they tell. Such a reading, I contend, broadens our understanding of religion, as well as our understanding of law. Specifically, in the case of Indigenous law and religion, we must take seriously what Indigenous law is, and how it differs from US law.[20] As law and religion scholar Winnifred Fallers Sullivan writes, "we need to widen our lenses and work comparatively, seeing how other folks do religion and law."[21] Anishinaabe legal scholar John Borrows explains Indigenous law thus:

> Law is us. And it's the animals, and it's our dreams, and it's our stories, and it's our relationships. It's the way we talk with one another and try to persuade one another, and that persuasion of course involves many different traditions now. But that persuasion is a part of our law, and it's not just for the parliaments and it's not just for the courts. We have a role in taking that kind of action.[22]

If law is "our stories," as Borrows argues, then Brantner's testimony should count as law just as much as the court's decision counts as law. Moreover, it should count as relevant and valuable knowledge, just as much as the testimonies of expert witnesses count—but more on this below. As Stark writes, it is through stories that "we can unearth the approaches and principles that enabled the development or restoration of proper relationships with others," including the land itself and the nation-state.[23]

Scholars of law and literature can offer useful insight into such a project when they propose, for example, to read legal text as literature and trial testimony as storytelling. Indigenous storytelling is part of a longer, broader, oral tradition through which knowledge and law are passed from one generation to another, writes legal scholar Kathleen Birrell.[24] We can therefore see it as a form of resistance to the colonial narrative of law. Both law and literature create and legislate the meaning of indigeneity. But while settler law constructs indigeneity as "authentic"—fixed, natural, pre-discursive— Indigenous literature and storytelling demonstrate that indigeneities are plural, that they are constructed through deep colonization, and that they also disrupt or deconstruct colonization. To appear before the law, the Indigenous subject must perform her indigeneity in a specific way—through attachment to the past—constructing indigeneity as static. Indigenous literature, on the other hand, portrays indigeneity as articulated or fluid.

It is easy for settler law to dismiss testimonies like that of Brantner's in the G-O Road case. As literary scholar Cheryl Suzack (Batchuana First Nation) argues, "colonial law and legislation limit Indigenous women's political, cultural, and social authority." Yet, the narrative advanced in Brantner's testimony, her identity and cultural knowledge, is foundational to social reform.[25] It can "advance our understanding of colonial-legal gender injustice" beyond the rights discourse promoted by legal texts.[26] Storytelling, then, intervenes in the "collective social imaginary"[27] and allows us to visualize justice anew. Stark gives us tools for doing so. "The study of Indigenous law," she writes, "in presenting alternative frameworks for the restoration of Indigenous–state relations, contains the potential to not only produce new methodological approaches but may also unearth alternate methods for living together differently."[28] If settler law, as she understands it, is the "creation stories" of the settler state (because it is through seminal decisions that the state narrates itself into existence and maintains its authority), then settler law must be contested through Indigenous stories. If settler law, including treaties signed with Indigenous peoples, established the rights discourse, then Indigenous stories will establish a discourse of responsibility:

We must speak for our relatives; we must uphold our commitments to the land, water, animals, flora and fauna. We have an obligation to protect creation. We are accountable for the damages being wreaked upon the land and water. Our survival necessitates we find ways to hold the settler state to the original spirit and intent of our treaties, which were and remain conditioned by our legal obligations to creation.[29]

Following Birrell, Suzack, and Stark, I therefore ask to read the testimonies in the G-O Road case as a way of resistance through storytelling.

The High Country

The proposed section of the G-O Road is 6.02 miles long, and, surprised that a case about a six-mile segment of a road reached all the way to the Supreme Court, I decided to go back and listen to the voices of Yurok, Karuk, and Tolowa members who reside in the area and use the High Country for religious purposes. Their voices are heard here through their testimony in the G-O Road trial and as consultants for the Theodoratus Report, which served as the central piece of evidence in the trial. They portray their religion as fundamentally land-based, as opposed to the approach of the courts to religion, which favors a Tillichian definition of religion as "ultimate concern." In other words, religion, according to the Yurok, Karuk, and Tolowa plaintiffs, is grounded in place, while according to the court, it is grounded in belief.

Chris Peters supported his testimony with a display of photographs of the sacred sites in the area, "to allow the Judge to see for himself the pristine qualities that existed there, and to help convey how the maintenance of quietude in the Sacred High Country was critical to the tribes' religious practice."[30] He began thus:

The Yurok, Karok [sic] and Tolowa Indian tribes live in the northwestern corner of California. These tribes share the use of a very special religious area. That area is located in the southern portion of the Siskiyou mountains, and referred to by the Indian people as the "High Country." Doctor Rock, Chimney Rock, Peak 8 and Little Medicine Mountain are located within this religious area and are some of the more sacred places within the High Country. They have been used throughout the years by Indian people who go there to pray for special purposes or special powers, or medicine. The High Country was placed there by the Creator as a place where Indian people could seek religious power.[31]

The Theodoratus Report similarly explains the use of the High Country, highlighting the search for spiritual power as permeating all daily life and Native culture.[32] Scholarship on Native American religions echoes these descriptions.[33] This means that religion cannot be separated from other aspects—either cultural or ethical—of everyday life. And the geographical area similarly cannot be divided into sacred and nonsacred areas; specific sites are not supposed to be singled out or isolated.[34] In fact, the Theodoratus Report explains the concept of "site" as more than "a limited measurable locality." A religious site can be a condition (psychological, visual, or otherwise sensory)—silence, for example. "In order to understand what a site means to Native American residents of this area," the report proposes, "a mental shift must be made away from the purely physical aspect of a site to an extended definition which includes various qualitative, psychological and sensory aspects."[35]

Treating specific geographic locations as separate, as well as treating some aspects of local Native lives as secular and others as religious, is a colonial practice that results in forcing a non-Western practice into a Western category (religion). But another thing that is important to me here is that if I am correct that the witnesses are asking to protect their home, then it makes sense that they would think of it holistically. One does not fight to protect only parts of one's home—only the important parts—as if it might be okay to destroy the living room but not the bedrooms. This distortion has to do with language as well. As Peters explains in his testimony, "it is difficult to talk about traditional types of things in translating it into the English language. I think the court will find [that] . . . converting Indian concepts into European language loses something in the translation."[36] Using English terms is nevertheless unavoidable when arguing a case in US courts, and it is worth asking, therefore, whether the legal route is appropriate in cases of Indigenous sacred sites. Niimiipuu literary scholar Inés Hernández-Ávila writes about the use of the English language by Native Americans as a site of resistance: as a result of boarding schools' silencing and denial of Native voices and languages, today Native peoples recognize their own sovereignty in English language literature.[37] We could view the arguing of a case about Indigenous sovereignty in the English language in settler courts as similarly subversive, even as it leads to the kind of problems Peters pointed out. As I mentioned before, it is not only language but also the dissonance between settler law and Indigenous law that contributes to these difficulties. But as we see with Birrell, Suzack, and Stark, there is also a disruptive, or subversive, potential here that is worth exploring.

The religious practice of the Yurok, Karuk, and Tolowa nations is described as focused on world renewal, aiming to stabilize and preserve the earth from catastrophe, and humanity from disease.[38] In trial, Peters explains that "world renewal" has both physical and spiritual aspects: "They are world renewal ceremonies, and most of the time when people think of world renewal, the general understanding, the image or the concept is making the physical world over again. The ceremonies do do that deed, but also they make a spiritual world over again, a spiritual bond that holds tribal people together."[39]

The religious practitioners believe that world-renewal ceremonies were initiated by prehuman spirits who inhabited the world and brought all living things and culture to humankind.[40] The Karuk call these spirits *ixkareya* and see them as guides for human behavior; the Yurok call them *woge* and believe that they are afraid of contamination by mortals.[41] Ceremonies of world renewal include the reciting of what the Theodoratus Report calls, following anthropologist Alfred Kroeber, "origin stories."[42]

The use of the High Country is described in detail in the Theodoratus Report. The knowledge related in the Report is valuable to Yurok, Karuk, and Tolowa members who may want to revitalize traditional practices, as a lot of the traditional knowledge has been lost in the era of assimilation policy (more on this later). However, it is also problematic, not only because of the reliance on Kroeber and other non-Native "experts" but also because, as one of the unnamed consultants quoted in the Theodoratus Report says, "one of our religious beliefs is that we don't expose our sacred practices. It is a personal thing."[43] Reading this sentence with Kahnawà:ke Mohawk anthropologist Audra Simpson's concept of "ethnographic refusal" in mind, one can see in this secrecy a political act. Simpson writes that such a declaration

> involves an ethnographic calculus of what you need to know and what I refuse to write. This is not because of the centrality of esoteric and sacred knowledge. Rather, the deep context of dispossession, of containment, of a skewed authoritative axis and the ongoing structure of both settler colonialism and its disavowal make writing and analysis a careful, complex, instantiation of jurisdiction and authority, what Robert Warrior has called "literary sovereignty."[44]

Ethnographic refusal is difficult, if not impossible, to practice in court. Once the Yurok, Karuk, and Tolowa peoples decided to take the Forest Service to court over the G-O Road and religious freedom, they in a way committed to revealing the details that are essential to proving the sincerity of their belief. But, as I mentioned in the introduction, this knowledge is not mine to share, and anyway, I find myself more interested in the meaning of the existence of a document such as the Theodoratus Report than in its specific content. The Theodoratus Report mentions a "bitter disagreement" between different Forest Service employees regarding the impact of the development plan. One of the employees is Arnold Pilling, who will later become an expert witness in the G-O Road trial. The Theodoratus Report was commissioned because of this disagreement. Anthropologist Thomas Buckley describes this disagreement at length in his chapter on the G-O Road in *Standing Ground*, his 2002 book that resulted from his extensive ethnographic work with the Yurok people.[45] Both Buckley himself and Arnold Pilling, when the Forest Service consulted them, objected to the completion of the road, but the Forest Service archaeologist, Donald Miller, having overseen a few interviews with local Yurok and Karuk members and consulted the Kroeberian literature, concluded that the Indigenous nations had no case against the Chimney Rock section. The disagreement between them, however, forced the Forest Service to start over. They hired a contract anthropologist, Dorothea Theodoratus, and gave her a free hand to design and execute her study as she saw fit, with only one condition: that she not consult Pilling and Buckley. "The 'Theodoratus Report' (USDA/FS 1979a) finally came in at nearly five hundred pages and cost the government over $200,000. While the report contained an invaluable wealth of information and new native testimony, its conclusions were rather simple: the GO-road should not be completed for precisely the reasons that both Pilling and Buckley had made clear by 1976," Buckley writes, adding that Pilling worked pro bono and Buckley himself was paid a total of two hundred dollars for his report.[46]

Conducting ethnographic work in the area, as well as relying on the earlier work of local salvage anthropologists, is problematic; using this knowledge in policymaking and in the courts is even more troubling. Given that the ethnographic insight into Indigenous lives portrays Indigenous peoples as "primitive" and as "dying cultures," thus justifying their colonization, dispossession, and genocide, relying on this knowledge in court can only lead to further justification of settler colonial dispossession. As Cutcha Risling Baldy writes:

> It was thought that the research and documentation being done by Western scholars were essential to preserving knowledge about Native cultures

before they disappeared into the annals of history. In the early twentieth century, following some of the most violent periods of colonial history, many anthropologists, archaeologists, linguists, and other scholars became interested in documenting Indian life to preserve what they perceived as a "dying culture." This phenomenon of salvage ethnography implied that Native cultures had been static in nature before contact, and therefore the once pristine, untouched Indian society would have no ability to survive the continuing intrusion of Western culture nor change or adapt to a new way of life.[47]

Baldy adds another aspect of salvage ethnography that is ethically dubious: though the anthropologists themselves usually rely on Native consultants, it is the anthropologists and archaeologists who are considered to be the experts and authorities on Indigenous peoples. "Subsequently, these scholars were depended on as expert witnesses, and their ideas, theories, and findings were given more weight and consideration than that of Indigenous peoples."[48] I keep all this in mind when I cite the Theodoratus Report here, and I give most of my attention to the Indigenous plaintiffs' testimony (I will refer to the expert witnesses' testimonies briefly in chapter 4), as a way to center Indigenous knowledge and sovereignty.

What, then, do we learn from the plaintiffs about their peoples' relationship with the High Country? We learn that people seeking power continue to go to the High Country to achieve personal medicine and curing medicine. Some Karuk members who use the Blue Creek area were originally trained somewhere else, but their sites were desecrated, so they have switched to this new area.[49] In trial, Peters estimated that about forty people physically or actively used the area at the time. But he explains that there is also a spiritual use of the area that does not require attending it physically. He calls it "a spiritual visitation . . . through the mind."[50]

In a letter to Judge Weigel, Kickapoo attorney Marilyn Miles, who represented the Indigenous plaintiffs, responds to the Forest Service's argument that the G-O Road would not have an adverse effect on the plaintiffs' religious practice because only very few people ever use the High Country. She explains that the number of people directly using the High Country is unknown—and probably very small—thus:

> only a limited number of people are called or chosen by the Creator or Spirits to be such persons. Thus, only certain people can go to the Doctor Rock area on behalf of the rest of the community, and only then for a proper purpose and at a proper time. But this is not unlike other religions; not all

members of a particular faith are permitted on the alter [sic], for the alter [sic] is reserved for the priest or spiritual leader.[51]

Miles explains that the few people allowed in the High Country use the powers that they get there in ceremonies that benefit the entire community. Miles adds and describes a photo to illustrate her point: "Enclosed for the Court's assistance is a photograph from a recent ceremony in Weitchpec. The medicine woman in the center of the photograph was required to go to the sacred high country for guidance and power to pray for the Indian child held by her mother and for others in the community, and all those in attendance are dependent upon the powers and Spirits of the area, and thereby 'use' the sacred region."[52]

Miles concludes her letter to Judge Weigel thus: "This is the best, and perhaps the only answer Indian plaintiffs can give the Court. The number of persons who physically go to the high country is not known, although Indian plaintiffs recognize that the numbers may not be large. As explained above, however, it is wrong to measure the religious values of this sacred area and the associated practices in terms of the number who set foot there."[53]

When asked about their religion, the Yurok and Karuk witnesses describe a religious system that begins with community and its relation to the natural world, rather than with the individual and her relationship with God. Witness Jimmie James (Yurok/Hupa) tells the court that "the most important thing was to have an understanding of nature. Love your people, and always remember to follow out the command of the Great Spirit, the Great Creator, and this up-to-date, I have tried to be obedient to those commands."[54] The most important religious virtue is an understanding of nature, because nature, or specific natural settings, is considered to be sacred. Sacred places are those in which communication with the Creator, or the Great Spirit, can be conducted. As Peters explains, "the High Country—Doctor Rock, Chimney Rock—is essential to our religious beliefs, and serves as the very core of our cultural identity." Therefore, Peters says, "this area is our church: cannot be moved or disturbed in any way."[55]

The witnesses often compare the High Country to a church, perhaps because they assume (probably justifiably) that it would be easier for the court to understand the importance or centrality of the area to their religion through this analogy: the High Country is to Yurok, Karuk, and Tolowa religion what a church is to a Christian congregation. But this analogy is misleading, because, as legal scholar Marc DeGirolami points out, "destroying Saint Patrick's Cathedral, dreadful as that would be, would not destroy or even severely impair Roman Catholicism."[56] And while moving a church structure to the other side of a street to accommodate a development plan is not unheard of, the peaks in the Six Rivers National Forest cannot be moved; moreover, one cannot simply declare another part of the forest a new place of worship (thus allowing for the Chimney Rock area to be developed). The witnesses explain that the specific area is central to their religious practice because it was given to them by the Creator. "This is where we meet with the Great Spirit, that area, and that's why we all get a call to go there."[57]

Questions about the specific ways in which the area is being used by religious communities and individuals are being addressed through specific stories. This is another advantage of reading the testimony rather than the Theodoratus Report. The report was conducted in consultation with the local communities, but the consultants' explanation of their use of the High Country is generalized, supplemented by academic accounts, and thus loses the quality that I am looking for, of centering the concrete and the specific instead of generalizing and abstracting. Beyond Chris Peters's general explanation that the area has "been used throughout the years by Indian people who go there to pray for special purposes or special powers, or medicine"[58] and that "the High Country is used by Indian people who have dedicated years for special training and preparation,"[59] Jimmie James tells about his grandmother, who "lived to be about 110 years old . . . and has fought the spirits of the devil for our people, she's well known": "And then she goes back to Elk Valley and stays there quite a number of days to give thanks, and you might say give praise to the Creator. Then, from there, she is all going to different areas wherever she is called, wherever she is called, she goes, regardless of what kind of weather. She charges nothing, and whatever they give her, she smiled."[60]

James has also visited the area himself:

> I had a beautiful experience there. I went up there because I felt that my family had a friction against me, and I went up there and I come out of there with a pleased answer, and it was not long when one of my boys was in a car wreck in the canyon, 300 feet down the mountain, in the car. There was nothing left to it. And his head was split, his shoulder was busted up, two fractures in his back, a chunk of his arm was taken off, and when the doctor

saw him, he said he would live only three days. I finally took him to another doctor. He said, that is all, he would live three days. But we talked with the Great Spirit about it, and that has been in '68, and he is still alive. I wish I brought him with me today. That area means a lot to me.[61]

As Michael Pfeffer, former director of the California Indian Legal Services, who litigated the case, recalls: "With each successive witness, the packed courtroom could sense a shift in Judge Weigel's attitude. At the time of the trial, Judge Weigel must have been in his late 70s at the least, and he clearly connected with most of our witnesses, who were of like age."[62] Sam Jones, another elder, testified. Pfeffer describes his testimony:

> In his disarmingly simple, straightforward way, Sam described how his mother, a medicine woman, directed him to go to the Sacred High Country for protection and guidance before he was sent off to World War II. Despite being a machine gunner in some of the most intense battles of the war, Sam returned unscathed. Those of us in the courtroom that day remember Sam saying, "Well all I know is, it works. It's always worked for us and has always worked for our people and if you destroy the center of the universe, I don't know what will happen."[63]

These stories of the High Country highlight family relations, suggesting that what the nations are seeking to protect is more than their religious practice; it is their home, their past, and their future. This may be why the witnesses describe the High Country through its function and through its invasion rather than simply through its geographical features.

Jimmie James says he is familiar with the area "because [his] grandmother was a Pomo Indian Doctor, and she went through very much before she could get the power from the Great Creator":

> Here is Doctor Rock, and this is where they start out their dancing, and Elk Valley is where they come first to meditate, to clean themselves, clean their hearts, so that they can thank the Great Spirit, the Great Spirit will be pleased before they can even talk to him. . . . Then they go down to the Doctor Rock and do their dancing, and they don't get involved with other voices but the Great Spirit, and from there, they are told what to do before they begin or are granted the power.[64]

While James's description is oriented by dances and interaction with the Creator, Chris Peters provides two descriptions of the area—a physical one and a spiritual one:

First, let me describe it physically. The area has had many intrusions already. There has been a Jeep road, there has been trails put there by the U.S. Forest Service. That intrusion has been limited when compared to the proposed harvesting plan and G-O Road development. The area still maintains significant acres of quality roadless, pristine environment. Significant strands of old growth still exist there. There is animal life there that is not found in other places, and in an abundant form. It is a wilderness area as closely defined in terms of wilderness areas set aside in other areas throughout the country. It's as close to a natural setting as exists in today's society.[65]

This description brings together the quality of the area that is most important to the lawsuit—the wild, or pristine, condition of it—and the fact of its invasion by the settler state. The first thing Peters tells the court when he is asked to describe the High Country is that "the area has had many intrusions already." This part of the testimony is surprising. The other components of Peters's answer sound much more like a physical description of the area (there are trees and animal life; it is pristine), but the most important point Peters has to convey is that the area has suffered intrusions. He then continues to provide a spiritual description of the area:

The area, in terms of my conversations with older generations, the area has spiritual qualities. It is a sacred area. The area is a place where people can engage in an emotional interaction with a spiritual world. A translation to that in the English language may be likened to a prayer, but a lot more significant than a prayer. It is said that that area is not even a part of this world that we live in here. That that place up there, the High Country, belongs to the Spirit and it exists in another world apart from us.[66]

The Burden of Invasion

Because *Lyng* is a religious-freedom case, those who read it tend to focus on the religious practice of the Indigenous plaintiffs. But when we free ourselves from this legal framework and listen to the witnesses, we hear a story about a place, a home, "a spiritual world . . . that holds tribal people together."[67] Similarly, if we are not bound by the religious-freedom framework, we are free from searching for the "substantial burden" that the government's development plan imposes on the Yurok, Karuk, and Tolowa's exercise of religion, and we can hear what the witnesses describe as more than such a burden. What they talk about is invasion, contextualizing the "adverse effects" on religious practice within the colonial structure of which invasion is an integral part. Once we hear the story as one about colonial invasion, the government's arguments—that the High Country is one of many areas the nations hold as sacred[68] and that very few people actually use the area[69]—become insignificant.

The notion of desecration of the sacred High Country is highlighted by the following analogy: "Empty beer cans and used condoms are about as appropriate on Doctor Rock as they would be on the altar of a cathedral; traditional Indian religion places great emphasis on abstinence from physical pleasures while seeking spiritual energy."[70] The nations are concerned that with increased access to the High Country, there is increased possibility that the area will be improperly used. Indeed, journalist Sarah Neustadtl describes one of the medicine caves in the High Country as "a soot-blackened grotto littered with beer cans."[71] A Yurok woman expresses concern that her children or grandchildren might be called to be doctors and that there might not be a place for them to go when they are ready to receive power.

The Theodoratus Report dedicates a short chapter to "contemporary attitudes toward non-Indian incursions."[72] It discusses the anticipated impact of the G-O Road on the High Country and the rituals that Yurok, Karuk, and Tolowa people conduct there. This discussion is presented within a more general context of Native-white contact, which suggests that the researchers understand that the problem is larger than the immediate impact of the construction of the road on the ability to perform specific rituals in specific locales. Because the Yurok, Karuk, and Tolowa view the environment holistically (the report refers to their approach as an "environmental viewpoint"), the question of mitigation is also irrelevant here—no matter where the road is built, it would pose a substantial burden on the local religious practice:

> The mountains, rivers, wildlife, and ocean are viewed as a whole in which each part is related to each other part. Thus, a discussion of the religious use of the high country around Doctor Rock leads to consideration of the effect that a road there might have on the visual and aural properties of the area, then to the effects of logging on the environment, especially natural plant growth, then to the effects on the streams, silting of the river and finally to salmon fishing.[73]

This approach to the environment teaches us something about religion as well. "*The religious aspect is not a thing apart*, it is part of the whole."[74]

Consultants have felt that the Forest Service had declared a systematic war on sacred sites. In their description of the impact of the development plan, they explain that they believe that the road would lead to logging regardless of the specific route chosen and that because of the religious characteristics of the area, it must be treated as a whole rather than as consisting of distinguished individual sites:

> Many consultants stated that because of the religious characteristics of this area, nothing should be removed. It is believed that living things, especially trees and other plants, should not be removed from the high country unless it is done following the specified procedures of Indian culture. To do so is considered irreligious. It is also believed, and reinforced by tradition, that "improper" removal is likely to bring extremely bad luck or disease to the offender (whether he/she be a believer *or* a non-believer).[75]

This passage highlights that the Supreme Court's understanding of "substantial burden" on religious practice cannot capture the harm to the High Country that the nations anticipate if the development plan is executed. The practitioners in this case cannot—as they could have in *Yoder*[76] or in *Sherbert*—disobey and avoid "extremely bad luck" in the cost of a fine, imprisonment, or loss of unemployment benefits.[77] Because the trees themselves are considered living beings, their removal would be irreligious. But if the trees are living beings, part of the community, then their removal is an attack on the community, and it should be thought of as a continuation of the genocidal policy I address below. In other descriptions, we can read a story that seems more in line with the prohibition interpretation: the construction of the road would result in heavier traffic, which would have an adverse effect on the audiovisual conditions of the area (which, as we have seen, are themselves considered to be a "sacred site"), which in turn means that the religious ceremonies that take place in the area would not be effective, which would lead to more adverse effects. When this is the story, one might say that the government's development plan does not prohibit the nations from using the High Country for their rituals (even though there is some adverse impact on the rituals). But the interpretation according to which the logging itself is a desecration of the sacred area does not lend itself to the interpretation of burden as prohibition or coercion.

When the witnesses in trial are asked whether (and why) the High Country should remain undeveloped, they give several different answers. Jimmie James explains: "Let me put it this way: if we took a bulldozer and run it through the white man's church, it is like if they went in there and felled the trees, it would be like pulling the lumber and everything off of the walls, and then destroy their Bible—it is the same as that."[78] Chris Peters adds that the pristine nature of the area is its main religious characteristic, and this would be destroyed with development.[79] In reference to the difference between the existing jeep road and the new proposed section of the road, he explains:

> The road is a dirt road, and it connects, it goes through the area. The use of the area disturbs the quiet and the solitude of the area, though the road itself, as discussed earlier in previous hearings, may not have a direct adverse effect. The use of the road has a significant and destructive impact on the ability to engage or maintain engagement with the spiritual world. . . . The new road would provide significantly greater numbers of people using the area. It is also the basis of whether further development will occur. . . . You know, in Indian customs generally, a decision of this magnitude is not only made for the current generation but is made for six or seven generations to come. The management plan may produce some immediate jobs and stimulate some economies today, but it will have a destructing effect on generations to come . . . . Cultures are not dying, they are coming back stronger.[80]

Peters's story is much more in line with Justice O'Connor's interpretation, according to which the road in and of itself does not substantially burden the religious practice. It is the use of the road that would disrupt communication with the spiritual world. But when asked directly how the 6.02-mile proposed section of the road would burden the religious practice he has just described, Peters explains:

> The whole area, the High Country, as I've indicated, the belief was that it's there for Indian people to prepare themselves and then go up into and communicate with a spiritual world. What we're talking about here is what I refer to as spiritual trespass, that is when people on the far extreme of manifest destiny can say they can manage something better than the Creator, and this is the Creator's land, and to build a road to intrude directly through that spiritual land is spiritual trespass, and that is what the Forest Service has perpetrated.[81]

This was an unexpected response to the question about burden, which demonstrated how different the witness's view of the conflict is than the court's. For Peters, the construction of the road was unacceptable because it interferes with the Creator's plan for the area and its use. Judge Weigel did not accept such an answer, and even though he was generally very sympathetic to the witness, here he told him that his answer has not been responsive. The witness, who probably knew well that this is not an answer that the court can accept, immediately agreed and returned to the question of burden:

> The road development in the area, once it is completed, would bring with it a lot of damage and more destruction. The road itself represents something down here in this world, asphalt for one, signs for another, and that intrusion in the area is significant. The dirt road intrusion has not been as significant as to what it would bring with it in terms of the new road, which is the asphalt.[82]

Again, the judge did not understand what the problem is with asphalt. The witness illustrated this point with a story: "Last night a woman . . . prayed for us, and to do that effectively, she had to take off everything that was a white man's stuff, jewelry and things like that, to engage the powers that she has. In the same respect here, you are bringing into a spiritual area something that is foreign to that area, and it is an intrusion."[83] This answer helpfully ties together religious burden with colonial invasion. The road does not belong in the High Country because white settlers do not belong in the High Country. It is the Yurok, Karuk, and Tolowa home that the government proposes to invade, and it is only in this context that we can fully understand the G-O Road case.

To fully understand the *Lyng* decision, we will need to go back to Chief Justice John Marshall's decision in *Johnson v. M'Intosh*, and I will dive into it in the next chapter. For the purposes of this chapter, I'll just say that the *Johnson* decision recognized that Native Americans had a right of occupancy, meaning that while it took away from them absolute title to the lands they inhabited at the time of contact, it did leave them with some property rights, albeit limited ones. What is important to me is that in granting Native Americans this occupancy right, Marshall acknowledged that these lands are their homes. And just like when I rent an apartment, my landlord's property rights are limited (to some extent) by the rights I hold as a tenant, as the person who treats the apartment as her home rather than a source of income, so Marshall recognized that Native title must limit the property rights (stemming from discovery) that the US government had to these lands.

The nineteenth-century Marshall Court—in addition to creating Native title—also sought to "domesticate" Native American nations, referring to them as "domestic dependent nations." When I talk about this domestication, I mean, following Niimiipuu scholar Beth Piatote, three things: (1) the discourse of domesticating or civilizing the "savage Indian" ("kill the Indian and save the man"[84]), which called for implementing policies that, despite their rhetoric of humanization, violated the dignity of Native Americans, infantilized them, and destructed their communities; (2) the attack on Indigenous sovereignty through the domestic sphere (including the practice of out-adoption, the forced removal of Indigenous children from their families to attend government-funded boarding schools, and the allotment of reservation land in severalty); and (3) the legal definition of Native Americans as "domestic dependent nations" in the Supreme Court in the nineteenth century.[85]

In *Cherokee Nation v. Georgia* (1831), the US Supreme Court recognized that the nationhood of Indigenous peoples was limited primarily by US military conquest. It defined the Native American political organization as "domestic dependent nations" and their members as "ward[s]" of the nation, existing in "a state of pupilage." According to the Supreme Court, "Their relation to the United States resembles that of a ward to his guardian. They look to our government for protection; rely upon its kindness and its power; appeal to it for relief to their wants; and address the [p]resident as their great father."[86] Piatote writes that "assimilation-era policies ... were driven by the notion that the tribal-national polity, as a competing national sovereignty, must be destroyed. And the way to break up the tribe was to break up the Indian family and to cultivate children's allegiance to the United States rather than to the tribe."[87]

The discourse of domesticity appears here as a special tool for domination, but as Pawnee attorney and legal scholar Walter Echo-Hawk writes, the status of "domestic dependent nations" also established the trust responsibility of the United States toward Indigenous nations:

> The protectorate relationship assumed by the US government under the *Worcester* doctrine ought to *require* the government to protect those places as the guardian of domestic dependent Indian nations. Because the culture, religion, and very identity of Indian tribes is often dependent upon worship at tribal holy places—as seen in the Yurok World Renewal Religion—the protectorate principle of federal Indian law should impose an affirmative

and enforceable obligation to protect those places from harm, as an integral part of the trust responsibility necessary to the well-being of the domestic dependent Indian nations.[88]

While the discourse of domestication was meant to support dominion over Indigenous peoples, the domestic can also provide a site of resistance. Piatote shows "the resilience of the tribal-national domestic by centering the intimate domestic (the Indian home and family) as the primary site of struggle against the foreign force of U.S. national domestication."[89] At this point, I bring religion back into the story.

Revitalization

The federal government began regulating Native religiosity during the era of the government's domestication policy—when the United States stopped signing treaties with Indigenous nations, treating them as foreign, sovereign nations, and started making policies for them, treating them as wards of the federal government. Together with limiting the movement of Indigenous peoples and invading every aspect of their domestic life, this policy also made religion an object of regulation. "Policies about religion were at the core of this invasion," Susan Staiger Gooding writes.[90] In the second half of the nineteenth century, all recognized Indigenous nations were assigned one of the thirteen recognized Christian denominations, and Christian boarding schools were institutionalized on a national scale. But these policies, Gooding argues, were the result of a concern not with Native Americans' belief but with their ceremonial practices. In 1883, Courts of Indian Offences were founded on all reservations to enforce the prohibition on traditional practices referred to as "the old heathenish dances, such as the sun-dance, scalp-dance, etc."[91] The prohibited practices suggest that the policy was aimed at eliminating the social and political communities created and maintained through them rather than at any religious belief.[92] I discuss this criminalization of Native ceremony in chapter 3.

Yurok attorney Amy Cordalis and legal scholar Kristen Carpenter (of Cherokee descent) provide context for the G-O Road case that invokes domestication. As part of the assimilation policy of the early twentieth century, Indigenous religion was outlawed and referred to as "the devil's religion." As a result, many Indigenous peoples stopped performing certain rituals or were forced to go underground. In the face of racism and discrimination, many Native individuals tried hard to conceal their "Indianness," undergoing a kind of identity crisis. The worst identity crisis was experienced by the generation of Native Americans sent to boarding schools run by the Bureau of Indian Affairs (BIA)—the most devastating manifestation of the assimilation policy. Native children from the Lower Klamath River (including Yurok, Karuk, and Hupa children) were sent to residential schools in Northern Oregon. According to Cordalis and Carpenter:

> These children left the Reservation speaking tribal languages, believing in their cultural covenants, and practicing the religion—only to be beaten and punished for exactly these traditional practices by boarding school teachers and administrators. These students became the first generation of Indian people from the Klamath River not to live in their aboriginal territory or participate in annual tribal religious ceremonies.[93]

One of the witnesses in the G-O Road trial, Earl Joseph Aubrey, Jr., a thirty-four-year-old Karuk timber faller, mentioned his schooling offhandedly in his testimony. When asked to describe his early training in the Karuk tradition, he responded:

> It started when I was about—well, when I was real young, but when I was twelve years old, it took affect [sic], I was shipped away to Chemaw Indian School for about seven years.
>
> Q. Could you tell us where that school is located?
>
> A. It's about one mile south of Salem, Oregon.
>
> Q. Is it a BIA school?
>
> A. It's a BIA school. I was shipped away for seven years, but in summer days I was let to come home for two months out of the year, and I was chosen by our grandmother, who was the carrier for Daisy Jacobs, who was our medicine lady at the time.[94]

Aubrey's story is unique in that he maintained his connection to the High Country, to medicine-making, and to dancing (albeit partially) throughout his years in boarding school. His testimony is therefore useful for a religious-freedom case that requires proving the continuity of the religious practice in the area (which, of course, erases the colonial effects of domestication policies on Indigenous identity in general and on Indigenous religious practice in particular). Aubrey's story nevertheless alludes to this policy, even when what he needs to prove is continuity rather than change. As Lakota historian Nick Estes writes, while the asserted purpose of BIA boarding schools was "civilization" or "domestication," "boarding schools served to provide access to Native lands, by breaking up Native families and holding children hostage so their nations would cede more territory."[95] Therefore, having Aubrey's story told in a settler court and becoming part of the public record is important, and I see it as a form of resistance through storytelling—of speaking truth to power, if you will.

When Aubrey's generation returned from boarding schools to the reservation, they found extreme poverty, no job opportunities, and alienation from their traditional ways of life. "Yet, even at this low point," observe Cordalis and Carpenter,

> hope was on the horizon—the civil rights era of the 1960s was headed to the Klamath River. The generation raised pre-contact was still alive. Although they were weary to "be Indian," they still knew their traditions. Children born in the 1940s and later were not sent away to boarding schools and in fact, they had been exposed to a better education in local public schools. Some of them had made it to college, graduated, and headed home.[96]

Their experiences at the university had politicized them, having exposed them to Indigenous activism at Alcatraz and Wounded Knee. They were eager to reassert their Indigenous identity and to engage their elders in a political movement. Nonprofit organizations in Northwest California, funded by the US government as part of its "war on poverty," [NICPA] were involved in organizing local Natives. "Remarkably," write Cordalis and Carpenter, "within a few years the people began to dance again."[97] Medicine women returned to the High Country. "These events were significant to revitalizing the tribal religion and many of the participants would later become plaintiffs in the *Lyng* litigation."[98]

In the G-O Road trial, when Judge Weigel asks witness Chris Peters about the impact that the development plan in the High Country might have on the revitalization of Yurok and Karuk ceremonies, Peters explains that the High Country is "where we get personal power that reaffirms our Indianness and our way of life. To disrupt it and to destroy it, as the Forest Service is proposing to do, would definitely have an impact on the regeneration of Indian people. Currently it would totally destroy any hope of our grandchildren from knowing what that area has for them."[99]

Conclusion

Peters's testimony begins to clarify that what the G-O Road plaintiffs are interested in protecting is their identity and their way of life. But if we pay attention to what the witnesses tell the court, we can see that what they mean by protection is revitalization rather than preservation—as preservation assumes continuation, which is what the framework of religious freedom requires them to prove (and recall here Goeman and Baldy's methods of (re)mapping and (re)writing).

An important component of this revitalization is access to knowledge about the tradition, the dances, and the centrality of the High Country to the livelihood of the Yurok, Karuk, and Tolowa nations. But relying on white anthropologists for recounting this knowledge—as both the Forest Service and the court did—is just another aspect of the colonial structure revealed in the witnesses' storytelling.[100] As Peters told Thomas Buckley when Buckley started his ethnographic work with the Yuroks, a few years before the commission of the Theodoratus Report: "We want to do our own anthropology now. We may not do it as well as white people from the universities, but we'll do it as well as we can."[101] For justice to be restored through the revitalization of Indigenous ceremony, the sacred area, just like the ethnographic knowledge, needs to be unsettled. Judge Weigel's exchange with Lowanna Brantner at the end of her testimony suggests that he understood this point:

> We [are] the people from Bluff Creek, which is no more now—that's where we had our Boat Dance or our White Deerskin Dance. Unbeknownst, unknown to me and my people, we didn't know that the BIA, even though we had a treaty which we didn't know later that it was not ratified—we gave all we had promised, way beyond the mountains for them and for the land that we were to have in there, to keep our homes. In that way we lost everything and now we are standing on the last peak, Doctor Rock, Chimney Rock. My neighbors have lost a lot of their ceremonial grounds due to mismanagement of the people, not because they were cruel, but because they didn't understand.
>
> The court: Not because they were what?
>
> The witness: They are not cruel.
>
> The court: Cruel?
>
> The witness: Or unkind. They just did not understand.

The court: Who was it that didn't understand?

The witness: The new people that came into the Indian country.

The court: By the "new people," who do you mean?

The witness: The white people.

The court: The white people? Well, you are generous in saying they aren't cruel.[102]

The judge was clearly affected by Brantner's testimony, and as she left the stand, he summarized it, to make sure he understood what she wanted to convey, promising her that she has been very helpful: "You see, the one thing that I got from your testimony very clearly is that . . . due to the deprivations occasioned by the whites, such as the pollution of the streams and the like, and the taking over of more and more land, that the preservation of this particular piece of sacred land has become all the more important."[103] Weigel understands, then, that to understand Indigenous sacred sites, he needs to remember the colonial invasion of Indigenous homelands.

Michael Pfeffer describes a moment in trial that is not reported in the trial records. According to Pfeffer, Brantner asked Judge Weigel to close his eyes and accompany her to the High Country. "The room was deathly still as Judge Weigel and Lowana Brantner embarked on their journey. As the clock ticked on and seconds became minutes, the silence deepened even further and the only sound was the occasional muted cough. Finally, Lowana opened her eyes and commanded Judge Weigel to return. She turned to him and said, 'Now do you know what we mean?' His response was simply, 'Yes, I do.'"[104]

But it is not the understanding of the judge in a settler court that can meaningfully restore justice and autonomy to Brantner or to her people. Because the attack on Indigenous lifeways and well-being was done through an attack on the domestic, the tool for restoration must come from there. As Yurok member Lawrence "Tiger" O'Rourke told legal scholars Ellen Alderman and Caroline Kennedy: "They might as well rewrite the Constitution. They teach us we have freedom of religion and freedom of speech, but it's not true . . . . This was our place first time, our home. It's still our home, but we don't have the same rights as other Americans."[105] The witnesses in the G-O Road trial talked about protecting their home, but the colonial domestic discourse never saw the Indigenous home as something worth protecting or preserving. Rather, it has been another front through which to control, assimilate, and dispossess Indigenous peoples.

Pfeffer describes the affect in the courtroom after Brantner's testimony: "For all intents and purposes, we had won! The courtroom, including the Judge and all his clerks, erupted into pandemonium—applause, cheers, crying and laughter. Judge Weigel, a most careful preserver of decorum, let the celebration go on for some time as he and Lowana smiled at each other. Those of us that were there that day will never forget it."[106] Judge Weigel indeed decided the case in favor of the Yurok, Karuk, and Tolowa nations—in favor of the High Country, their home. The road interfered with the religious practice of the Indigenous nations, and the national need for timber was not enough to justify such interference. "Audrey Jones had arranged a picnic supper for the victory celebration at the community hall beside the Klamath, and people brought salmon and venison and bowl after bowl of potato salad," describes journalist Sara Neustadtl.[107] "Lowana was asked for her story again and again, and to everyone she explained, 'It was the doctoring. The Indian doctoring.'"[108] Again, we see how stories of the Indigenous home are not separate from Indigenous medicine and how they can become not only Indigenous law but settler law as well.

What the celebrating community didn't know at the time is that five years later, the US Supreme Court would deliver a devastating decision, reversing the district court and the court of appeals' decision to protect the High Country from development. It is to this devastating decision that we now turn.

2

———•••———

LAND AS PROPERTY IN THE
LYNG DECISION

While the Indigenous witnesses in the G-O Road trial tell stories about land as home, Justice Sandra Day O'Connor, in her majority opinion in *Lyng*, tells a story about land as property, and the story she tells is not new. If what the witnesses asked the court to protect was their home, the lands in which they are residents, then O'Connor is here to remind them that they have a landlord and that this landlord has rights. If the Cherokee cases told a story of Indigenous peoples as "wards of the nation" and of the federal government as their "great father," here Indigenous peoples are represented as tenants and the federal government as their landlord. How did we come to this?

Legal scholar Carol M. Rose argues that when political and legal philosophers present their theories of property, they often turn from scientific, abstract, synchronic rhetoric to storytelling.[1] This includes John Locke's famous chapter on property in his *Second Treatise of Government* and William Blackstone, a century later, in his *Commentaries on the Laws of England*.[2] Both of them tell "pseudo-histor[ies]" of "property as an institution with an origin and evolution."[3] Not only theorists but also US Supreme Court justices participate in this tradition, of telling stories about property. Geographer Nicholas Blomley argues that sociolegal scholars need to think not only about the history of property but also about its geography.[4] We may say the same about Supreme Court justices. While in *Lyng* O'Connor ostensibly tells a story about religious freedom, one could argue that the real story she is telling is about property. Indeed, scholars such as Vine Deloria, Jr., (Lakota), Brian Edward Brown, and Chris Jocks (Kahnawà:ke Mohawk) observe that legal decisions about Indigenous sacred sites are "built on a keen understanding and appreciation for the civilizing effects of property."[5] Even Justice Brennan in his dissenting opinion in *Lyng* makes this observation:

> The Court does not for a moment suggest that the interests served by the G-O road are in any way compelling, or that they outweigh the destructive effect construction of the road will have on respondents' religious practices. Instead, the Court embraces the Government's contention that *its preroga-tive as landowner should always take precedence over a claim that a particular use of federal property infringes religious practices.* Attempting to justify this rule, the Court argues that the First Amendment bars only outright pro-hibitions, indirect coercion, and penalties on the free exercise of religion. All other "incidental effects of government programs," it concludes, even those "which may make it more difficult to practice certain religions but which have no tendency to coerce individuals into acting contrary to their religious beliefs," simply do not give rise to constitutional concerns.[6]

In this chapter, I offer a reading of O'Connor's "cruelly surreal"[7] majority opinion and propose that if it is indeed an understanding of land as prop-erty that drives this decision, then it should be read against the background of cases such as *Johnson v. M'Intosh* (1823)[8] rather than religious freedom precedent such as *Sherbert v. Verner*,[9] *Wisconsin v. Yoder*,[10] and *Bowen v. Roy*.[11]

Justice O'Connor's Majority Opinion

In *Lyng*, according to Brian E. Brown, the Supreme Court "forfeit[ed] its role as guardian of religious liberty by unworthily becoming the advocate of governmental proprietorship over land."[12] O'Connor, joined by Justices William Rehnquist, Byron White, John Paul Stevens, and Antonin Sca-lia,[13] acknowledged in her opinion that "it is undisputed that the Indian re-spondents' beliefs are sincere and that the Government's proposed actions will have severe adverse effects on the practice of their religion."[14] Never-theless, she disagrees with the respondents that the burden is heavy enough to violate the respondents' First Amendment free exercise right, unless the government can show a compelling interest in completing the road or exe-cuting the timber-harvesting plan. Her disagreement relies mostly on the court's previous decision in *Bowen v. Roy* (1986), where it was decided that:

> The Free Exercise Clause simply cannot be understood to require the Gov-ernment to conduct its own internal affairs in ways that comport with the religious beliefs of particular citizens. Just as the Government may not insist that [the Roys] engage in any set form of religious observance, so [the Roys] may not demand that the Government join in their chosen religious prac-tices by refraining from using a number to identify their daughter.... The Free Exercise Clause affords an individual protection from certain forms of governmental compulsion; it does not afford an individual a right to dictate the conduct of the Government's internal procedures.[15]

In *Roy*, the court rejected an Abenaki couple's suit to prevent the use of a Social Security number to process welfare benefits for their daughter. The Roys claimed that use of the number would rob their daughter of her spirit and prevent her from attaining greater spiritual power. According to O'Connor, "the building of a road or the harvesting of timber on publicly owned land cannot meaningfully be distinguished from the use of a Social Security number in *Roy*."[16] In both cases, she explains, government actions would interfere with a private person's ability to practice his or her religion. Nevertheless, in neither case does the government coerce any individual to act in violation of his or her religious beliefs. Similarly, in neither case does the government penalize a religious practice or belief. Therefore, in neither case is there a violation of the First Amendment's Free Exercise Clause.

O'Connor is able to equate the two cases because she understands the burdened practice or belief as personal or private. It seems, therefore, that challenging this understanding of religion as a private matter (as I do in chapter 3) would be useful in distinguishing between the cases. But none of the respondents in the case challenged this conception of religion as private. Instead, respondents focused on other aspects of the two cases. As O'Connor describes: "We are asked to distinguish this case from *Roy* on the ground that the infringement on religious liberty here is 'significantly greater,' or on the ground that the government practice in *Roy* was 'purely mechanical' whereas this case involves 'a case-by-case substantive determi-nation as to how a particular unit of land will be managed.'"[17] I argue that these are not the meaningful differences between *Roy* and *Lyng*. While in

Roy it is the spiritual development of an individual that government actions allegedly infringe upon, in *Lyng* it is a community's well-being that is violated when the Forest Service threatens to destroy its homeland. This might mean that the case is not really about religious freedom at all, at least as far as religion is understood as a private matter.

The State of California argued that *Roy* should be distinguished from *Lyng* because in *Roy* the government's actions took place in a remote location, the Roys did not have any real knowledge about them, and therefore the notion that the government's actions created a burden on the Roys' religious practice was merely subjective. In *Lyng*, on the other hand, the government's actions "physically destroy the environmental conditions and the privacy without which the [religious] practices cannot be conducted."[18] O'Connor rejects this reasoning. Any attempt to distinguish between the cases, she explains, would require the court to determine the truth of the underlying beliefs that led to objections to the government's actions, and this task is simply impossible to accomplish. Note that it is not the *sincerity* of the belief that matters according to O'Connor but the objective truth of the belief. This is an implausible interpretation of the Free Exercise Clause, one that renders all free exercise cases impossible to decide, unless we assume that Supreme Court justices are theologians with unique access to knowledge about the truth or falsehood of all religious beliefs (and O'Connor has already told us that this is not the case, that she is unable to determine the truth of Indigenous religious beliefs).[19]

Because the court cannot determine the truth of the religious belief underlying the Roys' objection to the Social Security system, it cannot evaluate the burden resulting from government actions. Nevertheless, O'Connor tells us, "respondents [in *Lyng*] insist . . . that the courts below properly relied on a factual inquiry into the degree to which the Indians' spiritual practices would become ineffectual if the G-O road were built."[20] O'Connor portrays the Free Exercise Clause as protecting not sincere religious belief or practice but outcome. Because she cannot know what would happen to the efficacy of the religious practice in question, she cannot offer it protection. But what the Yurok, Karuk, and Tolowa respondents argue here is that the practice of their religion itself would be burdened, not its efficacy. Indeed, they would be unable to practice their religion if the road is built (rather than arguing that they can continue the practice but it would not be as effective). Separating the practice from its anticipated results seems to misunderstand religion altogether.[21]

O'Connor's distinction between *Sherbert* and *Lyng* is unconvincing as well. While she agrees that the court "has repeatedly held that indirect coercion or penalties on the free exercise of religion, not just outright prohibitions, are subject to scrutiny under the First Amendment," she nevertheless determines that this does not mean that "incidental effects of government programs, which may make it more difficult to practice certain religions but which have no tendency to coerce individuals into acting contrary to their religious beliefs, require government to bring forward a compelling justification for its otherwise lawful actions."[22] The "hair-splitting"[23] differentiation relies on an understanding of the word "prohibit": "For the Free Exercise Clause is written in terms of what the government cannot do to the individual, not in terms of what the individual can exact from the government."[24] And what the individual—indeed, the Indigenous individual—might want to exact from the government are property rights, but those would be limited to Native title, or right of occupancy, as I discuss in the next section.

Does O'Connor mean that in *Sherbert* the government's refusal to pay unemployment benefits to Adell Sherbert, who lost her job because she refused to work on her Sabbath, amounted to a prohibition of religious practice while the construction of the G-O road did not? In any case, deciding free exercise cases cannot rely on the spiritual development of the religious objector to the government's actions, according to O'Connor.[25] O'Connor implies that free exercise does not equal spiritual development, and I agree. But the *Lyng* case is not about "personal spiritual development"[26] either, as we learn from the testimony and evidence in the trial.

"The Government does not dispute," O'Connor declares, "and we have no reason to doubt, that the logging and road-building projects at issue in this case could have devastating effects on traditional Indian religious practices."[27] This acknowledgment seems encouraging at first, but O'Connor explains the use of the High Country thus:

Individual practitioners use this area for personal spiritual development; some of their activities are believed to be critically important in advancing the welfare of the tribe, and indeed, of mankind itself. The Indians use this area, as they have used it for a very long time, to conduct a wide variety of specific rituals that aim to accomplish their religious goals. According to their beliefs, the rituals would not be efficacious if conducted at other sites than the ones traditionally used, and too much disturbance of the area's natural state would clearly render any meaningful continuation of traditional practices impossible.[28]

This explanation of the practice allows O'Connor to determine that it does not deserve First Amendment protection, despite the acknowledgment of the G-O Road's devastating effects on it. First, it is individuals rather than communities, or nations, who use the High Country for personal spiritual development, and O'Connor has already determined that personal spiritual development does not equal exercise of religion. Second, those practitioners believe that their rituals advance the well-being of the community and of the whole world. Unfortunately, the court cannot determine the truth of the claim that those rituals would not be effective if performed in other places. This focus on efficacy prevents the court from asking why it is important to the practitioners to practice their religion specifically in the High Country regardless of results. This question, I argue, calls for contextualizing the case more broadly, which in turn allows for an understanding of this case as one that is about more than free exercise. It seems more appropriate to argue that performing the same actions in other sites would render these actions not less effective but not religious: it is practicing them in the High Country that makes them religious. O'Connor has an answer to this argument as well.

"Even if we assume that we should accept the Ninth Circuit's prediction, according to which the G-O road will 'virtually destroy the Indians' ability to practice their religion,'"[29] O'Connor continues, the court cannot decide the case in favor of the respondents, because "government simply could not operate if it were required to satisfy every citizen's religious needs and desires."[30] The reasoning unfolds as a "slippery slope" argument, according to which many people would surely find some government action offensive, and some of these people would base their objection on sincerely held beliefs. Moreover, some people would find the opposite action offensive, and their objection may also rely on sincerely held beliefs. Because the constitution must apply equally to all citizens, no one can be given a veto over a public program that does not prohibit the free exercise of religion. And even though the respondents are not objecting to the current use of the area by tourists and other Native Americans (they only object to the development plan), "nothing in the principle for which they contend, ... would distinguish this case from another lawsuit in which they (or similarly situated religious objectors) might seek to exclude all human activity but their own from sacred areas of the public lands."[31] This analysis makes "ceremonies and rituals performed for thousands of years" sound like "personal fads or matters of modern, emotional, personal preference."[32] It assumes that religious belief and religious practice can be separated, as I discuss in the next chapter. O'Connor therefore understands the court's task as balancing between different citizens' demands on the government and holds that this task should be carried by the legislatures and other institutions.[33]

O'Connor moves on to briefly describe the religious practice as it is explained in the respondents' brief, and then reveals what seems to be the real reason behind her ruling: "No disrespect for these practices is implied when one notes that such beliefs could easily require *de facto beneficial ownership of some rather spacious tracts of public property.*"[34] The case turns, at this point, into one about land ownership rather than religion, even if the two issues are conflated in O'Connor's words:

> The Constitution does not permit government to discriminate against religions that treat particular physical sites as sacred, and a law forbidding the Indian respondents from visiting the Chimney Rock area would raise a different set of constitutional questions. Whatever rights the Indians may have to the use of the area, however, those rights do not divest the Government of its right to use what is, after all, *its* land.... Nothing in our opinion should be read to encourage governmental insensitivity to the religious needs of any citizen. The Government's rights to the use of its own land, for example, need not and should not discourage it from accommodating religious practices like those engaged in by the Indian respondents.[35]

O'Connor adds that the government has done everything that could be expected from it to minimize the impact that construction of the G-O road would have on the respondents' religious practice. She counts the commission of the Theodoratus Report, the steps taken to minimize audible and visual intrusions, and the selection of a route that avoids specific ritual sites (pointing this out suggests a misunderstanding of the sacred nature of the High Country, since it is the integrity of the area, rather than specific sites within it, that respondents ask to protect). These steps, O'Connor adds, are in line with the 1978 American Indian Religious Freedom Act (AIRFA), according to which, "It shall be the policy of the United States to protect and preserve for American Indians their inherent right of freedom to believe, express, and exercise the traditional religions of the American

Indian ... including but not limited to access to sites, use and possession of sacred objects, and the freedom to worship through ceremonials and traditional rites."[36]

A second section of AIRFA required an evaluation of federal policies and procedures in consultation with Native religious leaders, of changes necessary to protect and preserve the rights and practices in question. The Theodoratus Report satisfies this requirement. "Nowhere in the law is there so much as a hint of any intent to create a cause of action or any judicially enforceable individual rights."[37] O'Connor ends her discussion of AIRFA with a quote from the sponsor of the statute, Representative Udall, who defined it as "a sense of Congress joint resolution" that in fact "has no teeth in it."[38] What O'Connor, but also Brennan and the Theodoratus Report, does not ask is why this law has no teeth. Why bother make a law that is not meant to be enforced? If they had asked these questions, they may have discovered the role that the Forest Service, with the G-O Road in mind, played in rendering this act as toothless. I discuss this point further in chapter 3.

What the High Country Has to Do with Property

This is not O'Connor's only omission. She begins her story about the G-O Road case in 1977, when "the Forest Service issued a draft environmental impact statement that discussed proposals for upgrading an existing un-paved road that runs through the Chimney Rock area."[39] But this point of entry is arbitrary. What if we start at a different point in time? If *Lyng* is a case about property, we need not only read it against a different set of legal precedent than O'Connor has, but we also need to start it at a different point in time. We need to find out how Chimney Rock and Blue Creek became property of the federal government. We need to tell a story about dispossession, and especially of the eighteen unratified treaties between the United States and California tribes, to which witness Lowanna Brantner alludes in the G-O Road trial. Between 1851 and 1852, the United States ne-gotiated with hundreds of California Indians and signed eighteen treaties whose purpose was the peaceful transfer of lands from California tribes to the United States. The treaties set aside almost 7.5 million acres of land (7.5 percent of the State of California) for the different tribes to occupy. But settlers protested against these agreements, and Congress gave in and never ratified the treaties. Many Native peoples in Northern California, who had not been notified that the treaties were null and void, started living in the designated lands, only to be removed and relocated. "The result of the unratified treaties of California would continue to wreak havoc on Native tribes for hundreds of years."[40]

But the story about dispossession has not only a history but also a geography, and Blomley, following geographer Edward Soja, does not want us to let "an already-made geography set the stage."[41] The already-made geography that sets the stage for O'Connor's story of the G-O Road case is this:

> As part of a project to create a paved 75-mile road linking two California towns, Gasquet and Orleans, the United States Forest Service has upgraded 49 miles of previously unpaved roads on federal land. In order to complete this project (the G-O road), the Forest Service must build a 6-mile paved segment through the Chimney Rock section of the Six Rivers National Forest. That section of the forest is situated between two other portions of the road that are already complete.[42]

And describing Chimney Rock as a part of the Six Rivers National Forest that lies between two segments of a road, standing in the way of its completion, conceals the story about dispossession that can be told about this place. Shouldn't O'Connor ask, for example, what this place was before the Six Rivers National Forest was established in 1947? Shouldn't she ask to whom it belonged before it was government property, and how the government acquired it? In other words, shouldn't O'Connor ask about dispossession?

Environmental scholars Lynn Huntsinger and Sarah McCaffrey tell the story of the replacement of Yurok forest management regimes with Euro-American "science-based" forestry programs and its role in the loss of Yurok ownership of and access to their homelands. "The coming of Euro-Americans to the Klamath region dramatically changed the use, management, and ultimately the landscape of the Yurok forest," they write.[43] The government divested the Yuroks of their forest resources both by expropriation of their lands—ignoring their property rights and cutting off their access to gathering sites—and by managing the forest in a way that changed it ecologically. "Vegetation management and Yurok culture and economy were closely linked. The increasing unsuitability of the changed forest for Yurok subsistence helped push the Yurok to sell their land."[44]

During the Gold Rush, the government established reservations in the region to separate local Indigenous peoples from miners and settlers. But the reservations also separated the Yurok, Karuk, and Tolowa peoples from the High Country. In 1855, an Executive Order by President Franklin Pierce set aside one mile on either side of the lower twenty miles of the Klamath River as the Klamath River Indian Reservation. In 1864, the Hoopa Valley Reservation was established upriver, and, in 1891, by Executive Order of President Benjamin Harrison, the twenty-mile stretch between the two reservations was incorporated into one reservation that extended from the Hoopa Valley for one mile on either side of the Klamath river to the sea. This stretch of some fifty-six thousand acres became known as the Hoopa Valley Reservation Extension.[45]

With the passage of the 1887 Allotment Act, settlers pressured congress to open up timber-rich Klamath reservation lands to individual purchase. "About fifteen thousand of the twenty-five thousand acres of the original Klamath River Reservation were returned to the public domain and sold or homesteaded after the 161 Indian residents of the reservation received allotments averaging sixty acres in 1893."[46] Presidential proclamation established, in 1905, US Forest Reserves on Yurok, Karuk, and Tolowa Indigenous lands that later became the Six Rivers National Forest. The reservation superintendent noted in 1918 that "for some reason the land that was sold [to whites, after being returned to the public domain] contained practically all of the valuable timber and the land that was allotted to the Indians was what was left over."[47] As allottees were encouraged to move onto their own parcels, they abandoned their villages and lost access to their sacred sites. Kari Marie Norgaard and William Tripp (Karuk), authors of the Karuk Climate Adaptation Plan, refer to the results of the separation of the Karuk people from their lands as a loss of "knowledge sovereignty."[48]

Once the Forest Service was established in 1905, and the Bureau of Indian Affairs' Division of Forestry was created in 1910, even lands that were still considered Yurok lands were to be managed according to professional forestry practices of "science-based management." Professional forestry emphasized the protection of forests from fire. "Fire suppression was perhaps the first major form of ecological control exerted by professional foresters on Yurok lands, and it had the added benefit of expanding the domain of forest managers by expanding the acreage of forest."[49] Norgaard and Tripp write about reestablishing a traditional fire regime as part of the Karuk people's response to climate change as well as restoring Karuk sovereignty.[50] According to historian Netta Cohen, afforestation, justified "scientifically," was a means to appropriate Indigenous land in other colonial contexts as well, such as British and Zionist dispossession of Palestinian land.[51] What we see in this history of the Yurok and Karuk forest is that property and sovereignty are tightly related and that both are required to grant Indigenous peoples control over their lands.

Political theorist Robert Nichols argues that if we want to undo the conception of land as property (or commodity, or resource), using the idea of dispossession seems to be unhelpful—"contradictory and self-defeating"—because it claims Indigenous prior possession of the land. In settler states, Nichols writes, "Indigenous peoples have often been accused of putting forward a contradictory set of claims, namely, that they are the original and natural owners of the land that has been stolen from them, *and* that the earth is not something in which any one person or group of people can have exclusive proprietary rights."[52] Nichols explains that dispossession follows a recursive logic: it is dispossession that *constitutes* land as property. Blomley makes a similar point about the ambivalence of property, suggesting (in the context of resistance to gentrification in Vancouver, British Columbia) that "claims about property figure both negatively and positively; that is, the characterization of dominant forms of property as oppressive relies on a positive claim to community entitlements."[53]

The argument of this book—that land can be simultaneously understood as property and as other things that ostensibly contradict the idea of land as property—responds to this problematic. If we do away with the binary logic of rights, we would be able to see land as property, as home, as sacred wilderness, and as kin; we would be able to say without contradiction that the earth is not something that should be owned by a group of people, yet it has been stolen from Indigenous peoples; that dominant forms of property are oppressive, yet communities are entitled to their neighborhoods. We would be able to make sense of, to *celebrate*, the Yurok's recent purchase of more than fifty thousand acres of ancestral lands, including portions of the Blue Creek watershed, which flows from the High Country. "Like many sacred sites to the Yurok," explain Native American studies scholars Beth Rose Middleton Manning and Kaitlin Reed (Yurok), "this area fell outside of the boundaries of the reservation that the federal government had demarcated for the Tribe, and thus until the recent reacquisition of these lands ... the area remained outside of Yurok jurisdiction." Manning and Reed cite former Yurok Tribal Chairman Thomas O'Rourke, who explained, "The Blue Creek watershed is not only a significant salmon stronghold, it contains the path to our spiritual center, a sacred place where our medicine makers have travelled since time immemorial to bring the world back into balance."[54]

O'Connor's story about land as property makes it seem as if it is the federal government whose property rights need to be protected against the Yurok, Karuk, and Tolowa people, who are trying to take the land away from it (requesting de facto beneficial ownership of the High Country). To challenge this story, I am reading *Lyng* against a different set of legal precedent than the one O'Connor engages with, including *Sherbert* and *Roy*. I am especially interested in *Johnson v. M'Intosh* (1923), because O'Connor's words—"whatever rights the Indians may have to the use of the area . . . those rights do not divest the Government of its right to use what is, after all, *its* land"—echo Chief Justice John Marshall's creation of "occupancy rights" in *Johnson*. Marshall created this new, limited property right for Indigenous peoples whose lands were "discovered" by sovereign European nations, who were entitled to acquire those lands by purchase or conquest but had to allow Native peoples to use the lands as long as they inhabited them. O'Connor, like Marshall before her, does not take away the Indigenous nations' right to use the land; both subject this right to that of another sovereign nation (in both cases it is the United States), thus relativizing the sovereignty of Indigenous nations. Religious studies scholar Kathleen Sands explains that "*Johnson v. M'Intosh* was the first case in which the mythic role of Native Americans was judicially fixed." The question at its center was whether the tribes themselves could conduct the sale of Indigenous lands or whether only the federal government could broker such sales. The sales in question had taken place before the American Revolution and therefore were subject to British law. According to the British Proclamation of 1763, Native Americans could sell their lands directly only to the government, not to private parties. "In this sense, it was unnecessary to reach the question of whether the Indians actually owned their land, with the main question being the validity of the British proclamation in the American colonies."[55] However, at the time *Johnson* was decided, Indigenous ownership of land was an important, open question for both Native Americans and whites, and so Marshall addressed it, tying together property and sovereignty. Can a people be considered sovereign when inhabiting land that someone else owns? Legal scholar Joseph Singer ties sovereignty and property as racialized in US law:

Property and sovereignty in the United States have a racial basis. The land was taken by force by white people from peoples of color thought by the conquerors to be racially inferior. The close relation of native peoples to the land was held to be no relation at all. To the conquerors, the land was "vacant." Yet it required trickery and force to wrest it from its occupants. This means that the title of every single parcel of property in the United States can be traced to a system of racial violence.[56]

And legal scholar Cheryl Harris adds, after a reading of *Johnson v. M'Intosh*, that "if property is understood as a delegation of sovereign power—the product of the power of the state—then a fair reading of history reveals the racial oppression of Indians inherent in the American regime of property."[57] Harris argues that "whiteness shares the critical characteristics of property even as the meaning of property has changed over time. In particular, whiteness and property share a common premise—a conceptual nucleus—of a right to exclude."[58] Aboriginal scholar Aileen Moreton-Robinson calls this shared premise of whiteness and property "the white possessive."[59] As ethnic studies scholars Eve Tuck (Unangax̂) and K. Wayne Yang describe it, "in the process of settler colonialism, land is remade into property and human relationships to land are restricted to the relationship of the owner to his property. Epistemological, ontological, and cosmological relationships to land are interred, indeed made pre-modern and backward. Made savage."[60] But white settlers did not only make land into property; they also engaged in homesteading, making the land their home, civilizing it, domesticating it. According to settler logic, Indigenous peoples could not make land into property, but they also could not make the land into their home; they were too uncivilized to domesticate it.

Land dispossession was justified by a story about Indigenous peoples as savages who do not improve the land and therefore cannot own it. But then, allotment was justified by a story about how Indigenous peoples could only be civilized if they started to own private property. Indeed, if it were not for allotment (private property) and civilization (whiteness), extinction had been thought to be their unavoidable fate. This story persists today as well, as Cree legal scholar Val Napoleon and gender studies scholar Emily Snyder demonstrate when they quote a right-wing Canadian organization who claimed in 2002 that "without a system of authentic individual property rights to activate the wealth of the land, fuel native entrepreneurship, and encourage investment, Indian reserves will remain Indian ghettos."[61]

Allotment, according to the story told by those who considered themselves "friends of the Indians," was supposed to bring private property and civilization to Indigenous communities, but when allotment ended in 1934, Indigenous communities lost two-thirds of the lands they had owned fifty years earlier (before that, they had already lost 90 percent of their lands). Indigenous communities—Indian Country—were badly hurt. "Allotment failed, this modern story goes, because it attempted to impose private property on indigenous peoples who had no conception of the private ownership of land."[62] They soon lost their lands to "white settlement, fraudulent land transactions, and property taxes."[63] But locating the root of Indigenous suffering (or thriving) in private property conceals power relations and the lasting effects of settler colonialism on Indigenous communities. "What the vociferous assertions about private property fail to recognize," write Napoleon and Snyder, "is that if one accepts the private property premise, then one need not think any further about power or the ways that systemic forms of oppression such as colonialism, racism, and sexism circulate in law and economics. Instead, one can focus on the obstinate failure of most Indigenous people to buy into such an 'obvious' quick fix."[64] In the context of the G-O Road, we could say that settler colonial stories about land as property conceal Yurok and Karuk stories about land as home, the stories I aimed to uncover in the previous chapter. It also conceals stories about land as kin (the focus of chapter 5), as Sisseton Wahpeton Oyate scholar Kim TallBear notes: "Property literally undercuts Indigenous kinship and attempts to replace it. It objectifies the land and water and other-than-human beings as potentially owned resources."[65]

But some scholars interestingly ask to uncover Indigenous stories about *property*, and I would like to pay attention to them in this chapter. Historian Allan Greer, for example, challenges the idea that property is a single thing, "the hallmark of modernity and civilization." In the specific context of the Dawes (or Allotment) Act, the argument is that "allotment did not impose private property on people who had never seen it before. Rather, it replaces . . . myriad functioning and evolving tribal property systems with a single dysfunctional and unchanging system."[66] Legal scholar Kenneth Bobroff argues that in doing so, allotment destroyed the power of Indigenous communities to adapt their property laws to meet different social conditions.[67] Bobroff writes that "among tribes in what is now Northern

California, along the Klamath River and the nearby Pacific coast, property was held in individual private ownership and included ownership rights in other tribes' territories. For example, Hupas owned property inside Yurok territory. Ownership could be divided over time, with several individuals each having rights to the same fishing spot at different times of the year."[68] The Theodoratus Report mentions property a few times, for example, as part of its discussion of social life in the area: "In general the social life of Northwest Indian people has been assessed by ethnographers as centering around individual rights, property, and prestige."[69]

Just like Bobroff, the Theodoratus Report relies on Kroeber and other early-twentieth-century anthropologists, but in Yurok elder Lucy Thompson's *To the American Indian*, she mentions private property a few times, and when she describes the relationship between Yuroks and *woge*, she writes that nobody stole anyone else's land, or any other property.[70] Lowanna Brantner mentioned property in her testimony in the G-O Road trial as well, telling the court that dance regalia is owned by certain families. Hupa historian Jack Norton writes that anthropologist Alfred Kroeber characterized the Yurok as having "individualistic rather than communal attitudes toward the acquisition of personal property." Kroeber claimed this represented a minor capitalistic system. But he ignored "the Yuroks' special ability to live successfully in a decentralized, non-authoritarian political structure. Kroeber's training and cultural attachments did not allow him to recognize that such a structure was supported by an emphasis on reciprocal personal integrity in relationship to the society, as well as to the natural and cosmological world."[71] The question of private property is relevant to the G-O Road case because when the Forest Service evaluated the different possible routes of the road, in their Draft Environmental Impact Statement, they favored those alternatives that did not require the destruction of cultural sites or the transfer or sales of any property in the area.[72]

Lyng was argued as a case about religious freedom and decided as a case about property rights. Both discourses neutralize or depoliticize the question of who should decide the fate of the High Country. In other words, the question at the center of *Lyng* is about what is allowed to be done to the land, and while the Indigenous plaintiffs argue that their religiosity should be considered when answering this question, and O'Connor declares that it is property rights that should guide the answer to this question, I want to propose that the question is really about sovereignty. In *Johnson v. M'Intosh*, Marshall said that only sovereign nations had the right of discovery (and therefore of ultimate property). Pawnee attorney Walter Echo-Hawk writes that "once the English began purchasing tribal land throughout the colonies, it became impossible to deny that Indians owned the land." However, he continues, after the colonies achieved independence, "the Supreme Court of the new republic was free to take a second look at the question of Indian land ownership in the United States. A strong legal foundation was needed for acquiring Indian land if the aspirations of the young nation were to be realized."[73] Indeed, property and sovereignty are deeply intertwined, and when O'Connor says that the Indigenous respondents are requesting de facto beneficial ownership of the High Country, what she says is, perhaps, that they are asserting their sovereignty over the land. But does sovereignty mean the same thing for the United States and for Indigenous peoples? I explore this question in the next section.

Indigenous Sovereignty

The question of indigeneity in the US context (as in other settler colonial contexts) is a political question. While the *Lyng* decision depoliticizes it by analyzing the relationship between the Yurok, Karuk, and Tolowa nations and the High Country through the lenses of religion and property, recent scholarship on indigeneity emphasizes the political implications of indigeneity by closely examining it in relation to the question of sovereignty. Political theorist Karena Shaw, for example, thinks of the ways in which indigeneity as a form of difference challenges the discourse of sovereignty:

> Contemporary politics are framed by discourses of sovereignty. These discourses are neither natural nor neutral. They reproduce a space for politics that is enabled by and rests upon the production, naturalization, and marginalization of certain forms of "difference." Indigenous politics illustrate and challenge this in three ways: first, Indigenous peoples are among those both implicitly and explicitly produced and marked as "different" in and through sovereignty discourse, and this is one of the enabling conditions of sovereignty discourse; second, even as these discourses enable Indigenous peoples' political claims, they also continue to be marginalized by and through these same discourses; and, third, through their (necessary) engagement with this paradox, these movements are encountering, challenging, and reshaping the "limits" of contemporary politics. Thus, even as Indigenous politics are framed by these discourses and practices, they also,

in part because of their centrality to them, expose, denaturalize, and refor-mulate them.[74]

When indigeneity is understood (or produced) as Indigenous differ-ence, it "takes on an almost sacred character and becomes a compelling id-iom for articulating rights, values, and identities."[75] The rights discourse that goes hand in hand with the discourse of difference interpolates po-litical questions into legal ones.[76] This has become, argues legal anthro-pologist Jennifer Hamilton, the main tool for Indigenous peoples to make political claims, especially in Anglo settler states. Hamilton talks about "a double bind in the cultural production of indigeneity in which the very conditions that enable Indigenous peoples to make compelling legal claims based on *difference* can simultaneously lead those claims to failure."[77] She demonstrates how "the deployment of such culturalist discourse in law cre-ates a specific context in which broader political assertions, especially those concerning sovereignty and land rights, are potentially undermined."[78]

Political theorist Kevin Bruyneel asks where Indigenous peoples fit in relation to the US political system: "inside, outside, or somewhere in be-tween?"[79] This is a question about Indigenous sovereignty—if they are sov-ereign peoples, then they are considered "outside"; accordingly, if they are inside, then they are not sovereign (only the United States is sovereign). Bruyneel seeks to open up a "third space"—an in-between space—for In-digenous sovereignty, one that will allow Indigenous peoples to be at once inside and outside the US political realm. For Bruyneel, this is their posi-tion in reality, and his goal is to allow for a theory of sovereignty that would fit this reality. Bruyneel's analytical suggestion is refreshing and promising: he calls it "concurrent sovereignty" (a legal situation that exists in several states and that Bruyneel wants to adopt theoretically). Bruyneel points to the binary nature of sovereignty and looks for a way to break through this binary, which makes sovereignty into self-sufficiency.[80] Self-sufficiency is what the "friends of the Indians" who pushed for allotment thought In-digenous communities should strive for, a goal that can be achieved only through ownership of private property.

Thinking about sovereignty in the context of *Lyng*—a case that is os-tensibly about Indigenous religion—invites us to think of sovereignty in a nonbinary way, as bringing together law and theology, land and God. Here I am recounting some of sovereignty's features, in order to clarify its rela-tionship with indigeneity. Sovereignty is an ambiguous concept, classically defined as supreme legal authority, one that has both legal and theological bases—a legal authority based on divine right. The vast literature on Indigenous sovereignty focuses either on the theological dimension or on the legal aspects of it.[81] Neither, I believe, captures the complexity of the concept of sovereignty. In law, sovereignty is practiced through jurisdiction, as historian Lisa Ford points out, and so sovereignty is legalized and depoliticized.[82] In theology, we usually think of God as sovereign, and of political sovereignty as a feature of divine will, so politics is tied together with theology, not with positive law. Property plays a significant role in this binary: the settler's definition of sovereignty is tightly related to ownership of land, whereas Native American theology sees the matter through completely different lenses—the land is sacred, and therefore should belong to everyone. But this is a caricature of Indigeneity and its approaches to religion, sovereignty, and property.

Lyng remains a case about property and religion, leaving aside that which is explicitly political and neglecting the question of Indigenous sovereignty altogether. This happens because both O'Connor in her majority opinion and Brennan in his dissent think about property and religion as competing rights, and of the Yurok, Karuk, and Tolowa peoples as seeking protection of their right to exercise their religion freely, thus raising the question how this practice might affect the government property rights in the area. But if the political question of sovereignty is taken seriously, then the court should consider thinking of the conflict in *Lyng* thus: instead of seeing the court's job as balancing between the Yurok's, Karuk's, and Tolowa's right to free exercise and the federal government's right to manage its property as it sees fit, the court needs to adjudicate a conflict between nations who claim sovereignty over the same piece of land. Of course, this shift should dramatically change our view of the dispute, but it also sheds doubt on the US Supreme Court's jurisdiction over this case.

The US Supreme Court has struggled with the limits of Native sovereignty since the early nineteenth century and the Marshall Trilogy. The *Johnson v. M'Intosh* decision may be seen as secularizing sovereignty as it applies the doctrine of Christian discovery in the secular state, as I discuss later in this chapter.[83] The secularization of sovereignty by the Marshall Court involved transforming Native Americans from "pagans" to "savages" and from Indigenous peoples to a racial minority. The secularization of the terms of the dispute is significant because it led to the shifting of the focus of critique from questions of collective rights to land

and to self-determination to individual property rights, based on racial or ethnic identity. According to historian Patrick Wolfe, "on the passing of the frontier, U.S. Indian Policy sought to incorporate Indians into settler society not as so many separate tribes but generically, individually, and as a whole—which is to say, as a race."[84] While some scholars frame the problem as racism,[85] others believe that focusing on race and ethnicity conceals the real object of the dispute, namely, land. As literary scholar Jodi Byrd (Chickasaw) puts it,

> The conflation of racialization into colonization and indigeneity into racial categories . . . masks the territoriality of conquest by assigning colonization to the racialized body, which is then policed in its degrees from whiteness. Under this paradigm, American Indian national assertions of sovereignty, self-determination, and land rights disappear into U.S. territoriality as indigenous identity becomes a racial identity and citizens of colonized indigenous nations become internal ethnic minorities within the colonizing nation-state.[86]

When race and ethnicity become the focus of our critique, we are distracted from the real questions we need to ask and from the possibility of resisting US settler colonialism more effectively.[87] Wolfe reminds us that what he calls "the logic of elimination," which is tied with US settler colonialism, used race as its main tool. "Indigenous North Americans were not killed, driven away, romanticized, assimilated, fenced in, bred White, and otherwise eliminated as the original owners of the land but as *Indians*," he writes.[88] Our critique, then, should go back to recognition of Native Americans as Indigenous peoples rather than a racial or ethnic minority. Moreover, as literary scholar Mark Rifkin notes, both discourses of racial difference and equality and discourses of cultural recognition are deployed by the United States in ways that reaffirm its authority to determine the issues that would count as part of its political system. These discourses mask, according to Rifkin, "the structuring violence performed by the figure of sovereignty."[89] Native peoples are simply defined as those who are not sovereign. Thus, they help to define the state as sovereign.

Note that my argument here is not that Native Americans are outside the category of race and racism but that they should not be thought of as one (racial) minority in a multicultural society instead of as nations struggling for their sovereignty. As Lenape scholar Joanne Barker writes (referring to intersectional and assemblage theories), "a genuine accounting of indigeneity requires more than a presumed inclusion within the oppressed, as a racial difference that is ultimately the same as others racialized. And it has to do with the location and territory of power."[90] She then adds that "genuine respect of and alliance with Indigenous peoples" requires "a disaggregation of indigeneity from race and ethnicity."[91] Yet, the United States grants certain rights to Native Americans who reside in its territory based on their racial status: how much "Indian blood" they have in them. Barker writes elsewhere that the racialization of Native legal status by blood is a process that allows the state to individualize Native legal rights and so to defer attention to the collective rights to sovereignty and self-determination that Native peoples possess under international and constitutional law.[92] One effect of this racialization and individualization is ignoring the common good that defines Native peoples as communities, namely, their aboriginal relation to the land. It transforms them from communities of citizens with shared interests into a collection of individual citizens bearing liberal-universal rights. Osage theologian George E. Tinker criticizes this individualization using a slightly different terminology:

> The political and economic bias in the international discourse is to recognize only *states* as the fundamental actors in international political discourse. As such, the natural national entities that make up indigenous peoples' communities are seen today as merely ethnic minorities within state structures, who may have individual rights but who do not have any distinct set of community or cultural rights as an independent people. Hence, the sovereignty or autonomy of indigenous *nations* is *a priory* bracketed from consideration in any state discourse.[93]

The racialization and individualization of Native Americans by the United States has the effect of requiring one to prove that she is "authentically Indigenous" in order to be granted individual rights. This is the concern (and object of critique) of many scholars of indigeneity, including Eva Garroutte (Cherokee), Kathleen Birrell, Jennifer Hamilton, and Tisa Wenger.[94] Māori scholar Linda Tuhiwai Smith suggests that Indigenous peoples' critique of colonialism "draws upon a notion of authenticity, of a time before colonization in which we were intact as indigenous peoples. We had absolute authority over our lives; we were born into and lived in a universe which was entirely of our making."[95] However, the notion of authenticity has been vastly criticized. One of the problems with this notion is that performing "authenticity" successfully would mean that US settler colonialism did not do any harm to Native identity. Barker writes: "The United States escapes the consequences of its own historical sins by having real Indians situated in a far distant past before colonialism and imperialism mattered and embodying those cultures and identities today as though colonialism and imperialism have had no substantive or significant long-term consequences. Native peoples are confronted with the impossible task of representing *that* authenticity in order to secure their recognition and rights as sovereigns."[96]

This call for authenticity has devastating cultural implications, Barker continues. "Being authentic" often means in the eyes of the West that one adheres to "traditional" values, in a way that can create an identity crisis for Native Americans, who are expected to be homophobic and misogynistic, among other traits that the West considers to be "premodern." Legal scholar Ayelet Shachar adds that there may be "disproportionate costs imposed upon traditionally less powerful group members."[97] In many cases, accommodation of the different traditions and practices of minority groups depends on demonstration of "authentic" characteristics, and results in risking the weaker group member's citizenship rights.[98] Historian James Clifford writes about the relation between poverty and authenticity in the Native American context:

> Economic success . . . can bring significant increases in wealth. But it also encourages new hierarchies, communal divisions, and dependency on external markets and capital resources. Whatever material progress has been made over the past few decades is unevenly distributed. Indigenous populations in most contemporary nation-states remain poor, lacking adequate health and education, at the mercy of predatory national and transnational agents of "development." The modest, but real, gains in control over land and resources achieved by native groups in recent years are fragile, always susceptible to reversal by overwhelmingly more powerful majority populations. Intractable double binds—for example, an assumed contradiction between material wealth and cultural authenticity—are imposed on tribal people aspiring to something more than bare survival in settler-colonial states.[99]

This quote from Clifford demonstrates the absurdity created by the assumed close connection between sovereignty and property. On the one hand, you cannot be sovereign if you do not own land; on the other, wealth and ownership render you inauthentic, and then all you can hope for is to be integrated into the United States as a racial minority—you cannot demand recognition of your sovereignty. Religion plays a significant role in this equation as well, as this kind of continuity or authenticity is scrutinized when Indigenous communities fight to protect their religious freedom, as we will see in the next chapter.

Hamilton emphasizes the context of multiculturalism as the background against which we need to understand indigeneity as it is produced in the courtroom: "*Indigeneity* refers to the idea that the content and meaning of Indigenous difference is produced in particular contexts, in response to a variety of social, political, and economic forces," she writes.[100] In other words, cultural difference in general, and Indigenous difference in particular, is not essential, inherent, or natural. Therefore, it would be wrong to talk about indigeneity in terms of authenticity. Indigenous difference is produced, and law is one of the spheres where it is produced. Legal scholar Kathleen Birrell thinks of indigeneity in the context of law and literature. According to Birrell, "The narratives of law and literature both create and legislate meaning" in general, including the meaning of indigeneity. Birrell argues that "legal narratives conceive of indigeneity in terms of a putative 'authenticity'" and suggests that "the aesthetic of Indigenous literature disrupts and deconstructs the law." This potential disruption is the reason I opened this book with Indigenous testimony—storytelling—in the G-O Road trial. Birrell follows Wolfe in arguing that law embraces a notion of "the 'authentic' or whole Indigenous subject, framed and referenced by mythic time and complex kinship rather than by the impacts of colonialism." Birrell moves away from the discourse on authenticity and argues, following Michel Foucault and Judith Butler, that "in the context of Native title, the colonial schema in which the common law conception of indigeneity operates compels a particular performance from the Indigenous subject, in order to appear before the law at all."[101]

This is a crucial point in my reading of the decision in *Lyng*. When we conceive of indigeneity in terms of authenticity, we not only ignore the role that law plays in producing the Indigenous but also treat it as a fixed identity. Birrell, following Clifford, argues that literature dissolves this fixity, even if momentarily. Birrell talks about Indigenous literature, but attorney George D. Pappas shows how settler literature contributes to the legal image of the Indigenous as savage and primitive.[102] The point is that there is no such thing as "Native American" outside of the discursive powers that created it. But when a Native subject testifies in court, what she is up against is this legal fiction. The Indigenous subject that is produced in *Lyng* as requesting "de facto beneficial ownership" of the High Country is in relationship with the Indigenous subject that was produced in Marshall's opinion in *Johnson*—an Indigenous subject that cannot cultivate, and therefore cannot own, land. As Pappas writes:

> The discursive formations that helped to situate the privileged images of the Native Americans included discourses that portrayed them as noble savages, savages, helpless wards and finally as a "domestic dependent nation." The privileging of images about Native Americans in the Marshall rulings *excluded* any representation that cast the Native American as a farmer, a land owner or civilized human being. . . . These discourses were incorporated as findings of fact, or as *de facto* sworn statements in the John Marshall opinions.[103]

But popular culture is not the only discourse that informs legal decisions about Indigenous sovereignty. Theological discourses play a role as well. Political philosopher Jean Bethke Elshtain writes that "theological understandings had migrated into early modern political sovereigntism."[104] She thinks of the ways medieval ideas about God as sovereign have influenced early modern conceptions of the sovereign state and their relation to modern notions of self-sovereignty. Elshtain reminds us that sovereignty has not always been tied to territory[105] and that the idea of divine-right monarchy is also an early modern invention.[106] In terms of methodology, Elshtain warns us against over-abstracting our concepts, especially when it comes to political concepts such as sovereignty: "Without concrete history, political thought becomes a gnostic enterprise—all words, no flesh; all spirit, no body. Then, disastrously, that disembodied enterprise invites schemes and ideologies that are imposed over the living, incarnate tissue of human life."[107] If we step away from the abstraction of Indigenous sovereignty in the legal discourse, we can see that gathering acorns in the High Country is an act of what Native American studies scholar Cutcha Risling Baldy (Hupa, Yurok, Karuk) terms "bio-cultural sovereignty."[108] Or we can say, following Karuk author Julian Lang, that Indigenous sovereignty quite simply means "possess[ing] their own laws, history, language, religion, political structure, and lands."[109]

For political theorist Joan Cocks, sovereign power (or "sovereignal freedom") is not only a modern invention but also a delusion, and one that poses political dangers as well, especially when it is democratized.[110] Cocks casts doubt with regards to the aspiration to Indigenous sovereignty, asking about "the tendency of those oppressed by sovereign power to make counter-sovereignty bids to save themselves"[111]: "Human rights advocates and other progressives condemn the sovereign power of xenophobic majorities and defend the aspirations to sovereign power of vulnerable peoples, but what exactly makes the exclusivism of privileged citizenship a minus in the ledger of democracy, and the exclusivism of penetrated indigeneity a plus?"[112] This doubt is in line with political theorist Taiaiake Alfred's (Kahnawà:ke Mohawk) assertion that "sovereignty is not an appropriate political objective for Indigenous peoples, as the concept itself is essentially Western, and has served as a tool in colonizing Indigenous peoples."[113] I take this critique of the quest for Indigenous sovereignty seriously in my work, and I try to answer it because, even though I see the problematic the critics point to, I also see a great theoretical potential in this concept. But while I explore this theoretical potential, I also remember that both Abby Abinanti (Yurok), Chief Judge of the Yurok Tribal Court, and Tia Oros Peters (Zuni), executive director of the Seventh Generation Fund for Indigenous Peoples, have told me that they are not interested in sovereignty. Peters explained that while she uses the concept strategically, when talking at the United Nations, for example, she always remembers that it is a Western idea that is not her own or her people's. When I asked what they did care about, Judge Abinanti said that what she was working toward was healing. Perhaps healing is what lived sovereignty really looks like.

Kevin Bruyneel may have an answer to those doubts about sovereignty. The concept of state sovereignty presents us with what Bruyneel calls "a false choice."[114] Advocates of sovereignty for Indigenous nations often present us with a false choice between two possibilities only: (1) acknowledging Indigenous sovereignty with the consequence of destructing the sovereignty of the occupying state; or (2) continuing to deny Indigenous sovereignty. This is a false choice because both options accept the same (secular) conception of sovereignty. Shachar presents us with another problematic aspect of this binary: granting full jurisdictional power to the state, she argues, might be suitable to protecting the individual rights of the less powerful members of minority groups, but it does so at the expense of relegating their cultural identity to the private sphere, in a way that fails to acknowledge their cultural identities; granting full jurisdictional power to the group, on the other hand, would be suitable for protecting cultural diversity, but at the cost of enabling the systematic maltreatment of specific members by their accommodated group.[115] However, there is a third option. According to Bruyneel, "it is possible for both entities to enjoy concurrent sovereignty. The false choice here is that either indigenous tribes and nations must become sovereign states, thereby destroying the settler-states within which they reside, or their citizens must accept unambiguous inclusion in the settler polity, thereby denying their collective claim to sovereignty."[116]

Shachar proposes a model that avoids this false choice: the joint governance approach. According to this model, some people will jointly belong to more than one community and will accordingly bear rights and obligations that will derive from more than one source of legal authority. According to Bruyneel's and Shachar's frameworks, the Yurok, Karuk, and Tolowa do not have to become sovereign states in order to be considered (by the United States) as the ones who should decide the fate of the High Country, not as a byproduct of their right to freely exercise their religion but as the original, dispossessed, inhabitants of this land.

Property and Sovereignty

Legal scholar Bernadette Atuahene, writing about post-apartheid South Africa, connects land dispossession and property rights to dignity. She bases her definition of dignity on two central elements: equal human worth and autonomy. She defines dignity as "the notion that people have equal worth, which gives them the right to live as autonomous beings not under the authority of another. Consequently, individuals and communities are deprived of dignity when subject to dehumanization, infantilization, or community destruction."[117] Atuahene writes about what she calls "dignity takings" and "dignity restoration" in South Africa, but I find her theory useful in linking dignity and indigeneity. According to Atuahene, the term "dignity takings" applies "when a state directly or indirectly destroys or confiscates property rights from owners or occupiers whom it deems to be sub persons without paying just compensation or without a legitimate public purpose."[118] She argues that a comprehensive remedy for dignity takings entails what she calls "dignity restoration," which she understands as compensation that addresses both the economic harms and the dignity deprivations involved. According to Atuahene, dignity restoration has to do with the integration of the dispossessed into the dominant society, and this is where the South African case may differ from the Native American case, where Indigenous communities seek sovereignty rather than inclusion in a multicultural society.

But Atuahene's connection between dignity taking, property theft, and dehumanization is helpful in understanding the G-O Road case within the context of colonial invasion (and its religious aspects). This connection takes me back to *Johnson v. M'Intosh* and the doctrine of discovery. Two papal bulls, from 1455 and 1492, had declared the legitimacy of Christian domination over "pagans," sanctifying enslavement and expropriation of property, specifically in the lands "discovered" by Christopher Columbus. What was termed "the Doctrine of Christian Discovery" saw Indigenous Americans as subhuman because they were not Christian. Chief Justice John Marshall used the language of these papal bulls in his infamous decision in *Johnson v. M'Intosh* to justify state dominion over Indigenous peoples, replacing the terms "Christian" and "pagans" with "European" and "savages"—a term that similarly dehumanizes Indigenous Americans, even if this dehumanization was secularized.

Based on the notion that Indigenous peoples could not possess title to land, Native title was a colonial fiction, created by Marshall in order to grant Native peoples some property rights while allowing the US government to maintain control over land, especially its sale and distribution. Marshall ruled that Indigenous nations had only "the right of occupancy."[119] They can do whatever they want with the land while they occupy it, but they cannot sell it to anyone but the sovereign. According to Marshall, discovery of a given territory granted the European discoverer the right, against other European nations, to acquire Native land (by purchase or conquest) and then grant that land to non-Natives. On the one hand, the Supreme Court created a new property right for Native peoples, one that all parties, including the state, were bound to respect. On the other hand, the court took away absolute control of Native land by Native peoples.

The court said that Native peoples possessed an occupancy right that only the discovering sovereign could extinguish.[120] Thus, discovery did not vest title in the discoverer; it gave the discovering nation the right to extinguish Native title via purchase or conquest. The rights of the discoverer were against those of other European nations staking a claim to Indigenous land; they were not necessarily rights over Indigenous peoples. The court now said that Native peoples could convey their land to the discovering sovereign and to no one else. Thus, the sovereign's rights derived from discovery, and Indigenous peoples' rights came from occupancy. Residence in a given area conferred Native title upon an Indigenous nation (therefore, the claim to home does not amount to a property right).

We can ask how come such a revolutionary property expropriation did not do anything to the institution of property, and one possible answer would be that the people whose property was expropriated were already considered nonmembers of the community and therefore not worthy of property rights. In the Native American case, they were also considered too nomadic to own land and too unwilling to make significant improvements that would clarify their claim and give them moral weight.[121] Thus, to de-essentialize and re-politicize indigeneity, we can say with Atuahene that taking Native land required dehumanizing Native people and denying their sovereignty and autonomy.

And so the answer to legal scholar Jeremy Waldron's question, "why is indigeneity important?"[122] would be that taking Indigenous lands required Indigenous peoples' continuing dehumanization and the denial of their sovereignty and autonomy, which Atuahene sees as the violation of their dignity. The secularization of sovereignty by the Marshall Court was essential to the connection it made between sovereignty and property. It was as savages, not pagans, that Indigenous peoples were dispossessed. What does this secularization mean for Indigenous religions and religious freedom? This question is at the center of the next chapter.

3

·••·

LAND AS SACRED IN JUSTICE BRENNAN'S DISSENT

For reasons I have discussed in the previous chapters, the Supreme Court decided *Lyng* as a religious freedom case. The controversy about the G-O Road and the logging plan in the High Country had been moot because of the inclusion of the Blue Creek area in the California Wilderness Act of 1984. Nevertheless, the court has granted certiorari, agreeing to decide the (by then theoretical) question of protecting a land-based religious practice on federal land, because there had been a disagreement between the Sixth, Ninth, Tenth, and District of Columbia Circuit Courts on this question. According to the *Sherbert* test, in the case of incidental burdens on religious practice, the court first needs to determine whether the practice for which plaintiffs seek protection is based on a sincerely held belief and whether the government's action poses a substantial burden on the plaintiffs' ability to exercise this religious belief.[1] If these two elements are established, then the government must show that it is acting in furtherance of a compelling government interest and using the least restrictive means to pursue it. It seems that in the G-O Road case, from the start, there was no dispute over the sincerity of the Yurok, Karuk, and Tolowa peoples' religious beliefs, and this may have been the reason that "those beliefs [were] only briefly described" in the Supreme Court decision.[2]

However, the religiosity of Yurok, Karuk, and Tolowa uses of the High Country should not be taken for granted. As the Theodoratus Report itself tells us, "because of the particular nature of the Indian perceptual experience, as opposed to the particular nature of the predominant non-Indian, Western perceptual experience, any division into 'religious' or 'sacred' is in reality an exercise which forces Indian concepts into non-Indian categories, and distorts the original conceptualization in the process."[3] Lakota scholar Vine Deloria, Jr., on the other hand, writes that the religiosity of Indigenous practices can be inferred from its ongoing persecution as well as from its survival:

> Traditional [Indigenous] religions are under attack not because they are Indian but because they are fundamentally religious and are perhaps the only consistent religious groups in American society over the long term. If kidnapping children for boarding schools, prohibiting religious ceremonies, destroying the family through allotments, and bestowing American citizenship did not destroy the basic community of Indian people, what could possibly do so? The attack on religion today is the secular attack on any group that advocates and practices devotion to a value higher than the state. That is why the balancing test has been discarded and laws and ordinances are allowed primacy over religious obligations.[4]

In the previous chapter, I discussed how Native identity is produced through legal and political discourse. There is nothing natural, or pre-discursive, about Native identity and its relation to modernity or property. Similarly, there is nothing natural or pre-discursive about Native religiosity. Both Deloria and the Theodoratus Report are right in their evaluations that Native ways of life do not separate the "sacred" from the "secular" (in other words, that religion as a European Christian category is not a fit description of Indigenous ways of life) and that Indigenous religiosity has been attacked by the settler state (in other words, that religion is a colonial category), even if the two seem to contradict each other at first. Religious studies scholar Chris Jocks (Kahnawà:ke Mohawk) writes that "it is not until 1882 that Indigenous ways of living were recognized as religion by the U.S. federal government—recognized, that is, in order to outlaw them. The Code of Indian Offenses, announced in Interior Secretary Henry M. Teller's Annual Report of 1883, focused on traditional ceremonial dances as degrading relics of barbarism that promote idleness, sexual license, and—horror of horrors—the giving away of property."[5]

Yurok members have been ambivalent about applying the category of religion to their lifeways. Ethnographer Thomas Buckley explains that one source of Yurok frustration with infamous Berkeley anthropologist Alfred

Kroeber has to do with Kroeber's lack of interest in religion and with his dismissal of Yurok polity, which, according to Buckley, was largely implemented through ceremony but according to Kroeber was extreme anarchy.[6] Anthropologist Richard Keeling writes that Yuroks today feel that their "traditional spirituality has not been appreciated." The first thing an elder Yurok or Hupa would tell an outsider, according to Keeling, is that "for old-time Indians, everything used to be religion." Similarly, Yurok elder Geneva Mattz has told Buckley, "we are the praying people, that's who we are. In the old days everything we do is pray." However, when Buckley said he was interested in Yurok religion, a Yurok Brush Dance doctor told him ("with a grimace"): "I guess you could call it that." Buckley concludes: "Among Indian people of northwestern California who are concerned with such things, 'religion' tends to refer to Christianity, to belief and rituals that manifest institutionalized teachings. 'Praying,' privately or in communal rites like dances, is about something else: 'our sacred ways,' 'the Indian Way,' 'the old way,' sometimes, locally, 'spiritualism.'"[7] Buckley himself calls it "spirituality," which is a term that the courts have also adopted, and, as religious studies scholar Michael D. McNally shows, this is not to the benefit of Indigenous peoples trying to protect their religious freedom in settler courts.[8]

Reflecting on the G-O Road trial, Kickapoo attorney Marilyn Miles, who represented the Indigenous plaintiffs in this case, alludes to the power of religion when she says:

> I know as lawyers we always focus on the courtroom, but the G-O Road case was much more than that. I have always believed that it was because we focused on the spiritual, the religious, the power of the place and the people, that this particular case played out as it did—unlike prior legal challenges to the other sections of the road, which focused on statutes . . . none of the prior lawsuits even raised a First Amendment religious freedom claim, and it seemed to me to be so basic.[9]

Miles may be right to attribute the outcome of the trial to the religious freedom focus of the case, but one may also say that "the case played out as it did"—that it was lost in the Supreme Court—because of the framework of religious freedom. Religious studies scholar Jace Weaver (of Cherokee descent) writes that because Native religion is land based, all land claims carry in them religious claims.[10] I would add that all Native American religious claims carry in them land claims as well. Justice William Brennan's dissent is all about land as sacred, and according to him it is outrageous that the court is not protecting it as such, but in this chapter I argue that Brennan's focus on land as sacred depoliticizes religion and essentializes indigeneity. And so, even though I admit that Brennan's desire to protect Indigenous sacred sites is much better than O'Connor's willingness to sacrifice them for the sake of protecting government property rights, I also think that the discourse of sacred land he develops in *Lyng* is ultimately harmful to Indigenous struggles for sovereignty and justice.

For Justice Brennan in his dissent, the most important thing is that "for at least 200 years and probably much longer, the Yurok, Karok [*sic*], and Tolowa Indians have held sacred an approximately 25-square-mile area of land situated in what is today the Blue Creek Unit of Six Rivers National Forest in northwestern California."[11] Again, there was no dispute in this case about the sacredness of the land to the Yurok, Karuk, and Tolowa peoples. However, the sacredness of the land cannot be understood in isolation from its other features. In addition, the land has not been sacred in the same ways for two hundred years, as the witnesses in the G-O Road trial make clear. I understand Brennan's sentiment here. What he is saying to the justices of the majority is that the majority opinion is outrageous because a six-mile segment of a road cannot be significant enough to justify the destruction of a two-hundred-year-old religious practice. However, what I do in this chapter is show how destructive this notion is to Native thriving in the United States, because it plays right into the stereotype of the Indigenous as "primitive" and erases the specific history of genocide (through attempts to destroy religious practice, among other things) in Northern California and elsewhere.

Justice Brennan's Dissent

Justice Brennan dissents "because the Court today refuses even to acknowledge the constitutional injury respondents will suffer, and because this refusal essentially leaves Native Americans with absolutely no constitutional protection against perhaps the gravest threat to their religious practices."[12] Brennan acknowledges that "for Native Americans religion is not a discrete sphere of activity separate from all others."[13] One could argue that for non-Indigenous religious people, including Christians, religion cannot be separated from other spheres of life either. Attempts to portray Native American religiosity as fundamentally different from so-called Western religiosity is harmful in itself, as some legal scholars have recently argued.

Legal scholars Stephanie Hall Barclay and Michalyn Steele (Seneca) point out that "Justice Brennan articulated the truism that Native American religious practices are unlike those of other faiths, in part because of the 'site-specific nature' of Indigenous 'religious practice.' While the use of sacred sites is an integral element of worship for Indigenous peoples, the importance of sacred sites is not wholly unique to them."[14]

Legal Scholar Kristen A. Carpenter (of Cherokee descent) writes, "Ironically, perhaps, in the legal field both supporters and detractors of Indigenous claims in sacred sites cases, along with peyote, eagle feathers, and human remains cases, have claimed Indian spiritual practices are just too different from the religions contemplated for protection in the First Amendment."[15] Carpenter commends religious studies scholars, such as Michael D. McNally, for critically engaging with the category of Indigenous religions and acknowledging that the portrayal of Indigenous traditions as sui generis ultimately serves the majority religion, Protestantism. Along these lines, Barclay and Steele add that if Indigenous religions should be treated as unique, it is because of the extent to which they have been burdened by governments: "But what is perhaps unique about sacred sites for Indigenous peoples in countries such as the United States is the extent of the obstacles that government has created and maintains to inhibit Indigenous use of these sacred sites. These obstacles, both historic and contemporary, have resulted in catastrophic interference with Indigenous spiritual practices related to particular sites—often operating as an effective prohibition on these practices."[16]

I share this notion, and I wish Brennan's dissent had paid more attention to this history of the relationship between the state and Indigenous religions. Brennan quotes from the Theodoratus Report, saying that "any attempt to isolate the religious aspects of Indian life 'is in reality an exercise which forces Indian concepts into non-Indian categories.'"[17] This acknowledgment of Western intellectual imperialism seems politically progressive and is generally welcome in a Supreme Court decision, even if only as part of a dissenting opinion. However, I argue that we can take this logic a step further and think about religious freedom as an unsuitable category for the pursuit of justice by Native Americans altogether. Religious studies scholar Tisa Wenger discusses this issue in a different context, writing that the conflict over Native American religious freedom always involves the investigation of whether the practice in question is "authentically" religious. Religion as a set of beliefs, practices, and institutions that can be separated from other spheres of life is a uniquely European colonial concept, and Native Americans started to use it only after contact, to refer to Catholicism, referring to their traditional ceremonies as "custom." Adopting the concept of religion for pragmatic reasons in cases such as *Lyng* is a strategy that tends to fail. "Separated and abstracted from other spheres of life, 'religion' becomes the picturesque repository of tradition and sentiment, made irrelevant to what appear to be the more real-world concerns of land and government."[18]

What happens to Native religious practice in this process is that it is treated in US courts as at once individual and universal. McNally explains that the courts do so by translating Indigenous religions into "spiritual practice." Nevertheless, he sees potential in the legal framework of religious freedom for Native Americans, and he proposes that this framework can be used strategically (and successfully), as collective rather than individual right, thus helping to promote Indigenous sovereignty as well.[19] Jocks further explains that in many Indigenous communities, religious training and ritual practice are collective responsibilities more than individual freedoms.[20] However, he argues that "the concept of religion itself is intrinsically alien to Indigenous ways of life—practices, ontologies, epistemologies, and values. Those who use the word religion and think with it have proven unable to escape its categorical separation of 'matter' and 'spirit.' The result is that, as applied to Indigenous lives, the ideal of religious freedom cannot apprehend what it pretends to protect."[21] Even as I argue that framing *Lyng* as a case about religious freedom is problematic, as it leads to a depoliticized debate over the religious nature of the relationship between Indigenous peoples and lands, I can still see a potential in making *land* central to the debate, as Brennan does, as this necessarily makes the debate into one about indigeneity.

Brennan mentions stewardship—"the individual's relationship to the natural world"—as a "pervasive feature" of the Native American lifestyle, calling this relationship "the Indian religious experience."[22] He explains Native American religion at length, but for the purpose of this chapter, the following sentence is key: "Where dogma lies at the heart of Western religions, Native American faith is inextricably bound to the use of land. . . . Land is itself a sacred, living being."[23] Brennan later compares *Lyng* to the situation in *Wisconsin v. Yoder* (1972):[24] "Here the threat posed by the desecration of sacred lands that are indisputably essential to respondents' religious practices is both more direct and more substantial than that raised by a compulsory school law that simply exposed Amish children to an alien value system," he writes. "And of course," he continues, "respondents here do not even have the option, however unattractive it might be, of migrating to more hospitable locales; the site-specific nature of their belief system renders it nontransportable."[25]

But there is one similarity between *Yoder* and *Lyng* that Brennan misses. The parents in Yoder opposed "removing those children 'from their community, physically and emotionally.'"[26] The Yurok, Karuk, and Tolowa peoples are also opposing their own removal from the High Country. If we understand the nations' relationship to the High Country as a kinship relationship (as I do in chapter 5), we would be able to see the similarity to *Yoder*. Of course, in the case of Indigenous Americans, removal from ancestral land would be a continuation of the genocidal assimilation policies as I discuss in chapter 1. And so, it is not enough to recognize that the "site-specific nature of their belief system renders it nontransportable"; rather, being indigenous to this place, having a relationship to it as home and as kin, is what makes the High Country so essential to the continuing existence and thriving of the Yurok, Karuk, and Tolowa peoples.

Brennan's strongest words appear in the final section of his dissent. This case, he writes, represents yet another stress point in the long-standing conflict between two disparate cultures—"the dominant Western culture, which views land in terms of ownership and use, and that of Native Americans, in which concepts of private property are not only alien, but contrary to a belief system that holds land sacred."[27] The court, he continues, avoids addressing these "potentially irreconcilable interests," turning the task to the legislature. In his view, "Native Americans deserve—and the Constitution demands—more than this."[28] Let me point to one more aspect of Brennan's dissent and ask what his opinion teaches us about indigeneity. "Because of their perceptions of and relationship with the natural world, Native Americans consider all land sacred," Brennan writes. "Respondents here deemed certain lands more powerful and more directly related to their religious practices than others. . . . Adherents challenging a proposed use of federal land should be required to show that the decision poses a substantial and realistic threat of frustrating their religious practices."[29]

Here the problem in Brennan's enthusiastic embrace of the Theodoratus Report becomes apparent. Brennan's dissent becomes an exploration of indigeneity—Native Americans consider all land sacred—rather than a discussion of a specific area that, for reasons not mentioned in the dissent, ended up as part of a national forest rather than Yurok, Karuk, and/or Tolowa Country. The relationship between the nations and the High Country has a complex history (to which the Theodoratus Report dedicates one of its three chapters, to which Brennan does not refer in his dissent), and the category under which it should be thought of, I argue, is that of Indigenous sovereignty. I discussed Indigenous sovereignty theoretically in the previous chapter, and in this chapter I discuss the specific place religion has had in this history. But religion is only one dimension of the nations' relationship with the High Country. This relationship is also cultural, communal, and political. As Yurok elder Lowanna Brantner explained during her testimony in the G-O Road trial, the High Country has become so important to the Yurok, Karuk, and Tolowa peoples because of the desecration of other sacred areas throughout the years, a process that has left the High Country the last untouched area.[30]

As we have seen in the trial testimony, the Yurok, Karuk, and Tolowa nations have a unique relationship with the High Country, and each of the specific peaks within it has its own role for those peoples. Focusing on the general sacredness of land to Native Americans is therefore problematic. It does not distinguish between the three nations involved in the case and other Indigenous peoples; even though it does acknowledge that "certain lands" are "more powerful and more directly related to their religious practices" than others, this qualification is secondary; it is not as important as the sweeping characterization of Native Americans as people who consider the land sacred. Religious studies scholar Greg Johnson writes:

> The constituent parts of traditions cannot be disarticulated from on-the-ground circumstances. This means traditional practices take place—always and everywhere—in moments configured by political and legal realities. . . . Thus tradition cannot be analyzed or meaningfully described without historical, cultural, geographic, political, and legal contextualization. Likewise, in order to be protected . . . tradition must be recognized and protected in specific places, times, and jurisdictions. It is not enough for a state to profess to protect traditions in general; insofar as traditions do not exist in the abstract, neither does protection of them exist in the abstract, aside from mere gesture.[31]

As Johnson argues, protecting a tradition abstractly cannot be more than a gesture. If Brennan wants to protect Yurok, Karuk, and Tolowa religious traditions, then this protection has to be localized. An abstract notion of sacred land would not suffice. Moreover, contrasting the idea of land as sacred with that of land as property suggests that Native Americans could never "authentically" file suit as the original owners of this land. If the court essentializes indigeneity as a religious relationship to the land, and if it understands this religious relationship to exclude the possibility of owning the sacred land, then it means that claiming rights to land as its original owners always already marks one as an inauthentic Indigenous subject. However, to prevail with a free exercise claim, one has to prove that her indigeneity is authentic—that her Native American religious belief is "sincerely held."

What does it mean to appear before the court as "authentically" Indigenous? It means that the court produces, through its various rulings, a certain image of the Indigenous subject as essentially other. One of the characteristics of Indigenous difference as it is produced in legal discourse is the connection between Indigenous peoples and the past, making Indigenous identity static, ignoring its flexibility and evolvement with time, especially through its encounter with and survival of settler colonialism. Here is how Brennan does it in his final words in *Lyng*: "Today's ruling sacrifices a religion at least as old as the Nation itself, along with the spiritual well-being of its approximately 5,000 adherents, so that the Forest Service can build a 6-mile segment of road that two lower courts found had only the most marginal and speculative utility, both to the Government itself and to the private lumber interests that might conceivably use it."[32]

But the witnesses in the trial together made it clear that what would be destroyed if the High Country is developed is much more than a religious practice or the spiritual well-being of the religious practitioners. The context that they provide in the stories they tell is crucial to understanding the *Lyng* case as about Indigenous sovereignty rather than merely about free exercise. Thus, for example, Jimmie James, a witness we met in chapter 1, responded to a question about his traditional upbringing: "I was taught from both sides of my family, although the Bureau of Indian Affairs tried to take that away from us and tried to teach us to live as a white man, but I always went back, because I had a hunger for the Indian teaching. I followed that through life."[33] James's relation to the Yurok and Hupa traditions (or religions, if you will) cannot be understood without attention to the various attempts by the US government to sever this relationship, to make him and his people "live like a white man."

When witness Chris Peters was similarly asked about his own traditional upbringing, he described assimilation policies by which the witnesses, their parents, and their grandparents have been affected, including residential schools, and that effectively disabled cultural continuity. As we have seen in chapter 1, Peters located the plan to develop the High Country within this history:

> When the road was first proposed, in the late fifties, it was a time when Indian people were going through some changes. Those Indian people were sons and daughters of a previous generation that experienced major and massive holocaust in that area. The miners, the settlers, and the early loggers brutally killed and murdered significant numbers of Indian people. As a reaction to that or in addition to that, the Federal Government enacted laws and legislation that made it against the law for Indian people to practice their religion. They were scared by people on Gunther Island to carry on their ceremonies, because it had been documented that mass murders occurred by common citizens when Indian people would practice their religions in our area. They were sons and daughters of people who were herded onto reservations and rancherias in the State of California, and exposed to diseases and exposed to more murders—so Indian cultures in the past few generations have been weakened.[34]

Peters provides the court with so much context that is missing in the Theodoratus Report. His testimony demonstrates what anthropologist Ronald Niezen argues when he writes that "hidden from view in today's sweat lodge ceremonies or in the drumming and dancing of powwows are histories of religiously motivated massacres and atrocities, Christian proselytizing, state policies of assimilation, and, among Indian peoples themselves, forgetting, reinvention, and renewal."[35]

Against this background, we can understand the struggle of the three nations to protect their sacred land as part of a larger project to revitalize Indigenous ceremony and restore Indigenous sovereignty. As Peters said during the G-O Road trial, "Indian people now are removed from that [assimilation era]. We can stand up more aggressively and say, 'we want to continue our identity.' And large numbers of people are doing that now, not only here, but throughout the nation. There is a revitalization of Indians that is coming, and it is growing stronger each year."[36] Therefore, "Today Indian people are standing together to ensure that our children will have the rights and freedom to practice our religious customs."[37]

Johnson argues that the sincerity of a religious belief is proven exactly by this resistance in the face of the threat of the desecration of sacred sites. "In many indigenous contexts," he writes, "sacred places are often left unto themselves out of deference to their power and sanctity. If threatened, however, the opposite dynamic is triggered as practitioners exercise their kuleana (responsibility) to care for the sacred."[38] Peters's words prove the Yurok, Karuk, and Tolowa responsibility to care for the High Country. They also demonstrate the strong connection between Indigenous religious freedom and Indigenous dispossession, a connection that is missing from the *Lyng* decision, including Brennan's dissent. I believe that it is the religious freedom framework that causes Brennan to miss this connection, and in the following pages I examine the questions that courts (and scholars) had been thinking about over the course of a century of religious freedom jurisprudence prior to *Lyng*. With the exception of *Sequoyah v. Tennessee Valley Authority* (1980),[39] where the Sixth Circuit Court briefly mentioned the Trail of Tears, those cases provide us with questions (and answers) about religion and religious freedom that are pretty narrow. My argument is not that the way that courts have understood religion does not describe Indigenous ceremony or land-based ways of life, though this is part of the problem, but that the framework of religious freedom, and the way that religion is defined legally, does not leave room for an investigation of the settler colonial context in which Indigenous peoples are fighting to defend their sacred lands. After looking at the precedent available to the *Lyng* Court, I return to the *Lyng* case and to the context that is missing from Brennan's dissent, context that would center the connection between religious freedom, dispossession, and genocide, and thus politicize religion.

Defining Religion

As we have seen, O'Connor's interpretation of *Lyng* (and therefore Brennan's critique of it) is based almost exclusively on the then recent Supreme Court decision in *Bowen v. Roy*.[40] However, reviewing the century-long history of free exercise jurisprudence and the body of precedent available when deciding the case suggests that *Lyng* could have been decided differently if it were to rely on other cases. A review of free exercise jurisprudence and scholarship follows.

The religion clauses of the First Amendment to the US Constitution declare unconstitutional any prohibition on the free exercise of religion and laws respecting the establishment of religion. The consequence is that whenever a group demands to be recognized as religious and be granted the right to the free exercise of religion, courts must determine whether the religious practice in question is "legally" religious. This situation is problematic, because American law is essentially secular—the American people have chosen to live under the rule of law (as opposed to the rule of God)—and therefore, allowing (or requesting) law to define religion may have grave consequences for the category of religion. The consequences described by anthropologist Méadhbh McIvor in the British context are relevant here, too: "Judges dabble in theology as they seek to define and police the messy reality of claimants' religious worlds."[41] In the Canadian context, legal scholar Benjamin L. Berger thinks of the meeting of law and religion as "cross-cultural," because both law and religion are cultures, each with its own aesthetic, symbols, and normative commitments, but it is a cross-cultural meeting with a clear hierarchy: law has a coercive capacity that religion does not usually have access to.[42] Therefore, as religious studies scholar Winnifred Fallers Sullivan argues, "legal religion" (religion as it is imagined by the courts) is not really free.[43]

How does the court go about defining religion? Legal scholar Eduardo Peñalver argues that the case of religious freedom is unique, because, unlike free speech, where the legal definition of "speech" is clearly different from the colloquial use of the term, in the case of the free exercise of religion, the courts tend to use the term "religion" unreflectively, as if the everyday use of the term makes it clear what religion means.[44] But, as Sullivan argues, religion today is as difficult to define as truth is in *Rashomon*. In our everyday use of the term, everything may be recognized as religion, and nothing is exclusively defined as religion. This fact renders the courts' job of securing the right to religious freedom (but also of securing disestablishment) impossible, as Sullivan's book's title suggests.[45]

Legal scholars have suggested different definitions of—or different methods for defining—religion, hoping that courts would rely on their suggestions when deciding cases about religious freedom. Some have sought substantial definitions, relying on classic definitions such as those proposed by scholars of religion like Émile Durkheim[46] or Clifford Geertz,[47] and some have defined religion in a functional way: legal scholar John Sexton proposes to understand religion as Paul Tillich did,[48] functionally, and to declare anything of "ultimate concern" to a person as deserving constitutional protection.[49] Legal scholar Kent Greenawalt rejects the notion of a dictionary-style definition of religion and proposes a method—identifying religion through analogy, something similar to a Wittgensteinian "family resemblance"—for the court to use when trying to identify religion.[50] Peñalver supports the Wittgensteinian method and adds guidelines for the court to follow: First, seek to define only religion, rather than offering broader definitions that would include conscience as well, as has been done in some cases. Second, given the evolving nature of language, the definition has to be flexible and bear the potential to evolve alongside ordinary language. I should add here the evolving nature of religion as well, which courts consistently fail to account for, especially in the case of Indigenous religions, because of the expectation to prove "authenticity," as I discussed earlier. Third, compare the phenomenon in front of the court to as many phenomena that already count as religion as possible, in order to avoid bias toward a specifically Western definition of religion.[51] Berger suggests that judges cultivate indifference to difference, to allow more room for minority religions to be understood as inoffensive to the state. Turning away from the obsession with definition, then, Berger proposes a "phenomenological turn in the study of law and religion, one that seeks to privilege experience of the law as the analytic starting point, rather than legal concepts or ideal forms of theory."[52]

Assigning courts the task of defining religion has political implications. Political and legal theorists agree that the United States is a secular nation that cares deeply about religion. Legal scholar Paul Kahn refers to this feature of the American polity as "cultural pluralism" and argues that it raises a theoretical challenge as well as a practical one (how can we decide which minority practice is tolerable?)[53] Political theorist Bette Novit Evans adds that in a pluralist culture, defining religion becomes more and more difficult, because religious practice has become more diverse. Furthermore, religious organizations have started offering many services beyond the strictly religious service, and at the same time the government is regulating more and more areas of life. Therefore, the conflict between government and religion becomes inevitable.[54] The main problem that arises has to do with the principle of separation between church and state, because if separation (or disestablishment) is dependent on the state or the law defining what counts as religion, then how can we see the two as separate? Scholars have understood disestablishment as the state's neutral stance toward different religions and toward non-religion, but Evans notes the difficulty of providing a neutral definition that would not offend anyone. If we want a broad definition, it will probably be very superficial, and if we want a deep definition, it is doomed to be too narrow.

Evans worries not that politicians and courts would resent religion but that they would be ignorant about it. Sullivan adds to that worry that religion in the twenty-first century, when diaspora religion is the most common one and when most religious people in the West live in secular states, is "lived religion." This means that religion changes constantly according to circumstances, and therefore any theoretical definition would always be too static to capture the phenomenon.[55] Political theorist Elizabeth Shakman Hurd writes that "religion is too unstable a category to be treated as an isolable entity, whether the objective is to attempt to separate religion from law and politics or design a political response to 'it.'"[56] For her, then, the challenge is "to signal an interest in a category, religion, which is legible to many, while also arguing for a different understanding of it."[57]

I think about the definitional question in the context of *Lyng*, or of Native American religious freedom more broadly, because the practice of defining religion has its own motivations (colonial, protestant, academic). The courts (and Indigenous litigants) engage in practices of defining religion for their own reasons, and thus they become actors in the religious studies game, sometimes unknowingly and unintentionally. Uncovering these processes is important because in the academic field of law and religion the question of how courts define religion has been so central that it has overshadowed other questions, such as that of Indigenous sovereignty. Bringing Indigenous sovereignty back into the picture helps to demonstrate that the definition of religion is not an end in itself. While *Lyng* was the first case on Native American religious freedom to have reached the US Supreme Court, the court did not seriously engage in the definitional question in *Lyng*, because there was no dispute that the practice in question was religious. Let us look at the legal definitions of religion that the parties and the court had available to them in *Lyng*.

Free Exercise Jurisprudence Before *Lyng*

Like legal scholars, the Supreme Court has had to grapple with the question "what is religion?" throughout the years. Though it has not been as adventurous as the lower courts, it has allowed the First Amendment to protect a variety of phenomena as religious. In *Reynolds v. U.S.* (1878), the Supreme

Court defined religion for the first time, ruling that the First Amendment protects only religious belief and not the actions that it entails.[58] The *Reynolds* Court ruled that the Mormon defendant's belief that practicing polygamy was a religious duty did not exonerate him from criminal conviction.[59] According to the court, criminal statutes against polygamy enforce a social duty and cannot be attacked on free exercise ground, lest religion become the law of the land and every citizen become her own law. This Lockean differentiation between religious belief and religious conduct is problematic, commentators have argued.[60] This differentiation cannot be meaningful because states can only regulate conduct; they cannot regulate belief.[61]

This definition of religion as belief was rejected by the Supreme Court more than half a century after *Reynolds*, in *Cantwell v. Connecticut* (1940).[62] In *Cantwell*, the court unanimously reversed the conviction of Jehovah's Witnesses for soliciting money for a religious cause without prior government approval and common law breach of the peace. The court held that the religion clauses of the First Amendment applied to the states by virtue of the Fourteenth Amendment and interpreted the Free Exercise Clause as protecting against laws prohibiting both belief and "chosen form of religion."[63] According to Justice Owen Roberts, "the Amendment embraces two concepts—freedom to believe and freedom to act," even if the freedom to act is not absolute.[64] "Conduct remains subject to regulation for the protection of society,"[65] but deprivation of a religion's means of survival is considered an impermissible "censorship of religion."[66] In *Cantwell*, the court struck down a law as infringing free exercise rights for the first time, balancing the citizens' right to exercise their religion freely against the legislature's prerogative. In attorney Donald Falk's words, "states could not place the physical means of a religion's continued existence at the discretion of public officers. Further, general regulations that might infringe on religious practice had to have a permissible motive and could not inhibit free exercise more than was necessary to protect a substantial state interest."[67]

Cantwell's protections were sharply but briefly limited in *Minersville School District v. Gobitis* (1940).[68] *Gobitis* rejected a free exercise challenge by Jehovah's Witnesses to a statute requiring all schoolchildren to salute the American flag and recite the Pledge of Allegiance daily. The court exempted any "general law not aimed at the promotion or restriction of religious beliefs" from free exercise scrutiny,[69] and it limited free exercise protection to three narrow rights: subjective belief, conversion of others, and assembly in a chosen place of worship. The government thus could justify a broad range of burdens on religion unless the offended parties could show clearly that the government action lacked any rational basis. Legal historian Sarah Barringer Gordon explains that because the flag salute was a nonreligious exercise, the public saw the Jehovah's Witnesses refusing the salute as simply unreasonable: "By importing religion into a nonreligious exercise, they seemed superstitious and disloyal, as well as impolite and aggressive."[70] According to the District Court judge who heard the *Gobitis* trial, however, "the decision about what counts as religious should rest with the believer, not school officials."[71]

Three years later, *West Virginia State Board of Education v. Barnette* (1943) overruled *Gobitis* and refined the *Cantwell* test. *Barnette* rejected the toothless "rational basis" test for legislation and held that the First Amendment religious rights of the individual limited the scope of state power.[72] The court ruled such rights could be restricted "only to prevent grave and immediate danger to interests which the state may lawfully protect."[73] Three principles established in *Barnette*, which was decided on the grounds of free speech, are relevant to free exercise according to Falk: first, infringement upon the free exercise of religion is justified only for the sake of protecting a legitimate state interest from grave and immediate danger. Second, the court would not defer to other branches of government's judgment on Bill of Rights issues. Third, the government has no inherent power to act contrary to the Bill of Rights; all levels of government must respect the freedoms the Bill of Rights guarantees.[74]

In the 1960s, the court began to consider cases about government actions that indirectly burdened free exercise, and it also broadened its definition of religion. In *Torcaso v. Watkins* (1961),[75] the court declared a religious test for public office unconstitutional. In a famous footnote in his majority opinion, Justice Hugo Black wrote that the First Amendment protected not only religions that were based on belief in the existence of a creator but also nontheistic faiths, such as Buddhism, Taoism, and secular humanism.[76] Two days later, in a decision in *Braunfeld v. Brown* (1961),[77] the court, considering whether Sunday closing laws infringed upon the free exercise rights of an Orthodox Jew, established a framework for evaluating laws that had the purpose or the effect of burdening the free exercise of religion, unless the secular purpose cannot be achieved without this burdening. While the plurality opinion did not see economic burdens as amounting to the prohibition of religious practice, the dissent (filed by Justice Brennan) focused on the compulsory effect of forcing one to choose between religious belief or practice and economic survival. While the plurality opinion used a rational-basis standard, Brennan argued for using strict scrutiny.

Sherbert v. Verner (1963), two years after *Braunfeld*, sees such forced choice between religious belief or practice and economic benefits as imposing "the same kind of burden upon the free exercise of religion as would a fine imposed . . . for . . . Saturday worship."[78] According to the *Sherbert* strict scrutiny test, a government action that incidentally burdens religion is justified only by a "compelling state interest in the regulation of a subject within the State's constitutional power to regulate."[79] Moreover, where there is such compelling interest, the government also needs to show that "no alternative forms of regulation would combat such abuses without infringing First Amendment rights."[80]

Under the *Sherbert* test, as it was clarified in *Wisconsin v. Yoder* (1972) and in *Thomas v. Review Board of the Indiana Employment Security Division* (1981),[81] a plaintiff must show that a sincerely held belief is substantially burdened by a government action. The burden of proof then shifts to the government to show either that the religious practice poses a grave and immediate threat to society (in the case of direct burdens) or a compelling state interest that cannot be achieved using a less restrictive means (in the case of indirect burdens). While *Yoder* expands the strict scrutiny test of *Sherbert*, it narrows the definition of religion that was broadened in *Torcaso*. *Yoder*, which Justice O'Connor distinguished from *Lyng* in her majority opinion and Justice Brennan cited as a relevant precedent in his dissent, exempted Old Order Amish children from compulsory secondary education because high school attendance is contrary to Amish beliefs. The *Yoder* Court held that a facially neutral statute that advanced a substantial state interest is subject to the balancing test because it unduly burdened free exercise rights. But it required the plaintiffs to demonstrate that the practice in question is sincerely rooted in religious belief, thus narrowly understanding religion as belief rather than conduct yet again. Even though compulsory school attendance threatened the Amish way of life, this burden was declared unconstitutional because this way of life was rooted in religious belief (rather than understanding this way of life as religious in itself).

The court in *Thomas* clarified that the test applied to state actions that indirectly or incidentally infringed upon a religious practice: such infringement is justified only if it is the least restrictive means to achieve a compelling state interest. Even more important to my reading of *Lyng* is the court's holding that the religious belief of a group does not have to be accepted by, or even comprehensible to, nonbelievers. Furthermore, to invoke First Amendment protection, a belief need not be articulated with precision or shared by all members of a religious sect. In *Goldman v. Weinberger* (1986),[82] however, the court exempted the military from the compelling interest balancing test and excused the US Air Force from review of its rational justification. The court held that "the military's perceived need for uniformity," reasonably and evenhandedly applied, legitimized the infringement of Goldman's religious practice.[83] The dissent in *Goldman* noted that a regulation written from a Christian point of view could not be considered "neutral."

In *Bowen v. Roy* (1986), the court rejected an Abenaki couple's suit to prevent the use of a Social Security number to process welfare benefits for their daughter. The Roys claimed that use of the number would rob their daughter of her spirit and prevent her from attaining greater spiritual power. The court held that the Free Exercise Clause "does not afford an individual a right to dictate the conduct of the Government's internal procedures."[84] An individual could not use the clause as a sword to make the government "behave in ways that the individual believes will further his or her spiritual development."[85] The court was divided on whether the government could require the Roys to use their daughter's Social Security number to receive benefits. Chief Justice Burger distinguished the case from *Sherbert* and claimed that "mere denial of a governmental benefit by a uniformly applicable statute does not constitute infringement of religious liberty."[86] The opinion lowered the standard of Free Exercise Clause analysis in benefits cases. Government benefits programs would withstand scrutiny as long as the government's scheme was neutral and uniform in its application and was a "reasonable means of promoting a legitimate public interest."[87]

Justice O'Connor, joined by Justices Brennan and Marshall, concurred in part and dissented in part. Justice O'Connor found the *Sherbert* balancing test applicable to the question whether the Roys had to provide the number despite their beliefs and that the government had available less restrictive means to prevent welfare fraud. Justice O'Connor noted the lack of precedent for the reasonable means test, which would relegate free exercise claims to "the barest level of minimal scrutiny."[88] She believed such a lax interpretation of the clause would enfeeble the Constitution's "express limits upon governmental actions limiting the freedoms of . . . society's members."[89]

The last free exercise case decided by the Supreme Court before *Lyng* was *Hobbie v. Unemployment Appeals Commission of Florida* (1987),[90] which reaffirmed the traditional free exercise analysis of incidental burdens on religious practice. The court expressly rejected Burger's attempt in *Bowen v. Roy* to apply a reasonable means test to some "incidental neutral restraints on the free exercise of religion."[91] Thus, prior to *Lyng*, the court's Free Exercise Clause doctrine stood as follows: direct criminalization of religious activity and compulsion to act in a manner contrary to religious belief (direct burdens) were forbidden unless justified by a grave danger to a substantial government interest. Indirect burdens on religious practice had to be justified by a government interest of the highest order that could not be served by less restrictive means.

Native American Sacred Sites Cases Before *Lyng*

Before *Lyng*, the Supreme Court had never considered whether development of federal land could injure the free exercise rights of Native Americans. Lower federal courts, however, had considered several such claims.[92] The first appellate opinion on an Indigenous free exercise challenge to public lands development was *Sequoyah v. Tennessee Valley Authority* (1980).[93] The Cherokee Nation challenged the impoundment of the reservoir behind the Tellico Dam in Tennessee, claiming that the dam would flood their sacred homeland along the Little Tennessee River, inundating and destroying sacred sites, medicine-gathering sites, holy places, and innumerable ancestral grave sites and would otherwise "disturb the sacred balance of the land" by stopping up the last free-flowing stretch of the largest and best trout-fishing water east of the Mississippi River.[94] The trial court had rejected the plaintiffs' free exercise claim because the Cherokee lacked a property interest in the site. However, the court of appeals balanced the burden on religion against the government's interest, following *Sherbert* and *Yoder*.

The absence of a property interest was not conclusive in view of the history of Cherokee expulsion from the area at issue and the importance of geographic sites to the Cherokee religion. For the sake of such balancing, however, the Sixth Circuit required that the Cherokee prove (again, following *Yoder*), the "centrality or indispensability" of the area to be flooded to their religious practice. Ruling that the plaintiffs failed to show that the sites at issue were "central or indispensable to religious practice," the court determined that the plaintiffs' affidavits reflected "personal preference," which is unprotected by the First Amendment.[95] Absurd as this decision may sound, the reference to the Trail of Tears and the acknowledgment of its grave impact on the question of property is rare and welcome in a court decision about Indigenous sacred sites, and I believe that a similar move by Justice Brennan in *Lyng* might have redeemed his dissenting opinion. Without acknowledgment of the colonial, genocidal history of the place in question, religion is doomed to be depoliticized and indigeneity essentialized. Even when land is conceptualized merely as sacred, the historical and political contexts should be considered, as they were, even if briefly, in *Sequoyah*.

Six months later, in *Badoni v. Higginson* (1980),[96] the Tenth Circuit Court dismissed the appeal of Navajo plaintiffs similarly confronted with the disappearance of sacred land under invasive waters impounded from yet another government-sponsored dam. In opposition with *Yoder*, the court discussed the government's compelling interest in operating and maintaining the dam *before* discussing the question of whether this operation and maintenance burdens Navajo religion. Plaintiffs sought to prevent the flooding and desecration of sacred sites in Rainbow Bridge National Monument by enjoining the continued filling of Lake Powell and by forcing the government to institute stricter controls on tourist activities in the area. The court concluded that the government's interest in the dam was of the highest order and could not be served if Lake Powell was kept at a level low enough to protect plaintiffs' religious sites. Examining the burden that the dam imposed on Navajo religion, the court determined that plaintiffs had to show the coercive effect of government action on their religious practice, which they failed to do, because they were not denied access to the sacred areas. But while the court decided in favor of the government, it also subjected federal land management policies to Free Exercise Clause scrutiny.

In *Wilson v. Block* (1983),[97] the District of Columbia Circuit Court rejected Hopi challenges to the expansion of a ski resort in the San Francisco Peaks within the Coconino National Forest. While the plaintiffs established the indispensability of the San Francisco Peaks as a whole, they failed to establish "the indispensability of that small portion of the Peaks encompassed by the Snow Bowl permit area" or the site of the proposed expansion.[98] The court required that the particular land threatened would be "indispensable to some religious practice" and that "plaintiffs seeking to restrict government land use in the name of religious freedom must, at a minimum, demonstrate that the government's proposed land use would impair a religious practice that could not be performed at any other site."[99] While plaintiffs might have *believed* that the sacred quality of the Peaks was impaired by the ski resort development, they had not shown a cognizable burden on religious *practice*. *Wilson* thus focused free exercise inquiry on the link between a particular geographic area and a particular religious practice that could not be performed elsewhere. Though land development might erode religious beliefs, the Free Exercise Clause was not implicated unless the mode of worship was irreparably injured as well.

The *Lyng* lower courts followed this logic, and based on the evidence and testimony in trial, both the district court[100] and the Ninth Circuit Court[101] decided that the High Country was indispensable to the Yurok, Karuk, and Tolowa peoples' religious practice and that the government's interest in developing the area was not compelling enough to justify the burden it would impose on the nations' religious practice. Justice Brennan's dissent upholds the lower courts' decisions, but the price that Yurok, Karuk, and Tolowa religion must pay for this protection may just be too high.

What Brennan Missed

One could tell the story of *Lyng* in many different ways. It is remembered as a decision that interpreted religious freedom too narrowly and property rights too broadly; as a case that demonstrates the advantage of the political process of legislation over the legal route of litigation; and as a story about the attachment of Indigenous peoples to sacred lands despite colonization ("The tribal-centric story is a story of a community forced to defend itself against the assimilationist agenda of the federal government—and developing a contemporary political identity in the process," according to Yurok attorney Amy Cordalis and Cherokee legal scholar Kristen Carpenter).[102] While Justice O'Connor's majority opinion is infamous for sacrificing Native American religions for the sake of protecting the federal government's property rights, Justice Brennan's dissent may be celebrated as sensitive to cultural difference, acknowledging the differences between so-called Western religion and Native religion and the strong relationship between Native

Americans and the land they inhabit. However, while "courts have become increasingly fluent in 'culture talk,'" this discourse has been critiqued as "simplistic, essentializing, and incomplete."[103] This chapter asks to show how—albeit all the obvious advantages of Brennan's dissent over O'Connor's majority opinion—Brennan's "culture talk" participates in depoliticizing Indigenous identity.

Shawnee legal scholar Robert Miller writes, "If an Indian religious case was ever going to win in the Supreme Court, it was [*Lyng*]."[104] Yet, the three nations lost the case. "Given the fact that no . . . Native American plaintiff has ever prevailed on a free exercise claim before the Supreme Court,"[105] there may be a reason to doubt the effectiveness of the constitutional route for Indigenous peoples in settler courts. But, as my reading of Brennan's dissent in *Lyng* has shown, even if an Indigenous community does ever win a free exercise case, this win would come at a price. The court is doomed to produce (and reproduce) both Indigenous difference and religious difference, marking both indigeneity and religion as static categories. Protecting the Yurok, Karuk, and Tolowa nations' relationship to the High Country because "Native Americans consider all land sacred,"[106] as Brennan proposes to do, distorts our conception of both indigeneity and religion.

As the testimonies of Yurok and Karuk witnesses demonstrate, their communities (like other Indigenous communities in settler states) have survived, responded to, and adjusted to colonial invasion. These adjustments include their relationship with the sacred: as one of the witnesses explained, the High Country has become more sacred than it had been because other sacred sites have been desecrated by settlers. The Supreme Court ignores this history. Thus, while the court produces what legal anthropologist Jennifer Hamilton called "Indigenous difference," it similarly produces religion as a static, apolitical category. In this way, the category of religion is constructed to help maintain the interests of the settler state, and any claims to religious freedom are always already weighted in favor of state power.

So what would be a better way for the court to talk about Indigenous religions? What context is missing? One thing to keep in mind is that religion was often used by settlers to conceal the violence and dispossession of Native lands, as Christian settlers represented their goal as Christianizing (and thus civilizing) Indigenous peoples rather than taking their lands. As religious studies scholar Jennifer Graber writes about Protestant ministers, missionaries, and reformers who deemed themselves "Friends of the

Indian," "in bringing the Christian God to Indian Country, these Protestants obscured their role in violent and coercive expansion and constructed an image of themselves as benevolent believers who imparted life-saving gifts to Indian people." Graber adds that Native peoples (she focuses on the Kiowa people) also relied on religion ("practices of making kin, giving gifts, engaging in diplomacy, as well as their rites for engaging sacred power") to resist dispossession, or "American efforts to reduce their lands, change their way of living, and break their tribal bonds."[107]

Similarly, in the Canadian context, religious studies scholar Pamela Klassen writes that "'since time immemorial' diverse Indigenous nations have organized themselves quite literally as peoples with laws and ceremonies shaped by the understanding that 'the Great Spirit has planted us on this ground where we are.'" Settlers have used religion, or what Klassen calls "churchstatedness" to assert jurisdiction over those Indigenous lands. "Sometimes that meant advocating for the separation of church and state as a sign of enlightened governance; at the very same time this could also mean combining forces between church and state to declare Indigenous peoples savage, uncivilized, and ignorant of the laws of property." And Klassen concludes: "Either way, colonial understandings of Indigenous spiritual jurisdiction—ways of speaking the law rooted in sacred authority derived from a relationship to land and place—were often unenlightened, mistaken, or willfully uncomprehending."[108]

It is also essential to keep in mind, when making decisions about Indigenous religions, the criminalization of Indigenous ceremony that lasted for half a century, from 1883 until 1934, the year the Indian Reorganization Act passed. As part of its assimilation policy, the federal government outlawed Indigenous religions, with a particularly brutal focus on what it perceived to be "heathenish" ceremonial dances. In a letter to Commissioner of Indian Affairs Hiram Price, Secretary of the Interior Henry M. Teller expressed a concern that among many tribes there persisted "certain of the old heathenish dances" and other ceremonial and traditional practices that he felt were both "intended . . . to stimulate the warlike passions" and contribute to the general "demoralization of the young."[109] In 1883, Price issued "Rules for Indian Courts" (known as the Civilization Regulations) that defined a number of "Indian Offenses," including participation in the Sun Dance. The "usual practices of so-called 'medicine men'" were also prohibited, as were ritual acts of property destruction carried out in accordance with tribal mourning customs (the code was revised in 1892 and again in 1904). To enforce this new Code of Indian Offenses, the 1883 Rules directed the Commissioner of Indian Affairs to establish Courts of Indian Offenses at each federal Indian agency, staffed with judges appointed by the local federal agents.

While the Courts of Indian Offenses were not entirely successful at their tasks, Indian agents did suppress religious ceremonies through various means, including the destruction of dance houses, the denial of food rations, imprisonment, and the threat of military intervention. According to tribal elders, Indian agents in Northern California rigorously enforced the prohibitions on religion. While many Indigenous dances continued, practitioners were forced to go underground. For the first time in tribal memory, certain ceremonies were not performed on an annual basis. While Yurok and Karuk doctors were harassed and ridiculed by Indian agents, Christian missionaries preached that the tribal religion was the "devil's religion." Religious studies scholar Susan Stager Gooding writes that "the list of Native American practices prohibited by these federal regulations suggests this policy was aimed not at the beliefs of Indian peoples but at the networks of social and political relations produced in the context of indigenous ceremonial practices."[110] Legal anthropologist Justin B. Richland adds that the list of "offences" demonstrates the extent to which these courts "were explicitly designed to promote the assimilation goals of the federal government."[111]

Neither Justice Brennan nor the Theodoratus Report mention any of this. The section of the report dedicated to the relevant years (1883–1918) focuses on allotment and then goes on to fulfill the aim of demonstrating the continuing existence of Yurok, Karuk, and Tolowa religious practice in the High Country, rather than documenting any disturbances. Under the title "Religious Diversity: Indian Religion and Christianity," the report tells us that "during the late nineteenth and early twentieth centuries while Indian lands were being allotted and the boundaries of the Hoopa reservation were being extended, Indian people carried on their religious observances and ceremonies in the [H]igh [C]ountry."[112] At the same time, "the reservation system in the United States was greatly influenced by Christian missionary groups who often held Indian Department jobs" and "tried with mixed success to convert Indians to Christianity."[113] Northern California was "under the guidance" of the Methodist Episcopal Church, then by the

Presbyterians, and after them the report tells us about Pentecostal and
Baptist presence in the area.

At the same time, the Theodoratus Report tells us, "there was also a continuing Indian religious presence." The report cites a Hoopa Valley Agent
whom, in 1918, wrote that "the native Indian dances are still continued but I
see no particular evil in them [except] that they take the Indians away from
their employment at times during the busy season. It is doubtful that they
can be eliminated to advantage."[114] In 1925, a Baptist missionary in Requa,
at the mouth of the Klamath River, was concerned about the persistence of
Yurok ceremony. He wrote to the superintendent, "Next Saturday Sept 5th
will be Indian Brush Dance at Jimmy Jenson's place outside of the house."
He expected a lot of attendees and a lot of whiskey. "Indian doctors here
already," he wrote.[115] The missionary hoped that the superintendent would
come down to Jenson's to stop the dance. The report does not mention
whether the ceremony took place or whether (and how) it was prevented.
All that mattered for the sake of the Theodoratus Report was that this was
proof that the Yuroks were still dancing in 1925.

The neutrality with which the report handles Christian presence is not
in line with Indigenous experiences. Hupa historian Jack Norton writes:
"In 1872, the Hoopa Valley Reservation fell to the control of the Methodist
Church. Complaints of 'paganism and indolence' soon appeared in reports
to Washington. J. L. Bruddus, superintendent of the Hoopa Valley Reservation, 1872, wrote in his annual report that 'the majority of Indians were
idle, careless, improvident; they would not work unless compelled to. They
were also addicted to gambling, and their native dances had a demoralizing
effect.'"[116] Even when the Theodoratus Report does refer to Indigenous
responses to white Christian settlers, it sounds very different from Norton's description. The report tells us about Karuk ceremonial activity in
1928, based on a letter written by Fin Jacobs (Karuk), "complaining" that
the whites are not respecting Karuk guidelines as to how to behave on their
holy grounds. "Our Pick-ya-wish ground is like school or cemetery to white
people," Jacobs writes. "No one should go around it until it is necessary."[117]
Jacobs reports that white people are building fences that block the path the
medicine men are supposed to take during ceremony and that they make
illegal Karuk fishing and hunting that is essential to their way of life. But
for the Theodoratus Report, all that Jacobs's statement does is establish
that the dances were still taking place every year in 1928. "Thus the Karok
[sic] religious ceremonies and use of the [H]igh [C]ountry continued into

the period when knowledge of their use could have been transmitted to Indian people now living."[118]

The neutrality with which the Theodoratus Report tells us about what Norton evaluates as tragic, indeed, as genocidal, is understandable, given that it was commissioned by the Forest Service to "identify cultural properties and evaluate their significance to Native Americans in the area of potential environmental effect of the Gasquet-Orleans Road, Chimney Rock Section; to describe the various impacts which may be expected from proposed changes in the area; to discuss mitigation alternatives if adverse effects are found to be involved; and to offer recommendations relative to the management of the cultural properties."[119] It is the framework of religious freedom and the type of consultation it requires from the government in the case of developing areas sacred to Native Americans that control the design of studies like the Theodoratus Report. Of course, we do not need the official legal code that criminalized Native ceremony to know that dancing in Northern California was dangerous, as is demonstrated by Chris Peters's mention in his trial testimony of the 1860 Indian Island Massacre, where settlers killed between 150 and 250 Wiyots during their world renewal ceremony.[120] All of this was available to Justice Brennan when he wrote his dissent. But whether or not this California history belongs in Brennan's dissent, the *legal* history related to Native American religious freedom is striking in its absence.

Similarly striking is the absence of acknowledging the role the G-O Road controversy has played in the weakness of the 1978 American Indian Religious Freedom Act (AIRFA).[121] Cheyenne and Muscogee activist Suzan Shown Harjo connects AIRFA with the Civilization Regulations when she writes that the passing of AIRFA was necessary in 1978 "because Native peoples were still suffering the ill effects of sorry policies of the past intended to ban traditional religions, to neutralize or to eliminate traditional religious leaders, and to force traditional religious practitioners to convert to Christianity, to take up English, and to give up their way of life."[122] Historian Theodore Catton explains that the Forest Service was seen as the most resistant of all the federal agencies to Native perspectives that would tend to restrict public-land use. The Forest Service's strong commitment to timber production at the time made it especially protective of its prerogative to build more logging roads and carry on intensive forestry. The G-O Road case became the test case for whether AIRFA gave protection to Indian sacred sites on public lands.[123]

Catton writes that in the run-up to AIRFA's passage, the Forest Service raised concerns that the legislation might lead to undue constraints on the use of public lands.

> The agency provided information to Congressman Tom Foley, Democrat of Washington, who then went to the bill's sponsor, Congressman Morris Udall, Democrat of Arizona, and said he would oppose the measure unless Udall would publicly allow that his bill had "no teeth." Udall gave in to Foley's demand, stating for the record that AIRFA's intent was merely to express the "sense of Congress." Section 1 of the act did just that, while Section 2 directed federal agencies to review their policies affecting Indigenous sacred sites and religious practice in consultation with Native traditional religious leaders. The president was to report back to Congress on the findings of the policy review in one year.[124]

Harjo, in her position as special assistant in the office of Secretary of the Interior, coordinated the multiagency review that the law mandated. She also produced, together with Vine Deloria, Jr., and Walter Echo-Hawk, the final report. She left the government the day after the report was delivered to Congress in 1979. Nine years later, she was called as a witness by the Senate Select Committee on Indian Affairs for its hearing on how to improve AIRFA. In her testimony, she gave "a blistering account" of the Forest Service's efforts not only to prevent AIRFA's passage but also to obstruct the policy review. It was, she said, the "least cooperative" among some fifty agencies that participated in the review after the law was passed.[125] This was a whole decade after the enactment of AIRFA. Harjo was, by then, the executive director of the National Congress of American Indians, and the G-O Road was still at the center of debate over Indigenous sacred sites. This was the year the Supreme Court handed down the *Lyng* decision.

Conclusion

It is the depolitization of indigeneity and of religion that allows *Lyng*, I believe, to remain the law of the land even after the Religious Freedom Restoration Act (1993)[126] was enacted to reverse *Employment Division v. Smith* (1990).[127] Indigenous sacred sites cases that have been lost since *Lyng* include *Navajo Nation v. U.S. Forest Service* (2008)[128] and, most recently, the fight against the Dakota Access Pipeline[129] and the Thirty Meter Telescope on Mauna Kea in Hawai'i,[130] as well as the attempt to defend Oak Flat from development.

In early 2021, a federal district court denied temporary injunctive relief to Apache plaintiffs seeking to stop the federal government from trans-ferring sacred lands to a foreign mining company, on the grounds that it would violate the First Amendment and RFRA.[131] This land is within Apache traditional territory, recognized as such under treaties, but it is also part of the Tonto National Forest, which the federal government claims to own and manage. Chi'chil Bildagoteel, known in English as Oak Flat, is the site of religious practices, including women's coming-of-age ceremonies. Similarly to *Lyng*, the court acknowledged that "the land in this case will be all but destroyed to install a large underground mine, and Oak Flat will no longer be accessible as a place of worship."[132] And citing *Lyng*, the court allowed the government to do that. Kristen Carpenter notes that in cases related to the construction of the border wall project, the government similarly failed to consult Indigenous nations "before blasting sacred sites and burial grounds."[133] According to Carpenter, the problem of Indigenous sacred sites is that many of them are located on federal public land now, having been taken from Indigenous peoples long ago. Therefore, "there is no 'private' place for those religions to go."[134]

And Indigenous religions should not be understood as "private." As Carpenter writes elsewhere about *Sequoyah v. Tennessee Valley Authority*, "Cherokee claimants explained in litigation over a sacred site, 'When this place is destroyed, the Cherokee people cease to exist as a people.' They may not have meant that each individual tribal member would literally die, but rather that the loss of such sacred sites would make it difficult or impossible to maintain Cherokee worldviews and lifeways."[135] And as I discussed earlier in this chapter, though the Sixth Circuit Court of Appeals did not see the place as central enough to Cherokee religiosity, its contex-tualization of the case within the history of the Trail of Tears is important in demonstrating that Indigenous religion is not "private." Brennan's dissent in *Lyng* fails to do so.

Brennan's generalization perhaps attempts to promote the protection of the High Country, but it erases Yurok, Karuk, and Tolowa presence in the area. Congress's protection of the High Country as wilderness in 1984 and in 1990 has actually protected it from development, but as I argue in the next chapter, the discourse of wilderness similarly erases Indigenous peo-ples and supports their dispossession from their lands. Jack Norton tells the post-*Lyng* story in a way that connects Indigenous ritual, wilderness, and the protection of the High Country:

> In the summer of 1988, after the Supreme Court decision, a unique event occurred. Quietly, several Karuk spiritual leaders prepared a ceremony to balance and heal the energy within the sacred area. They sent word to the dance leaders of the five High Dance tribes, and that summer, in Elk Valley just below Chimney Rock, a special Jump Dance or Mountain Dance was held. Two years later, Congress added the disputed lands in the sacred area to the California Wilderness Act that had been passed earlier. The paved two-lane road from Gasquet on the north side of the Siskiyou Mountains, and a similar road from Orleans on the south side, abruptly stopped at the edge of the sacred High Country. The entire area was, at least for the moment, free from disruption and harm.[136]

4

───◆───

LAND AS WILD IN THE CALIFORNIA
WILDERNESS ACT

In the previous chapter, we have seen that to support a free exercise case, Native Americans need to prove continuity: the court wants to see that the Indigenous nation has been practicing its religion in the same way, in the same place, for a long time (for hundreds or thousands of years, or "since time immemorial"). In this way, the courts construct indigeneity as fixed and immutable, ancient, and therefore primitive. This idea of indigeneity also erases the effects of settler colonialism on Indigenous communities and Indigenous lands: Indigenous peoples have not been practicing their religion in the same way for hundreds of years, because their ceremonies had been criminalized for more than half a century; they have not been practicing those ceremonies in the same places, because a lot of the lands have been stolen from them by the settler state, most notably through the national park and forest systems. Nevertheless, for the Indigenous subject to appear before the law, she must prove an unsevered connection to the past.

This chapter focuses on the idea of wilderness, which requires what seems to be the opposite: to prove that a place is worthy of protection as wilderness, one needs to prove that the area has not been affected by human activity, that it is pristine and wild. What we have in the G-O Road case is an argument that in order to protect Yurok, Karuk, and Tolowa religious freedom, the High Country must remain in its pristine condition. In other words, in this case, religious practice is claimed to have not made an impact on the environment—the Indigenous subject claims to have been in this place "since time immemorial" without impacting the environment of the High Country. They seem to have proven everything they are asked to prove, against all odds (because what they are asked to prove—a consistent presence in a place without leaving any trace—contradicts itself). The fact that the court was able to hear these two contradictory claims as coherent—the continuity of religious use of the place is heard as consistent with the description of the place as pristine—tells us a lot about how the court understands Indigenous use of land: the Indigenous does not leave a mark on the land even when she is there. As we have seen in chapter 2, this understanding of indigeneity justified the dispossession of Indigenous peoples from their lands.

After all this, after proving the impossible, the Yurok, Karuk, and Tolowa nations lost the G-O Road case. However, the High Country has not been developed. Congress offered it the protection that the court has failed to provide. This chapter tells the story of the High Country's protection in the California Wilderness Act[1] and in the Smith River National Recreation Area Act.[2] I show how, despite the problematic history of the discourse on wilderness for Indigenous peoples, the Yurok, Karuk, and Tolowa have succeeded in utilizing this discourse for their own benefit; once again, resistance to an oppressive discourse comes from within this discourse itself.

The High Country as Wilderness

In their complaint, the plaintiffs portray the High Country as wilderness: "This is an action for a declaratory judgment and injunctive relief challenging certain actions of the Forest Service in planning and approving road-building, clear-cutting, and related development activities in a remote and wild portion of the Siskiyou Mountains in northern California known as Blue Creek."[3] They then move on to describe the religious value of the area to the Yurok, Karuk, and Tolowa peoples, but they quickly return to wilderness: "Blue Creek is also highly valued by plaintiffs and others for its wilderness character and natural beauty, for the primitive recreational opportunities it provides, for the diversity and rarity of its wildlife and plant life, and for its exceptional anadromous fish habitat."[4]

What does wilderness mean to the plaintiffs? Why is the wild nature of the High Country valuable to them? In the complaint, they mention natural beauty, primitive recreation, wildlife, and plant life. The remote and pristine characteristics of the High Country are essential to the ceremonial use of the area, but as we will see in the next chapter, the tribes also have a kinship relationship with the nonhuman environment of the High Country. Therefore, protecting the wild nature of this place means more than keeping recreational opportunities open to them. It is doubtful that the State of California's "wilderness expert," Larry Moss, can convey the complex meaning of the High Country to the court when he is called to the stand.

Moss introduces himself as "a resources consultant and author." His CV, which was read into the transcript, includes in his professional experience that from October 1982 until January 1983 (just a couple of months before the trial takes place) the witness "traveled in the Himalaya mountains in Nepal, partially to contrast these high mountain areas with existing and proposed wildernesses on the national forests and parks of the United States."[5] Before that, he served as representative and consultant of the Wilderness Society, the Sierra Club, and various State of California offices and agencies, and he worked to establish wilderness areas in California. After listing his degree (BA in English literature) and graduate education (certificate in executive management), the CV reads: "I have hiked and camped in designated or *de facto* wilderness areas in the States of Georgia, Florida, Minnesota, Wisconsin, Arizona, New Mexico, Nevada, Utah, Colorado, Wyoming, Washington, Oregon, Alaska and California, as well as in western Canada."[6]

Deputy Attorney General, Edna Walz, representing the State of California in the G-O Road trial, explains that the Blue Creek area "was not . . . classified as primitive in 1964 [according to the Wilderness Act]. However, in 1970, the National Environmental Policy Act was enacted.[7] And pursuant to that, the Forest Service recognized that it had an obligation to evaluate the wilderness characteristics of all roadless areas, potential wilderness areas, for consideration whether they should be recommended to Congress for their wilderness consideration."[8] Walz explains that the area is a roadless area and qualifies for inclusion within the wilderness preservation system. However, if the Forest Service goes ahead to construct the Chimney Rock section of the G-O Road, the area would lose its wilderness qualification. Note that even if an area meets the criteria for wilderness designation, the Forest Service does not have to recommend it for this designation. However, Congress has the authority to include it in the wilderness system even without Forest Service recommendation. The only obligation of the Forest Service is to evaluate any roadless area within national forests for wilderness designation.[9]

The State of California challenges the evaluation process. The Blue Creek area's wilderness potential has not been evaluated properly because it was evaluated separately from the contiguous Siskiyou area, the State of California argues. The area should be considered as one, undivided area, because the existing dirt road should not count as separating them; the planned asphalt road would, however, separate them, and would ruin the wild, pristine nature of the High Country. The purpose of Moss's testimony is to show that "if they were properly evaluated as one contiguous area, as they should have been, that they would have received a much higher wilderness rating."[10]

Forest Service attorney Rodney Hamblin's objection—"what is wilderness, I'm sure, to 50 people is 50 different things"—is apt, and so it should not be the subject of expert opinion.[11] Further, even if there is such a thing as expertise in wilderness, the witness has a degree in English, which does not make him into a wilderness expert. Walz's response is priceless: "I would like further to note that there is no such thing as a degree in wilderness."[12] The court nevertheless allows for the testimony to proceed, but only as far as it describes the characteristics that make Moss believe that the area could be treated as wilderness. Testifying as to whether or not an area is wilderness within the meaning of the statute counts as legal opinion and is therefore prohibited. The purpose of the witness is to show that the existence of the jeep road is not a sufficient reason to separate Blue Creek from the Siskiyou wilderness study area.

Moss summarizes the definition of wilderness in the Environmental Impact Statement: "Wilderness area generally appears to have been affected by the forces of nature; little or none of man's imprints; has outstanding opportunities for solitude or primitive and fine type of recreation with at least 5,000 acres. It may also contain ecological or other significant values."[13] And he continues to evaluate Blue Creek: "The Blue Creek area, in my opinion, meets this statutory definition in that it is a natural area that is primarily affected by the forces of nature. It has outstanding opportunity for solitude which I have experienced several times in the area myself. It is at least 5,000 acres. And it also contains ecological, geological and other features of values stated under the act."[14] Blue Creek is also unique among other roadless areas, according to the witness, because of "the lower elevation, Douglas fir, hemlock forest." And he continues: "A significant example of this forest covered the coastal band in Northwestern California and Oregon. And that forest had mainly been cut on private land, on Forest Service land. And this is the largest remaining example of that particular forest type."[15]

The general wilderness characteristics of the Siskiyou area are, according to the witness:

> It consists of glaciated basins, clear streams, higher elevation peaks, mountain meadows.... The Blue Creek area is, in my opinion, part of the contiguous roadless area. It is different in nature than the higher Siskiyous. It consists of the slope of the Siskiyous as it reaches down for the Klamath River. It is mainly forested with different types of forest cover[,] the higher elevation[,] fir forests; the lower elevation, hemlock, Douglas fir. It has open, grassy meadows, oak woodland, and Blue Creek tumbles its way to the Klamath River in an elevation very close to sea level from approximately 5,000 feet in its headwaters.[16]

What follows is a lengthy testimony to support the argument that Blue Creek and Siskiyou should have been inventoried as one area and that when they are joined together, they have greater value as wilderness. The testimony ends with a description of the existing road: "Walking from west to east, it is a very low standard jeep trail that is not suitable for use for a highway vehicle. I would, under no condition, take my normal station-wagon [sic] Datsun across that road. Although I do drive across a substantial number of Forest Service roads. As it climbs up from the west going through a steeper portion, it goes along the ridge line."[17] The road is wide enough for one vehicle, it has a dirt surface with some natural rocks, it is slightly less than seven miles long, and there is no structure on it, such as a bridge or a plunk.

The government's attorney has questioned the witness's expertise on wilderness, but his testimony raises an ethical question as well. In chapter 1, I discussed general critiques of the use of white anthropologists as expert witnesses in legal cases about Native lands. But here, specifically, the witness's visits to the High Country are problematic. Take, for instance, the testimony of Arnold Pilling, a white anthropologist who has studied Yurok life in the area and was called to testify by the Indigenous plaintiffs. Asked when the last time he had visited the High Country was, Pilling said: "I have never been up there. Informants that I have worked with are, I feel, of the belief that only a person that has been personally trained and from the right families should go up there, and I have abided by that view."[18] The court is supposed to know this by the time of Pilling's testimony, which comes after a few Native witnesses have already discussed the inaccessibility of the High Country to anyone who has not been properly trained to use it. It is therefore appropriate to ask why Pilling's testimony is needed at all. However, what Pilling's testimony does to Moss's testimony is that it shows the extent to which Moss is unqualified to testify in this case. His testimony is based on his great familiarity with the area, following several visits, and the legitimacy of these visits is not questioned by any of the attorneys. What is demonstrated here is that the activity required to designate the High Country as wilderness is not in line with the protection of the area as sacred.

Pilling's testimony also demonstrates that the area should not count as wilderness, in the sense of a place that has not been impacted by human beings. He explains that early in the nineteenth-century, the area "used to have its separate ceremonial grounds and things were changed drastically by Indian hunting by whites."[19] And he continues: "In the 1850s, the whites went into the Blue Creek area with guns and they did it in other places on the river. But in the case of the Blue Creek villages, it was very effective and the area was cut down very much."[20] Pilling describes the documents he has worked with, but he also "worked with survivors, descendants that were taken up there by old people that have lived there to show the caved-in houses where the old people have been raised. These people I am speaking of are people who would have been born before 1800, because the Blue Creek area has, in terms of its traditional role in Yurok society, changed drastically during the first decade of major white contact."[21]

I bring Pilling's testimony here for two reasons. The first is that it casts doubt on the validity of Moss's testimony and of the "wild" characteristics of Blue Creek. But his testimony also demonstrates an ambivalence that Native American studies scholar Cutcha Risling Baldy (Hupa, Yurok, Karuk) describes, according to which ethnographic knowledge is sometimes valuable to Native communities, in her case Native communities who are trying to revitalize their traditions, and in our case, perhaps, information on the settler colonial history of Blue Creek.[22] However, we have already heard such testimony from Yurok elder Lowanna Brantner, and her testimony is now part of public record, just like Pilling's is, as I have

discussed in chapter 1. As Yurok/Karuk leader Chris Peters says, it takes a
white man or woman, it takes a PhD, to legitimize what Yuroks themselves
say about the High Country. Pilling's testimony makes its way into the
district court's decision only as far as it determines that Yurok, Karuk, and
Tolowa people have used the High Country for ceremonial purposes since
early in the nineteenth century. It does not find its way into the Supreme
Court's decision. His testimony was not offered in opposition to the wilderness designation claim, and the district court's decision declares that the
G-O Road violates the Wilderness Act. And even if we find potential in
Pilling's testimony, I am not sure this potential is realized at all.

Not only did the district court find that the G-O Road violates the
Wilderness Act of 1964, but in 1984—a year after the court handed down
its decision in the G-O Road case—the California Wilderness Act protected twenty-six thousand acres of the Blue Creek Unit from development as wilderness. Yurok elder Walt Lara, Sr., writes that following the
Lyng decision,

> we met with Congressman Doug Bosco, who attached the preservation of
> Chimney Rock area to the Siskiyou Wilderness Bill. I am happy that to
> this day, our sacred area is protected. However, I can't help but be frustrated
> and hurt at the epistemicide, the threat to our way of knowing and under-
> standing the world. I find injustice in the implication that a Wilderness Bill
> can protect animals, but the U.S. Constitution is not "required" to protect
> human beings. Furthermore, the decision on the Gasquet-Orleans Road set
> precedent and became the "Supreme Law of the Land."[23]

Lara is disappointed with the protection of the High Country by the
California Wilderness Act. He is disappointed not because he didn't want
the High Country to be protected but because it took a wilderness bill
to protect it. For Lara, protecting the High Country is protecting Yurok,
Karuk, and Tolowa people. Wilderness preservation is not meant to protect people. It is there to protect animals. It is the US Constitution that
is supposed to protect people, and in the case of *Lyng*, it failed. Moreover,
even though the G-O Road has not been completed and the High Country
has been "preserved," Lara does not forget the big picture: *Lyng* has become
the law of the land, which means that other Indigenous sacred sites—other
Indigenous peoples—are not safe.

While Walt Lara attributes the inclusion of the High Country in the

California Wilderness Act to the meeting with Congressman Bosco, Chris Peters implies that it has to do with the ceremony they held a few days earlier:

> On September 24, 1984, just a few short days after the completion of the Finish-up Dance of the revitalized Wela'welagah [earth-healing ceremony] at Pecwan, the U.S. Congress passed the California Wilderness Act ... [which] created the Siskiyou Wilderness area that encompassed a significant portion of the Chimney Rock section of the Gasquet-Orleans Road. With this action, Congress removed the main purpose for constructing the GO Road by officially stopping the Forest Service's plan for timber cutting and associated logging road building in the Puhlik-lah High Country. However, despite all of the favorable provisions of the California Wilderness Act, the construction of the GO Road was still under review by the U.S. Court of Appeals for the Ninth Circuit, so the Wilderness Act left a strip of land needed to build the controversial road out of the wilderness designation.[24]

The California Wilderness Act protected the High Country from logging but not from the G-O Road. It took a few more years, and an appellate court's decision in favor of NICPA, for the rest of the High Country to become protected.

> U.S. Congress, in 1992 [sic], passed legislation to establish the Smith River Recreation Area. The legislation not only preserved a pristine region of the Smith River, but also included a provision that would incorporate the six-mile strip of land initially set aside to construct the GO Road into the Siskiyou Wilderness Area. With this legislation, the plans to construct the GO Road would be stopped and our sacred lands would be preserved in perpetuity. This was a major victory for Native Peoples in Northern California and for a unique Earth Based Spiritual Theology. However, the legal precedence established in the GO Road case would still adversely impact Sacred lands throughout the Nation. Also, it should be noted that the decision to include the closure of the GO Road in the Smith River Recreation Area Bill was absent of significant consultation with Native Peoples, and it proved effective in quashing all community organizing that would lead to direct action or a consolidated resistance to oppose the genocidal Supreme Court decision rendered in the GO Road case.[25]

Shawnee legal scholar Robert J. Miller adds that the inclusion of most of the High Country in the California Wilderness Act was problematic and might have led to NICPA ultimately losing *Lyng*: Congress meant to preserve this area "of critical importance to Native Americans for cultural and religious purposes" because it was "highly suitable for year-around primitive recreation."[26] Miller recognizes two problems here: one is that Congress prohibited logging in the High Country but left a twelve-hundred-foot wide corridor in case the G-O Road was ever approved. Yet, Congress meant to take no position on that decision.[27] The second problem is that the passage of the act rendered moot the issues that led to the intervention of the State of California and the environmental plaintiffs who supported the Native claims in the G-O Road case, and therefore, by the time the case reached the Supreme Court, the Indigenous plaintiffs (now respondents) were left to argue the case on their own.

Risling Baldy reads the designation of this area as wilderness as "built upon the idea that Native peoples . . . had not interacted in any meaningful way with significant portions of California." It is part of "systematic attempts to attack the very existence of California Indians," which "were a means by which white settlers set out to exterminate, control, and dominate the land, flora, and fauna of Native California. It also meant attempting to destroy Native knowledge and epistemologies as a way to claim rightful ownership over the land."[28] This reading leads us to the more general problematics presented to us by the wilderness discourse.

The Problem with Wilderness

What does it mean to protect the High Country as wilderness? While wilderness is an important American idea with spiritual significance, it also brings to mind the doctrine of terra nullius and the doctrine of Christian discovery, two doctrines that have served to justify the conquest of many lands in North America and elsewhere. By designating an area as wilderness, we define it as pristine—one that has not been touched by human beings—thus erasing Indigenous existence in, and impact on, the area before its "discovery" by Europe. As the Wilderness Act of 1964 declares, lands designated as wilderness are

> an area of undeveloped Federal land retaining its primeval character and influence, without permanent improvements or human habitation, which is protected and managed so as to preserve its natural conditions and which (1) generally appears to have been affected primarily by the forces of

nature, with the imprint of man's work substantially unnoticeable; (2) has outstanding opportunities for solitude or a primitive and unconfined type of recreation; . . . and (4) may also contain ecological, geological, or other features of scientific, educational, scenic, or historical value.[29]

According to legal scholar John Copeland Nagle, the supporters of the enactment of the 1964 Wilderness Act wanted to promote spiritual values. Wilderness leaves the land as it was created by God and provides us with the opportunity to encounter God, be in solitude, and experience spiritual renewal. Yet the Wilderness Act itself fails to note the spiritual values of wilderness.[30] Geographer Linda H. Graber reminds us that wilderness is not necessary for the enjoyment of outdoor recreation or for the preservation of wildlife habitat. Perhaps what she is saying is that the secular justifications for wilderness preservation are not convincing. "Whether we realize it or not," she concludes, "an influential portion of the American public treats wilderness as sacred space."[31]

However, when we listen to what Yurok and Karuk members have said in response to the Forest Service's development plan in the High Country, we can see that the designation of the area as wilderness does not necessarily respond to their concerns. Take, for example, this testimony by a Karuk member, explaining what the problem is with developing the area and making it accessible both to the logging industry and to tourists:

> These areas need to be there when a new Indian person gets the "calling" to become a medicine person. Suppose the "calling" is received and the person arrives to find an army of tourists to take pictures and make tape recordings of a real live medicine person in the process of training. Also the trees are gone, the whole area logged off. The solitude and atmosphere for meditation is totally lost. How will that person train properly? . . . The culture has been torn apart by progress and now people are asking for the pieces to be torn in smaller pieces.[32]

While I acknowledge that the protection of the area from development is a positive outcome, indeed, a much better outcome than the Supreme Court decision *against* protecting this area, I am interested in exploring and critiquing the discursive implications of designating this area as wilderness, given the history of this idea and its role in dispossessing Indigenous peoples from their lands. The implications of the wilderness idea are not only discursive, of course. They are material. Kānaka Maoli food studies scholar Hiʻilei Julia Kawehipuaakahaopulani Hobart writes about the role a discourse on emptiness played in the Thirty Meter Telescope (TMT) controversy on the Mauna Kea in Hawaiʻi. While animacy has been central to Native Hawaiʻian resurgence and to the resistance to the TMT and to Western colonialism, "much of Maunakea's development, from earliest Western contact to the present day, has been predicated on an idea of its emptiness."[33] Discourses of absence and emptiness, she continues, "have systematically produced the Mauna as a place without humans, spirituality, nation, or even atmosphere."[34] Imposing "Western spatial imaginaries" of emptiness upon Indigenous geographies has justified development projects, from uranium mines and nuclear test sites, to pipeline construction.[35] Therefore, the same notions that inspire wilderness preservation also justify development.

Anishinaabe jurist John Borrows examines the role that the doctrine of terra nullius played in the case of *Tsilhqot'in Nation v. British Columbia* (2014), where the question at the center of the case was whether, at the time of discovery, the Tsilhqot'in Nation's social organization was of a sufficiently high level to establish aboriginal title.[36] Supposedly, if the Tsilhqot'in Nation was too nomadic, or not self-governing, then the territory of which they claim aboriginal rights had been legally vacant. "Social organization can be a synonym for self-government. When a nation organizes itself over an entire territory and controls land, makes decisions about its use, and excludes others in accordance with its laws, we should be clear about what we are saying—such a nation governs itself."[37] As we have seen in the previous chapter, according to Alfred Kroeber's description, the Yuroks had no political organization. Does this mean that at the time Europeans arrived in Yurok Country, the area was "legally vacant"?

Depicting the land as empty erases not only the presence of Indigenous peoples on the land but also the agency of the place itself. According to the Yurok, the *woge* spirits reside in the High Country, and so even if the Yurok cannot prove that they have been using it, according to their cosmology, the High Country has not been empty. As noted in chapter 1, the Yurok, Karuk, and Tolowa peoples believe that world renewal ceremonies were initiated by prehuman spirits who inhabited the world and brought all living things and culture to humankind. The Theodoratus Report describes one Yurok origin story retold by Alfred Kroeber:

The Yurok myths . . . belong to a time period when the earth was inhabited by a race of beings called woge . . . small humanoid beings who reluctantly yielded the earth to mankind. There is an eerie sense of nostalgic sadness and loss whenever the woge are mentioned . . . the woge withdrew into the mountains or across the sea or turned into landmarks, birds, or animals in order to escape close contact with newly created man. Yet the woge are still present in some sense, and they are depicted as being glad to be called upon (in ritual formulas and the like).[38]

The medicine people who go to the High Country to communicate with the spirits recite set narratives at specific places in a fixed order. A complicated process of purification is required before attending the High Country: abstaining from water, sex, and profane activity, fasting, isolation in the sweathouse, and using tobacco and a specific medicine made at a specific site in the High Country.[39] Medicine women must not be menstruating at the time of the ceremony, and neither can any other woman participating in the ceremony (e.g., the mother of a sick child for whom the ceremony is being conducted). About twenty girls and boys participate in the Brush Dance, the girls prohibited from dancing once they get married or have a child.[40] Elements of the traditional ceremonies (hereditary rights, loaning of regalia, reciprocal assistance across tribal lines, responsibility to feed visitors, and payment to mourners) continue to be an integral part of present-day ceremonies.[41]

Ceremonial dances are performed at the sites where the *woge* are said to have first brought certain gifts to humans. The dances are considered to be the reaffirmation of the gifts and to have the power to remove evil from the world and to restore balance to the earth. While in the past ethnographers argued that the Yurok dance regalia is merely a marker of status and wealth, Yurok people themselves disagree, seeing the regalia as both symbolic and sacred and also as living beings. They say that the ethnographers' focus on material wealth has led to misinterpretation of their culture. A Yurok member quoted in the Theodoratus Report said that "dances are our religion," while another specified that "when ceremonies are held, the people pray about everything, for the salmon to come, for the acorns to grow, for the presence of all kinds of game, and for children to grow up to be good."[42]

The mountains are the focal source of curative powers because this is where the *woge* spirits went when humans came to the earth, according to the creation story described above, and in death, the doctors' souls follow the path of the *woge* spirits to the mountains. Chris Peters writes about Yurok creation stories, according to which "human life is the product of the creative energies of the Earth along with the countless Wo-gay, Spirit Beings, who joined together with earthquake, lightning, thunder, water, and fire and gave life to humanity."[43] Peters continues to explain that "the Spirit Beings, including the spirits of plants and animals, combined their most dynamic and formidable qualities with the rich soil of Earth to form human life.... Humanity evolved or descended from the Wo-gay and ... we still have some of their creative energies within our DNA."[44] It is not only that the spirit beings reside in the High Country but that the land itself is a living being. According to Yurok earth-based theology, "the Earth is alive and has a spirit, and that humanity has a vital responsibility to help maintain such harmony. In fact, that is our primary purpose in life: we are Earth-healing and Earth-renewing peoples."[45]

Even though the land is alive and the *woge* reside in the High Country, settlers used the idea of terra nullius—legally vacant land—at the time of the G-O Road era as they did at the time of the California frontier and the Gold Rush. But ecologist M. Kat Anderson writes that "traditional management systems have influenced the size, extent, pattern, structure, and composition of the flora and fauna within a multitude of vegetation types throughout the state. When the first Europeans visited California, therefore, they did not find in many places pristine, virtually uninhabited wilderness but rather a carefully tended 'garden' that was the result of thousands of years of selective harvesting, tilling, burning, pruning, sowing, weeding, and transplanting."[46] Indeed, Karuk cultural biologist Ron Reed ties this management with social responsibility and political sovereignty.[47] Anderson adds, "The first European explorers, American trappers, and Spanish missionaries entering California painted an image of the state as a wild Eden providing plentiful nourishment to its native inhabitants without sweat or toil. But in actuality, the productive and diverse landscapes of California were in part the outcome of sophisticated and complex harvesting and management practices."[48]

"Far from the stereotypes of savage hunters and gatherers," Native American studies scholars Beth Rose Middleton Manning and Kaitlin Reed (Yurok) explain, "Yurok people have a highly sophisticated and complex understanding of the ecology and natural resources throughout their territory." According to Manning and Reed, "Indigenous stewardship facilitated sustainable economies and enhanced the growth and diversity of

California's resources."⁴⁹ Yurok tribal council attorney Amy Cordalis and legal scholar Kirsten Carpenter (of Cherokee descent) add that "long before the United States Forest Service or California Department of Fish and Game existed, the Tribes managed these resources according to a complex set of societal rules founded in Indigenous science, technology, religion, and law that produced a landscape quite different from the appearance of the Klamath River Basin today."⁵⁰ They have done this through a combination of traditional forest-management practices: gathering, burning, transplanting, and habitat modification.

The Religiosity of Wilderness

A lot of the critique of *Lyng* (including Justice Brennan's critique of the majority opinion) focuses on the incommensurability of Indigenous religion as land-based and Protestant Christianity as otherworldly and focused on inner faith.⁵¹ To say that a religious tradition is based on land can mean different things: it can mean that a religious tradition can only be practiced in a specific location or that its continuation is dependent on the integrity of a specific place, even if the place is not easily accessible. It can mean that certain deities or ancestors reside in a specific place or that a meaningful event has taken place there (Vine Deloria, Jr., talks about "revelation"). It can mean that medicinal plants that a community uses grow in a certain place. All these cases indicate a special relationship between a religious community and a specific place; indeed, they indicate a relationship between a people and its homeland. Is it really the case that Christians cannot relate to such a relationship to land?

Even if Protestantism is fundamentally detached from land (it is often said that Christians associate religion with built environments, with churches, while Native Americans see the land itself as sacred), perhaps wilderness is the one context in which the sacred becomes localized, or place-based, for Christians, especially in the United States. It is therefore useful in bridging the gap between Indigenous religions and so-called Western religiosity. And that might be the reason that Judge Weigel agreed to hear the wilderness expert's testimony during the G-O Road trial. As environmental studies scholar Nicolas Howe writes, "like religion, wilderness is a touchy subject. *Because* of religion, wilderness is a touchy subject. Of all the ideas associated with American environmentalism, it is the most heavily shrouded in the rhetoric of religious experience. Wilderness is the place of divine revelation, of spiritual communion, of personal devotion, of moral purity. It is where humanity is humbled by the sublime mystery of creation."[52]

This relationship between wilderness and religion has interested many scholars and environmentalists. According to author John Brinckerhoff Jackson, wilderness has been considered by the nobility "an environment where they alone could develop and display a number of aristocratic qualities"[53] and also where one could have the experience of "religious brotherhood."[54] However,

> strictly speaking, the wilderness experience is not mystical, for the relationship revealed is not with the divine but with unspoiled nature; but its effect is to subdue the omnipresent clamor of the ego and to reveal to us that we, along with all living things, are inseparable parts of the cosmic order. For all its intensity, it is a temporary thing; we return to the everyday world, though spiritually transformed.[55]

Wilderness, according to Jackson, is where religious sentiments, secular romanticism, aristocracy, and masculinity come together. Perhaps this has been the experience of Larry Moss, the wilderness expert witness in the G-O Road case. While he does not speak about the area in religious or spiritual terms at all, the comparison he suggests between the High Country and the Himalaya implies an assumption of spiritual significance.

Howe complicates things for us when he writes that environmental law has been critiqued for creating sacred spaces by designating them as wilderness; it is not that sacred places are protected as wilderness but that they become religious once they are defined as wild or pristine by environmentalists:

> Environmental law has always had a fraught relationship with landscape. Despite its close reliance on science, it has always been vulnerable to the charge that its interest in landscape is "merely aesthetic" or, worse, "merely spiritual." Especially when it comes to wilderness preservation, critics have long dismissed environmental litigation as a pretext for sanctifying pristine places, a technocratic excuse for re-creating Eden by force. Behind its charge lies a much more troublesome assumption: that environmentalism is nothing more than fundamentalism in disguise, and wilderness is its temple.[56]

Linda Graber put it more succinctly in 1974: "Why should wilderness be chosen as sacred as opposed to, say, city sites or heroes' graves? The

unsatisfactory circular answer must be that wilderness is sacred space because people have taught themselves and others to perceive it that way."[57]

But in Western traditions, wilderness is both a spiritual and a secularized legal concept. Representative Morris Udall, sponsor of the Wilderness
Act, echoed religious sentiments when he said that "there ought to be a
few places left in the world left the way the Almighty made them."[58] John
Muir found in Alaska the "perfectly natural effect of simple and appreciable
manifestations of the presence of God."[59] Roderick Nash generalized this
idea when he wrote that "wilderness symbolized divinity."[60] Henry David
Thoreau famously proclaimed that "in Wildness is the preservation of the
World."[61] Indeed, wilderness is central in the Hebrew Bible. For example,
most of the Pentateuch takes place in the desert, where the Israelites wan-
der for forty years before reaching (and conquering) the promised land.
These stories, which are highly influential in American political thought
in particular and in settler colonial thought more generally, portray wilderness as sacred and development as secular or even sinful (Moses's successful attempt to produce water from a rock in the Book of Numbers is
punished harshly; because of Moses's attempt to "develop" the wilderness,
he is banned from entering the promised land).

On the other hand, when we read *Lyng* and its aftermath, we can see
the protection of the High Country as wilderness as a secular alternative
to its protection as sacred. Cutcha Risling Baldy argues that what the California Wilderness Act protects in the High Country is not wilderness at
all but recreational use, which follows a capitalist logic. Wilderness is man-
ufactured in this act to enable use, which contradicts the wilderness ethic
expressed by wilderness supporters.[62] It is worth it, then, to ask about the
colonial implications of the spiritual power assigned to wilderness and its
secularization, which I do in the next section. Yurok Chief Judge Abby
Abinanti, in an open letter to Justice O'Connor after the *Lyng* decision,
helps to make connections between the spiritual and colonial aspects of
wilderness and the preservation versus development discourse:

> I hope heaven has no harvestable timber; or, if it does, I hope your people
> never have the ingenuity to find heaven and sail there. (I know how import-
> ant that place is to many of you.) Because if you can get there, and if there
> is any economic benefit to be had, heaven will surely be harvested, mined,
> developed, parceled out or otherwise required to yield a profit.[63]

The Coloniality of Wilderness

Abinanti's critique of the American obsession with development is valid, and the idea of wilderness drives this obsession: "Landscapes understood to be natural are . . . understood not only to be untouched but also to be waiting for civilizing instruments to develop them, as if that is their inevitable fate: a virgin prairie ready for the plow."[64] However, preservation is also not inherently good. Métis historian Mark David Spence reminds us that "wilderness preservation went hand in hand with native dispossession."[65] Environmental historian William Cronon critiqued the idea of wilderness as a pure manifestation of the sublime for concealing its roots in nineteenth-century frontier ideology and validating a long history of dispossession and conquest.[66] In other words, both development and preservation have worked as tools for settler colonial dispossession.[67] Perhaps the conclusion is that environmental discourse is useless to Indigenous communities altogether. As Vine Deloria, Jr., writes, "Inherent in the very definition of 'wilderness' is contained the gulf between the understandings of the two cultures. Indians do not see the natural world as a wilderness."[68]

Ecologist Ramachandra Guha's postcolonial critique of deep ecology and wilderness preservation acknowledges that the shift from an anthropocentric approach to a biocentric approach to the environment is welcome both in religious discourse and in scientific discourse. However, the idea that only the environment's integrity—and not human needs—should guide any intervention in nature is unacceptable, according to Guha. Indeed, the idea of wilderness is "positively harmful" when applied to the developing world.[69] In countries such as India, Guha tells us, "the setting aside of wilderness areas has resulted in a direct transfer of resources from the poor to the rich."[70] Designated wilderness areas are managed for the benefit of tourists and the needs of the locals are never considered. In the United States itself, "the function of wilderness is to provide a temporary antidote to modern civilization. . . . For most Americans it is perfectly consistent to drive a thousand miles to spend a holiday in a national park."[71]

The #LandBack movement has argued that the United States can begin correcting some of the wrongs it has done to Indigenous peoples by returning national parks to the Native peoples to whom they originally belonged. Ojibwe author David Truer writes about the national park system:

More than a century ago . . . Muir described the entire American continent as a wild garden "favored above all the other wild parks and gardens of the globe." But in truth, the North American continent has not been a wilderness for at least 15,000 years: Many of the landscapes that became national parks had been shaped by Native peoples for millennia. Forests on the Eastern Seaboard looked plentiful to white settlers because American Indians had strategically burned them to increase the amount of forage for moose and deer and woodland caribou. Yosemite Valley's sublime landscape was likewise tended by Native peoples; the acorns that fed the Miwok came from black oaks long cultivated by the tribe. The idea of a virgin American wilderness—an Eden untouched by humans and devoid of sin—is an illusion.[72]

Imagining land as wilderness goes hand in hand with imagining its inhabitants as primitive, childish, and savage. As Chief Justice John Marshall put it in *Johnson v. M'Intosh* (1823),

> the tribes of Indians inhabiting this country were fierce savages, whose occupation was war, and whose subsistence was drawn chiefly from the forest. To leave them in possession of their country, was to leave the country a wilderness; to govern them as a distinct people, was impossible, because they were as brave and as high spirited as they were fierce, and were ready to repel by arms every attempt on their independence.[73]

The idea of the Indigenous as savage contradicts the idea of empty land. As Native American studies scholar Dina Gilio-Whitaker (Colville Confederated Tribes) points out, there is a paradox inherent to how the United States has thought about Indigenous peoples and wilderness: "The virgin wilderness construct presupposes a landscape unadulterated by human intervention, which imagined the Indigenous inhabitants incapable of (or unwilling to) alter their environments. At the same time, paradoxically, it implied a landscape largely devoid of human presence."[74] This inherent contradiction has to do with a historical ambivalence of European settlers toward Indigenous peoples. On the one hand, they desired to be like the Indigenous people they encountered—free and authentic—and, on the other hand, they needed to extirpate them. As Gilio-Whitaker writes, "Virgin wilderness narratives are a way to discursively eliminate Indigenous peoples from the land as a form of erasure or extirpation."[75] The idea of wilderness, then, follows what historian Patrick Wolfe called "a logic of elimination": it erases Indigenous existence so that settlers can replace them. The paradox Gilio-Whitaker points to is not coincidental.[76]

———

As this chapter has shown, the discourse of wilderness has been harmful for Indigenous peoples. It has been used to dispossess them while advancing an ideal of a spiritual American man who can encounter the sublime only as he conquers a wild land on his own, in solitude. At the same time, it is as wilderness, not as sacred, that the High Country has been eventually protected. Can the master's house be dismantled with the master's tools, after all? Let us not celebrate prematurely. For wilderness designation further attaches the High Country to the federal government, not to the Yurok, Karuk, and Tolowa peoples. If the question of sovereignty is who can make decisions about—determine the fate of—the High Country, then wilderness designation makes the United States, not the Yurok, Karuk, and Tolowa peoples, the sovereign. Indigenous sovereignty will take us away from federal law and into the sphere of Indigenous law. It will take us away from ideas about wild land and place us in relationship with the land, not as owners, or developers, or preservationists, but as kin. The next chapter explores Yurok law and sovereignty on the Klamath River, as it developed after *Lyng*.

5

---•••---

LAND AS KIN IN THE KLAMATH
RIVER RESOLUTION

In May 2019, the Yurok Tribal Council passed a resolution to extend rights to the 'We-Roy, which is known in English as the Klamath River: "The Yurok Tribal Council now establishes the Rights of the Klamath River to exist, flourish, and naturally evolve; to have a clean and healthy environment free from pollutants; to have a stable climate free from human-caused climate change impacts; and to be free from contamination by genetically engineered organisms."[1]

In this chapter, I argue that this resolution demonstrates a kinship relationship between the Yurok and the Klamath River, a relationship that calls Yurok people to take responsibility for the struggling river and to help it heal. I also see in this resolution an assertion of sovereignty. While the US government has regulated Native lives by determining Native identity on the basis of blood quantum, the Yurok here define their community as including not only those who are enrolled members of the Yurok Tribe but also the Klamath River, who is their kin and for whose well-being they are responsible. As Plains Cree scholar Robert Alexander Innes tells us about the Cowessess First Nation:

> Cowessess has undermined the imposition of the Indian Act's definitions of Indian by acknowledging kinship relations to band members who either had not been federally recognized as Indians prior to 1985, or were

urban members disconnected from the reserve. This acknowledgement defies the general perception that First Nations people have internalized the legal definition of Indian, and in the process rendered traditional kinship meaningless.[2]

Here, too, despite all that the settler state has done to undermine Native kinship, the Yurok demonstrate that their relationship with the Klamath River has not been severed. This chapter asks what it means to extend rights to a nature entity, to treat it as a person, and not just any person but as one who is next of kin. I explore the significance of such treatment for the rights discourse that is usually focused on human beings and also for our understanding of land.

The idea of Yurok kinship with nature has been hinted at in anthropologist Alfred Kroeber's work, in the Theodoratus Report, and in the G-O Road trial, when the High Country was portrayed as the place of residence of the *woge*, or prehuman ancestors, but I explore this notion of kinship as it is expressed by the Yurok themselves, rather than by lawyers and expert witnesses. While the extension of personhood to corporations and to human fetuses has been cynically used against marginalized groups, and especially against the reproductive rights of women, and therefore legal personhood may be justly critiqued by feminist thinkers, this chapter shows that the recognition of the Klamath River (as well as of other nature entities) as a person is different, and the difference has to do with the notions of kinship and of responsibility that drive this recognition.

Central to an Indigenous understanding of kinship, and to Indigenous knowledge systems in general, is the concept of relationality, as aboriginal scholar Aileen Moreton-Robinson writes.[3] But kinship does not necessarily refer to biological families. As Potawatomi scholar Kyle Powys Whyte clarifies, "By *kinship*, I don't mean relationships shared only by members of small families or of biological lineage groups." Instead, he writes,

> kinship refers to a category of relationships that people have with one another. Specifically, kinship relationships fall under the category of relationships grounded in responsibility. Responsibility refers to bonds of mutual caretaking and mutual guardianship. When members of a society practice responsibilities to one another extensively, there's a high degree of interdependence. Such interdependence serves the purpose of facilitating a society's responsiveness to changes that affect its members' safety, well-being,

and self-determination. Whether faced with a hurricane, a pandemic, or a trade embargo, a high degree of interdependence in the form of shared responsibilities can be a crucial coping strategy.[4]

Kinship relationships are reciprocal, trusting, consensual, and transparent. Those relationships take time to develop—they must be ongoing. The Klamath Resolution, therefore, is a declaration of the ongoing kinship relationship between the Yurok and the Klamath River, a relationship that has not been severed by settler colonialism.

The story of the *Lyng* case features land as its protagonist, characterizing it sometimes as property, sometimes as home, sometimes as sacred, and sometimes as wild. The plot is about a competition between all these characteristics of land, and each of the previous chapters has imagined how the story of *Lyng* might end were one of them to win the battle. If land is understood primarily through its property aspect, then the Forest Service should be allowed to develop it in any way it thinks would be most profitable. On the other hand, if land's sacred nature is its prominent feature, then the Yurok, Karuk, and Tolowa nations' opposition to the Forest Service's development plan should be respected and the land should remain untouched. If the land is considered wild, the outcome would be similar to that of sacred land, but other uses of the area would be permitted, beyond religious ceremony and medicine-making (the Wilderness Act allows for some recreational activities to take place in wilderness areas).[5] What if the land is understood as the Yurok's, Karuk's, and Tolowa's home? In that case, the outcome might *look* similar to that of the sacred land story finale, but in truth it would be very different: the Yurok's, Karuk's, and Tolowa's opposition to the development plan would be respected, not because they have the constitutional right to worship on government property but because the place is recognized as their traditional home, which in turn gives them the authority to decide how it will be used. All these characteristics seem mutually exclusive—after all, wilderness is defined by not being anyone's home; the sacred cannot be owned by human beings.

In this final chapter, I would like to propose a fifth characteristic of land, to demonstrate two things. First, the first four characteristics of land (home, property, sacred, and wild) do not have to be understood as mutually exclusive. Second, the human relationship to the land does not have to be (actually, it *shouldn't* be) defined through the idea of rights. In a sense, what this chapter does is accept the notion of land as home presented by the Yurok and Karuk witnesses during the G-O Road trial and demonstrate what it looks like when the complementary notion of kinship with nature guides them in living in this home. Yet, the notion of land as kin is different from the notion of land as home: while I have a host of rights associated with the place I call home (even if I do not own it), it is obligation, not rights, that I have toward my family. My relationship with my children, for example, is not contractual; their well-being is my well-being.

This chapter explores the notion of land as kin, and it takes us from *Lyng* to its aftermath and from the High Country to the Klamath River. But even though I want to take us away from the rights discourse that has ruled the human relation to land, this chapter does take us through rights-based relationships between human beings and nature. We start with the idea that human beings have a right to nature (to use it or own it), which implies that human beings are not a part of nature, that they are somehow separate from and superior to it, and move toward the idea that nature itself has rights (to its integrity, for example) and that it is human beings' *responsibility* to protect those rights of nature (this notion implies that there is no binary and no hierarchy between humans and land). Ideally, from here we would move on to the idea that it is not human beings who protect nature or its rights; rather, it is nature who takes care of us humans. The discourse on responsibility (instead of rights) brings us closer to the idea according to which nature protects us rather than we nature, or perhaps that the relationship is mutual—that we take care of each other as kin. But this chapter will not fully explore this right-less kinship relationship with nature—this project must be left for future pursuit. First, we have to do away with rights.

Water Rights Around the World

In recent years, we have seen, around the world, movement toward the acknowledgment of nature entities as legal persons to whom rights are granted. What can we learn from these different cases? In 2008, Ecuador became the first country to enshrine the legal rights of nature in its constitution.[6] Bolivia passed a similar law in 2010.[7] New Zealand and the Indian state of Uttarakhand granted legal rights to specific rivers in 2017.[8] In Bangladesh, since July 2019, all rivers count as legal persons, and an environmental council can take to court anyone who harms the rivers.[9] That same year, the city of Toledo, Ohio, passed the Lake Erie Bill of Rights to protect its shores.[10] In 2021, the Magpie River in Quebec, Canada, was granted official rights and legal personhood. It was assigned nine rights, as well as potential legal guardians responsible primarily for ensuring these rights are respected. This is the first such case in Canada.[11] Activists in Bangladesh and New Zealand say they see the rivers as their ancestors, while Indian activists talk about sacredness as the reason for acknowledging the river's personhood.[12] In Toledo, it was simply too much pollution that drove the bill of rights. In Canada, the desire to preserve both recreational and traditional activities was declared as the reason for granting rights to the Magpie River.

Many of these laws met with resistance from industry, farmers, and river communities who argue that giving nature personhood infringes on their rights and livelihoods. We will see similar resistance to different attempts to heal the Klamath River. The question of responsibility is a complicated one, and in practice it comes down to the question of who has the money to sue, though the epistemological shift from rights to responsibilities is much more significant than the practical legal questions. As Tanana Athabascan poet and scholar Dian Million writes,

> nation-states and international humanitarian orders offer up promises of recognition, equality, and rights while reducing our non-human relations to resources. As subjects of these human "rights," the Indigenous are positioned at the end of a long line of those who seek "rights" in the form of care that never disrupts the violence of the racial-capitalist-settler-colonial order. Meanwhile, our non-human relations are quantified, commodified, and extracted—our relations in places are reduced to *things*.[13]

This epistemological shift, then, disrupts the settler colonial order and transforms the nonhuman environment from commodity or resource to kin. Enforcement is inherently difficult because of the trans-boundary nature of rivers, but the trans-boundary nature of rivers also makes them an apt site for critique of the binary notion of sovereignty.[14] At the same time, rivers' wild, raging, unpredictable nature makes them a fitting site for critique of governmentality: can humans really control rivers? Ethnic studies scholar Charles Sepulveda (Tongva and Acjachemen) writes about the efforts to "domesticate" rivers, comparing these efforts to the domestication of women: "Both domestication projects were produced for the expansion of empire and the growth of capital. The purpose and operating logic within both of these projects was to produce authority and (dis)possession over the land/water. And ultimately, to domesticate the 'wilderness.'"[15]

What I want to take from the global examples of rivers' rights are the questions that they raise about what it means for us to think of rivers as legal persons. "What does it mean for a river, and its associated natural elements, to have rights? What does it mean for them to have rights as a 'person'? How would such rights be implemented, given that rivers and other elements of nature would not be able to themselves claim and defend such rights?" ask environmental activists Ashish Kothari and Shrishtee Bajpai following the 2017 Uttarakhand High Court's decision to grant rights to the Ganga and Yamuna rivers as living beings. Mostly, they are interested in the implications for the relationship between humans and the rest of nature.[16] They ask about dams—should building them be allowed? Can the water be diverted to such an extent that water is no longer flowing in long stretches of the river? In addition, who would sue in the name of the rivers? And who would be the beneficiary of potential compensation?

These questions have been asked by legal scholar Christopher Stone in his groundbreaking 1972 essay "Should Trees Have Standing?" where, comparing environmental entities to others who had been previously considered not fully human and therefore rightless (Black people, women, children), he argues for the recognition of environmental personhood and rights.[17] However, what I am interested in is Kothari and Bajpai's observation that "rights are the obligations that the society and state have for establishing sustainable relationships. Fundamental rights, in that sense, are the most basic of obligations because they emanate from the idea that they are present even if no law exists." If the most fundamental right is the right to life, what does that mean when we talk about a river? Does it include the right to flow freely? Does it include the rights of other species? Kothari and Bajpai suggest that

the river has a right to exist, right to maintain its identity and integrity. This does not put an end to fishing or other human activities related to the river, but rather pushes for a healthy relationship that maintains the essential conditions of a river: its flow, its constituent plants and animals, its catchment, where snow or rain sustains its water intake, the rocks and soil and other elements of the landscape it flows through. Consequently, what could be challenged in the recognition of such a right are activities that badly or irreversibly damage the above conditions, including dams and diversions, industrial and urban pollution, fisheries using explosives or trawling methods, etc.[18]

I am less interested in the practical questions that these cases raise than in the epistemological shift they require from us. As environmental studies scholars Nicole Wilson and Jody Inkster write, "at the very least, [they] complicate concepts of governance as [they] call into question the ability of humans to govern or act on behalf of water. [They] may even call into question the extent to which water as a more-than-human is even 'governable.'"[19] Kothari and Bajpai explain that "any rights-based movement, especially one that is arguing for fundamental and inalienable rights, challenges not only the legal system, but also the culture on which this system is built." This observation is in line with Muscogee scholar Daniel Wildcat, who writes that Native thinkers, unlike Western thinkers, "include as a part of their political communities many other-than-human persons, including persons that swim, winged persons, four-legged persons, and so on." Therefore, Native thought and practice "have defined politics and ethics as involving a much broader conception of persons."[20] Religious studies scholars Suzanne Crawford O'Brien and Inés Talamantez (Mescalero Apache) write that in Anishinaabe cultures, "an animate being is a *person* by virtue of its membership and participation in an actual network of social and moral relationships and practices with other persons. So moral agency is at the core of the Native conception of personhood. This means that one cannot be a person in isolation."[21]

Therefore, instead of anthropomorphizing nature, Native epistemologies open the category of personhood to include nonhuman beings. What is changed is mainstream non-Native perceptions of both nature and personhood. Sisseton Wahpeton Oyate scholar Kim TallBear writes against the "animacy hierarchy" that places some beings below others: "Strictly speaking, the ideas of being *animate* and *inanimate* posit categorical divides between entities—those seen to be alive and those deemed as not living, a divide defined organismically in dominant thinking." And she reminds us that "the animacy hierarchy also de-animates many humans, including Indigenous and Black people, by placing them below the Western and often male subject."[22]

Lakota scholar Vine Deloria, Jr., adds that "human personality was derived from accepting the responsibility to be a contributing member of a society. Kinship and clan were built upon the idea that individuals owed each other certain kinds of behaviors, and that if each individual performed his or her task properly, society as a whole would function."[23] And so we could say that the challenge Kothari and Bajpai write about is a challenge to Western legal cultures, which focus on rights rather than on responsibilities and whose communities include only human beings.

Legal scholar Lawrence Tribe, building on Christopher Stone's work, proposed a new basis for environmental law, one that would start with human obligation. Thinking of our relationships (with one another as well as with the physical world) as almost sacred, Tribe recognized that it is easier for us to grant personhood and rights to animals than to tress, for example. However, "what is crucial to recognize is that the human capacity for empathy and identification is not static"[24] and that "choosing to accord nature a fraternal rather than an exploited role . . . might well make us different persons from the manipulators and subjugators we are in danger of becoming."[25]

Lenape scholar Joanne Barker is not convinced that environmental personhood is the answer. According to her,

> nowhere is the capitalism of rights clearer than in the extension of human rights to other-than-human beings, including water. The revolution has truly failed when the only way for water, air, or the land to remain unpolluted is by legally assigning it the status of human. Genuine revolution means genuine alterity. Vine Deloria Jr. suggested that for Indigenous peoples, responsibilities capture the core ethic of this alterity: "The basic problem is that American society is a rights society, not a responsibilities society."[26]

Barker presents here the biggest challenge I face in this chapter. And the challenge is to accept, simultaneously, that the extension of personhood and rights to rivers preserves and justifies the rights discourse that I critique in this book and that the Klamath River Resolution does not participate in the perpetuation of the rights discourse. The key to solving this seeming contradiction is found in the question of jurisdiction—this book began with sovereignty and it will end there as well. The resolution declares that the Yurok Tribal Court will have jurisdiction over cases against those who violate the rights of the Klamath River, and thus it addresses Deloria's concern about an Indigenous ethic of responsibility and an American rights society. The Yurok Court operates according to Yurok values and an ethic of responsibility. It replaces the punitive goal of the US criminal justice systems with a goal of reconciliation. It cares about healing the community and therefore refuses the principle of impartiality. But more on this later.

In response to the acknowledgment of the legal personhood of the Whanganui River in Aotearoa/New Zealand, historian Miranda Johnson argues that "this beguiling notion cannot capture the plural and heterogeneous expressions of attachment, practices of belonging and care, economic interests, and complex notions of identity that Whanganui people bear in relation to the ever-changing river." And she continues: "The simplistic idea that the river is a person does not accord with the complex record produced over a century and more of protests, petitions, and litigation on the part of several generations of Whanganui leaders who wanted to control the use of the river by individual settlers and government bodies." Finally, she concludes: "In this case, the fiction of legal personality singularizes diverse and heterogeneous understandings of the river in a form that, it is claimed, actually recognizes Māori beliefs and practices."[27] I want to take this critique seriously, but I also see the Yurok resolution as doing the opposite of singularizing diverse understandings of the river. What is important to me is the Yurok's relationship with the Klamath River as kin rather than the river's personhood independent from this relationship.

Gerard Albert, the lead negotiator for the Whanganui *iwi* explained it similarly: "We have fought to find an approximation in law so that all others can understand that from our perspective treating the river as a living entity is the correct way to approach it, as an indivisible whole, instead of the traditional model for the last 100 years of treating it from a perspective of ownership and management." What is important to my argument is that now the Whanganui river is considered, legally, to be part of the Whanganui people. Albert continues: "Rather than us being masters of the natural world, we are part of it. We want to live like that as our starting point. And that is not an anti-development, or anti-economic use of the river, but to begin with the view that it is a living being, and then consider its future from that central belief."[28]

The Yuroks begin with the view that the Klamath River is a living being as well, and it is more than just a living being; it centers their worldview, their identity. Yurok means, in Karuk language, "downriver people." What Native American studies scholar Cutcha Risling Baldy (Hupa, Yurok, Karuk) writes about Hoopa is true to the Yurok as well: "'Worldview' is 'water view,' a view *from* the river not a view *of* the river. We move upriver, or downriver, to the river, or from the river. So our theoretical standpoint is one that foregrounds *water view*, (re)claiming knowledges not just for the people, but also for the water; not just looking at our relationship to water, but our accountability to water view."[29] But the journey from this starting point to the recognition of the river's personhood and rights passes through the history of Indigenous water rights in the United States, which is different from that of the global contexts I presented in this section. I turn now to this history.

Water Rights in Native America

This section looks at the *Winters* doctrine of reserved water rights and then at legal scholarship critiquing it. For example, legal scholar Michelle Bryan looks beyond state and federal law to international law to find ways of protecting Native American access to waters they consider sacred, beyond fishing rights or reserved water rights. However, in some cases there is no clear distinction between fishing and sacred uses of waters. The nonbinary nature of the relationship between Indigenous peoples and water makes the rights discourse unsuitable for addressing such problems. Bryan argues that "tribes can and should argue for both on- and off-reservation treaty rights for sacred waters when the governing language of treaties, statutes, Executive Orders, or other federal instruments support such rights."[30] But I see this use, and I think she would agree, as purely strategic. More importantly, since it is highly unstable—the protection of treaty rights is not always guaranteed—it is necessary to find a different path, a different language, toward honoring the relationship between Indigenous peoples and water. Cases such as the recent protests against the Dakota Access Pipeline may begin to give us insight into such potential paths and languages, especially as the words "water is life," which have become associated with these protests, help us to think about the relationship between Indigenous (and non-Indigenous) peoples and water in non-dichotomous ways.

Religious studies scholar Natalie Avalos (Mexican Indigenous descent) argues that "the Oceti Sakowin (Lakota/Dakota) peoples' opposition to the Dakota Access Pipeline was a sovereignty issue. By responding with ceremony, the people affirmed their sacred relationships to the lands and the spiritual power within them that make them sovereign."[31] American studies scholar Nick Estes (Lakota) adds that "for the Oceti Sakowin, the affirmation Mni Wiconi, 'water is life,' relates to Wotakuye, or 'being a good relative.' Indigenous resistance to the trespass of settlers, pipelines, and dams is part of being a good relative to the water, land, and animals, not to mention the human world."[32] According to Risling Baldy, our treatment of water is about human kinship not only with water but with the whole natural world: "The water that we drink is the water the salmon breathes, is the water the trees need, is the water where Bear bathes, is the water where the rocks settle. Many of our stories foreground relationships to water. These stories show us that water is theory; theory that is built from relationality to the land, the earth, everything."[33]

And water does not adhere to state, municipal, or reservation boundaries. Bryan explains that although some sacred tribal waters are located on reservations, most of them are not. Moreover, "even when sacred waters are located within protected areas, they remain vulnerable. Waters can originate upstream of a reservation boundary and thus be affected in terms of both quality and quantity by the time they reach a tribe. And on many reservations, tribes may be deemed to lack jurisdiction to regulate certain activities on non-Indian lands within the reservation."[34] Neither does water adhere to boundaries between religious and nonreligious use. As Frank Ettawageshik puts it, "the true treaty right" his Odawa people have to Lake Michigan fish is not a quantifiable property right but a right to continued relationship to the fish: "Our ancestors didn't say 'those are our fish.' Rather, they reserved the right to fish. That meant they reserved a right to sing to the fish, to dance for the fish, to pray for the fish, to catch and eat the fish but to live with the fish, to have a relationship with the fish."[35]

The US Supreme Court first affirmed the water rights of Native American reservations in 1908 in *Winters v. United States*.[36] Environmental studies scholar Lloyd Burton writes about the huge impact this decision (known as the *Winters* doctrine, or reserved water rights doctrine) has had on resource management since then. By 1991, when Burton published his important book, *American Indian Water Rights and the Limits of Law*, more than forty Native nations had initiated administrative hearings and court battles, "claiming their share of the water resources on which the entire economic future of [western states] depends."[37] According to Burton, the "quantities of water in controversy are huge, as are the economic benefits accruing to whichever parties eventually win."[38] Historically, Burton explains, there have been three trends in the development of Native American water rights: the federal courts have generally treated Native nations as individual, autonomous nations, bearing ancient rights to natural resources, as they are implicitly treated in the US Constitution. However, policymakers (congressional and executive) have treated Native Americans collectively, as one ethnic minority struggling for their share in the national wealth. Finally, similarly to the process of creating reservations in the nineteenth century, when Indigenous communities were pushed to relinquish "theoretical sovereignty over vast areas in return for federally protected control over much smaller amounts of land," now we see the federal executive branch, the states, and private corporations encouraging those communities to give up their (theoretical) water rights claims in return for federal delivery of much smaller amounts of water.[39]

Two competing theories of water rights had been at play before the *Winters* case went to court: the first is the English common law of riparian rights, which the eastern states followed, according to which landowners had the right to the natural flow of all waters coming through and bounding their lands for "reasonable use." According to this doctrine, the rights of all riparians are correlative, and none of them may alter water flow or quality to a degree that would harm another riparian's use. These are the only limitations on each riparian's right—the amount of water is not quantified or limited otherwise, and the right is inherent to riparian land and is not lost if not used. The second doctrine is that of prior appropriation, in which there is a strict hierarchy of rights based on the chronological order in which users first began to appropriate a resource. Ownership of riparian land is not required, but the right is limited to an amount of water approved for beneficial use, and nonuse results in loss of the right. Finally, in times of shortage, rights are honored according to the hierarchy described above, and so senior appropriators may receive their full share while junior appropriators may get little or nothing.[40]

In *Winters*, the court did not rely on these doctrines as much as it did on an interpretation of the federal government's responsibility to the Native community when creating the reservation. According to the court, when the government creates a reservation, it commits to setting aside the amount of water necessary to fulfill the purpose for which the reservation was established.[41] The Supreme Court agreed that in keeping with the western states' water rights, the date a reservation was established would be considered as the date the water was reserved, thus making Native Americans the senior appropriators in most cases (since most reservations were founded between the 1850s and the 1880s).[42] However, unlike state prior appropriation doctrine, the water should not be quantified, and nonuse did not cause the loss of Native water rights. While reserved rights have generally referred to surface waters that abut or run through the reservations, the Supreme Court has affirmed reserved water rights in the Colorado River for a reservation that is not adjacent to the river.[43] Note that while there is an interpretation here of the purpose of creating reservations as one that requires the reservation of water as well as land, there is no questioning of the justification of the reservation system at all.

Indeed, the reservation system left Native American peoples with the least-desirable lands, but the reservations did include valuable implied rights. The reserved water rights of the *Winters* doctrine are, according to Legal scholar Robert T. Anderson, the most well-developed implied property rights, along with access to fish and wildlife, while rights to general environmental protections lag behind.[44] Indigenous water rights are property rights held in trust by the United States for the benefit of Native nations.[45] However, *Winters* supports reserving waters for agricultural purposes, which "reflects colonial desires to assimilate Indians into an agrarian economy and lifestyle," in contrast with water rights reserved for fisheries, which reflect government commitments to advancing Indigenous traditional values.[46] More recent cases indeed aim to protect uses of water other than agriculture by recognizing tribal water rights to instream flows.

While irrigation informs questions such as whom can use what water (and how much), the strength and purity of instream flows affect the quality of bodies of water used for fishing and for ceremonial purposes, for example. *United States v. Adair* (1983) addresses rights of the Klamath Tribes to instream flows, and the Ninth Circuit determined there that "one of the 'very purposes' of establishing the Klamath Reservation was to secure to the Tribe a continuation of its traditional hunting and fishing lifestyle."[47] Water rights for fisheries include the right to keep water in lakes and rivers to provide places for fish to spawn and for salmon to travel to and from the ocean. Most recently, in February 2021, the court "affirmed the senior priority date of the Klamath Tribes' water rights in the Klamath Basin, and upheld the need to maintain a healthy and productive habitat to meet the Tribes' treaty right to fish, hunt, trap, and gather."[48] According to the court in *Adair*, some Indigenous peoples' water rights have a priority date of "time immemorial," in cases where the community was using the water in its aboriginal territory before the reservation was created.[49] Acknowledging Indigenous presence in these places "since time immemorial" is generally positive. However, according to Bryan, the doctrine of prior appropriation stems from a worldview that is utilitarian, consumptive, and extractive, and therefore it is at odds with sacred Indigenous waters (including ceremonial waters, water understood as spirit, and waters in sacred places).[50] Nevertheless, Bryan calls for a regime change, in which sacred waters would be acknowledged by western states through the doctrine of prior appropriation, not only because of the legal protection it may afford but also as a symbolic step.

How can our current water law system meaningfully embrace both the utilitarian logic and the reality of sacred waters? As this book has shown, these worldviews are not necessarily mutually exclusive, and I am therefore sympathetic to Bryan's project. Bryan pushes her readers to innovate and collaborate in order to protect the multiple values we place on water today. We should focus, she writes, "on those controlling state rules that run most counter to sacred water: beneficial use, diversion, seniority, abandonment for non-use, and an economically driven 'public interest' requirement."[51] Traditionally, water rights that have been protected are related to domestic use (drinking water, gardening) and productive use (mining, irrigation). The list has expanded to include growing municipalities, railroads, and power companies, but leaving water in place has always been considered nonuse, and thus it is not protected as a water right.[52] As Anderson explains, water reserved for fisheries and hunting is associated with traditional Indigenous values, but this is not enough for Bryan: "Sacred waters are presently outside of the beneficial use lexicon. Indeed, the very word *use* connotes a value that may be at odds with a tribe's conception of water as living spirit, birthplace, or other source of the sacred."[53]

Bryan's focus is on water that is not protected by any treaty or other federal agreements, but she does offer a list of federal legislation that may be useful in protecting sacred Indigenous waters, even though federal law "does not offer protection for sacred tribal places just because they are sacred."[54] Bryan mentions the American Indian Religious Freedom Act,[55] the National Historic Preservation Act,[56] the Archeological Resources Protection Act,[57] the Native American Graves Protection and Repatriation Act,[58] and the National Environmental Policy Act.[59] However, these laws do not provide absolute protection of sacred Indigenous resources and instead offer limited procedural safeguards. Sacred resources are in the hands of agencies who may exercise their discretion to prioritize other interests.[60]

Another category of federal laws relates to Indigenous ownership and regulation of waters within reservation boundaries. The Clean Water Act authorizes some federally recognized tribes to adopt their own water quality standards, including standards for ceremonial waters.[61] The *Winters* doctrine could potentially be used to protect sacred waters, Bryan writes. The Zuni Tribe's water rights settlement restores water to Kohu/wala:wa, a sacred site known in English as Zuni Heaven, a center of Zuni ceremonial, burial, and cultural activities, which had been dried up by upstream water projects and diversions. Similarly, the Taos Pueblo negotiated a settlement for water rights to recharge the sacred Buffalo Pasture in New Mexico. However, settlements like these, which mention the protection of sacred waters as their purpose, are exceedingly rare.[62] Bryan hopes that if western states start articulating a sacred water value, federal agencies would begin placing more weight on Indigenous spiritual interests when managing federal lands.[63] We have seen cases in which federal agencies did take spiritual interests seriously, in Mato Tipila, known in English as Bear's Lodge, for example.[64] But Bryan, as mentioned, is interested in including such interests in state water law of prior appropriation. Two shifts need to take place for this to happen: (1) considering sacred water in the states' public interest tests for new or changed water rights; and (2) adding sacred tribal water as an express beneficial use capable of protection as a water right.[65]

I am sympathetic to Bryan's project because what it essentially asks is to do away with the binary sacred/property. However, Bryan remains within the logic of rights that I want to transcend. Thinking of water in terms of rights is thinking within a settler colonial framework. It does not challenge the state's authority over the land and the water, and it commodifies the water itself. As Barker writes, "there is a real problem in framing the water crisis through rights-based discourses. This framework confines our understanding to binary relations, both in terms of what the struggle is and what reform is desired. . . . Rights, while appealing to extra-state or global humanitarian ideals, are articulated through legal ideologies and discourses that have been developed to serve imperialists."[66] Let us look at the struggles for water rights in Yurok country, to find a way out of this binary logic.

Water Rights in Yurok Country

The Yurok reservation mimics the shape of the Klamath River: a thin snake, stretching along forty-four miles of the river, from the fork where the Trinity River joins it all the way to the Pacific Ocean. Just like their reservation, the Yurok struggle for sovereignty has been entangled with the fate of the Klamath River since their contact with white settlers in the 1830s. For example, the struggle for Yurok sovereignty took the form of a US Supreme Court case on fishing rights in the 1970s.[67] The court finally acknowledged Yurok fishing rights on the Klamath River, but decades of mismanagement, damming, and over-allocation of water had decimated the fish stocks. The struggle for tribal sovereignty then took the form of a lawsuit (followed by the Klamath Agreements) to remove dams from the river in the early 2000s. But while the status of salmon as an essential and sacred resource to Yurok life was acknowledged in the agreement, it was only a marginal reason for the decision to remove the dams. Nevertheless, the largest dam removal in US history is now planned for 2023, after a new agreement was signed between the Yurok and the Karuk, the states of Oregon and California, and PacifiCorp, the utility company who runs the dams, and PacifiCorp is now set to transfer its hydroelectric license jointly to the nonprofit Klamath River Renewal Corporation, Oregon, and California.[68]

The struggle for sovereignty and for healing the Klamath River has been fought on another front since the establishment of the Yurok Tribal Court, following the recognition of the Yurok as a tribe by the US government according to the Indian Reorganization Act.[69] While at its early days, the court was open only once a month, mostly to adjudicate fishing violations, it has grown to hear more than six hundred cases a year. The Klamath River and its fish play an important role in the tribal court. To restore the fish to the river, the Yurok declared a voluntary ban on commercial fishing, and the tribe tightly regulates personal fishing on the river. The Yurok Tribal Court hears cases that are related to this regulation, but it also often orders that monetary fines or child-support payments be paid in salmon, both in cases directly and not directly related to fishing or to the river.

This section tells the story of Yurok sovereignty, a story that is inspired by Yurok efforts to heal the Klamath River, to which they refer as their "bloodline." In federal Indian law, sovereignty might mean recognition of Yurok treaty rights by US courts; but, perhaps more meaningfully, to the Yuroks themselves sovereignty means the ability of the tribal court to make decisions about Yurok everyday life based on traditional values, and with close attention to the river and its fish that play a vital role in the economic, cultural, and spiritual identities of the Yuroks. Let me focus on one example of the entanglement between tribal sovereignty and the Klamath River: what is known in Yurok Country as "the fish wars." I will then present a new development, transforming rights *to* the river into rights *of* the river, and propose that tribal sovereignty requires not only that the Yurok people have recognized, protected rights but also that the river, as their kin, has rights. While this book is offered as a critique of the rights discourse as incapable of capturing the various layers of meaning of land, the story of the fish wars is a reminder that, at the same time, those rights cannot be taken for granted. Hoopa Valley Tribe's Fishery Department director Michael W. Orcutt writes that "it is with proper respect that we acknowledge the courage and fortitude of those Klamath tribal people who stood up for the preservation of their fishing rights, even in times of extreme adversity."[70]

The Klamath River runs east to northwest through the Yurok reservation boundaries. It has been the life source of the Yurok people both physically and spiritually. The river represents "time" in Yurok prayers. It is central to rituals such as the Flower Dance and to the initiation of medicine people. It is responsible for the continuance of humankind. The preamble to the Yurok constitution acknowledges the special relationship between the Yurok and the Klamath River:

> In times past and now Yurok people bless the deep river, the tall redwood trees, the rocks, the mounds, and the trails. We pray for the health of all the animals, and prudently harvest and manage the great salmon runs and herds of deer and elk.... This whole land, this Yurok country, stayed in balance, kept that way by our good stewardship, hard work, wise laws, and constant prayers to the Creator.[71]

Yurok elder Walter J. Lara, Sr., writes about the respect one must have on or near the river's edge. For example, you cannot refuse to help a person on the river, even if they are your enemy. You are responsible for their safety. This is out of respect for the river while you are on it. "Unkind words, unnecessary yelling, and fighting are against 'Indian Law,'" writes Lara.[72] We need to remember this rule as we talk about the fish wars. We should also remember that many lives were lost to the river over the years and think of it as a political entity because of the deaths it has witnessed. "Relationality is not always positive, because relationships are complex. Just as with our human relatives, the acknowledgment of kin relationships with water does not imply that kin always get along. For example, water is considered the giver of life, but it can also take life away," write Wilson and Inkster.[73] Even though the relationship with water can be deadly, the Yuroks explain much of their survival in relation to the spiritual power of the river and their own traditional knowledge and responsibility to it. They tie their fate with the river's fate, explaining that the Creator allowed them to reside on it and enjoy all that it offers them and, in return, required that they take care of the river.

The fish wars occurred all along the Klamath and Trinity Rivers. Yurok elders talk about them as a kind of ceremony, because each person played a critical role and worked together without any formal rehearsal.[74] Part of thinking of the fish wars as ceremony has to do with the obligation to engage with water according to protocol, to ensure mutual survival. Political theorist Glen Coulthard (Yellowknives Dene) writes that "ethically, humans held certain obligations to the land, animals, plants, and lakes in much the same way that we hold obligations to each other. And if these obligations were met, then the land, animals, plants, and lakes would reciprocate and meet their obligations to humans, thus ensuring the survival and well-being of all over time."[75]

Lara tells the story of the fish wars that started around 1945, when two Yuroks were arrested for fishing at Snake Rock. According to the State of California, Yurok people were allowed to fish only up the Klamath River at Tecta. They were allowed three fish a day, which meant that if you lived at the mouth of the Klamath River, you would have to travel by boat, fourteen miles up the river, to catch three fish and then paddle all the way back. For many elders, children, and disabled community members, this was nearly impossible. And so, some people would fish on the reservation down the river from Tecta, or get more than their three allocated fish, for other family or community members, with the risk of getting arrested.[76]

From the moment of that first arrest in 1945, over a span of more than thirty years, until the most violent battles on the river occurred in 1978, the State of California continuously harassed the Yuroks for fishing. In 1969, the community decided to bring a case all the way to the US Supreme Court, in the hope that the court would acknowledge their fishing rights. A Yurok fisherman named Raymond Mattz volunteered to lead the case. One day, Mattz's mother wanted to cook fish heads, and so she sent him and a few of his friends to the river to fish. When they were caught, Mattz claimed all five gill nets were his own and was cited for fishing illegally. In court, when the judge told Mattz to pay a one-dollar fine to get the nets back, Mattz refused to pay, claiming he had Indian rights. This was the time of the civil rights movement, and in Berkeley, California Indian Legal Services agreed to represent Mattz in court.

Mattz lost in all state courts, according to whom the Allotment Act had opened up Indian land for white settlement. Reaching all the way to the Supreme Court, Mattz argued that the nets were seized in Indian Country and that the State's laws prohibiting their use did not apply to him. *Mattz v. Arnett* was decided in 1973 in favor of Raymond Mattz, concluding that the Klamath River Reservation was never terminated and is still considered Indian Country. *Mattz v. Arnett* confirmed the status of the Lower Klamath River as Indian Country and Indian fishing rights there and laid the groundwork for asserting sovereignty. Yurok elder Lavina Bowers says this decision was transformative: "Once the fishing rights were given back, people could be *Indian* again. It made people stronger. People had rights, rights to be Indian again. People could pray out loud and in public."[77]

After the *Mattz* decision, the Yuroks happily continued to fish. State and Federal officials, as well as tourists and local non-Indigenous fishermen, continued to harass them. The harassment continued and violence escalated. I'll omit some of the most gruesome details but affirm that Yuroks compare these incidents to the violence that occurred during the Gold Rush and consider them a continuation of genocide.[78] Here is how Yurok elder Robley Schwenk remembers it:

> My most prevalent memory of the fish wars was the federal officers coming down the river in a boat. They were whooping and hollering, slapping their hands on their mouths, like stereotypical "Indians." This behavior was a norm for them and a way to intimidate or belittle us.... Each time, they would harass us and tell us that we needed to stay off the river. We would remind them that we had the right to fish. In one interaction, [an] officer pulled a pistol on me and said, "I told you that you're not allowed to fish here anymore." At that moment I thought that I might be killed in the next few minutes. It's hard to describe how I felt. It should be remembered that we (Yurok people) didn't have weapons during the fish wars. Only the "feds" had weapons.[79]

Such incidents occurred regularly, and some of the younger Yuroks started photographing them. The fish wars culminated in 1978, right at the time that Dorothea Theodoratus was conducting her research for the Forest Service in the area.[80] In response to one of the most violent incidents (officers sunk a boat with two teenage boys who were photographing them), the community all went together to fish down the river and shortly after, officers arrived in boats full of weapons. The community started to retaliate. When the officers pulled out guns, they used oars to defend themselves. They dismantled the motors on the officers' boats so that they could not get away. They were planning to wrap a net around one of the boats, with the officers on board, and drag them to the ocean, as the officers had done to the Yurok youths.

But the elders were opposed to such violent actions, out of respect for the river. The community was convinced. They decided instead to found a grassroots organization—the Klamath River Indian Conservation Wildlife Association—and advocate for fishing rights. They took a journey to the Bureau of Indian Affairs' (BIA) offices in Washington, DC, but the BIA said they didn't have fishing rights because they were not an organized tribe. The BIA was pushing the Yuroks to organize according to the 1934 Indian Reorganization Act, but the Yuroks had refused to organize until the settlement of the *Jessie Short* case, a federal case in which thousands of Yuroks claimed to be owed revenues from timber sales. The case started with a lawsuit in 1963 and was settled thirty years later, in 1993.[81] In 1988, distinct reservations for the Yurok and the Hoopa were created through the Hoopa-Yurok Settlement Act.[82] The act called for the organization of the Yurok Tribe and provided a mechanism to form the first federally recognized Yurok government. Five years later, in 1993, after the *Jessie Short* case was settled, the Yurok nation had its own constitution, government body, and tribal court, and the struggle to heal the Klamath River has since taken a different form.

Robley Schwenk says that "it's important for the next generation to be aware of this history. Our young people should think about things like why we ended up with a mile on each side of the Klamath River when our natural homelands extended south to Little River passed [*sic*] Trinidad, California and north to Damnation Creek, approximately ten miles north of Klamath, California. Most importantly, remember that nobody gave us fishing rights. Fishing rights were retained by the people of our tribe!"[83] Orcutt similarly writes that these are inherent rights given to Indigenous peoples by the Creator.[84] It is therefore important, even as I offer critique of the rights discourse as inappropriate to capturing the multifaceted nature of land, to remember that the Yuroks have fought hard to secure those rights and that it is not the state who has the authority to grant them or to take them away.

Nevertheless, the state has done a lot of harm in its war against Indigenous water rights. "Although the Klamath people (along with the Hupa, Karuk, and Yurok further downstream) have retained their water and fishing rights throughout the worst of U.S. policy toward Indian people, the question remains as to whether they will have enough water to support the suckers," wrote activist Winona LaDuke (Mississippi Band Anishinaabeg) in 2005, and this question could not be more relevant today, as a major juvenile salmon kill is unfolding on the Klamath River.[85] The issue that LaDuke so succinctly expresses is at the heart of this chapter: that securing water and fishing rights does not ensure the well-being of the river, the fish, or the people who live with the river and the fish as their kin.

Kinship and the Klamath Resolution

The deep relationship between the Yurok people, the Klamath River, and its salmon is expressed in different ways and in various sources. For example, in *To the American Indian: Reminiscences of a Yurok Woman*, Lucy Thompson writes that "salmon was the staple of the Klamath Indians, who prayed for its bounty, feasted on it fresh, and dried it for later use. Their lives revolved around the coming of the salmon; their myths told of its origins."[86] Author Stephen Most recounts a Yurok creation story as told by Geneva Mattz (Raymond Mattz's mother): "In the beginning of time, the Creator came to the mouth of the Klamath. He stood on the beach and thought: 'This is a great river. I want to leave my children here. But there's nothing for them to eat.' So the Creator called to the spirit of the river, Pulekukwerek . . . Pulekukwerek answered, 'I can feed them. I can send fish' . . . Greatest of all, Nepewo entered the river each fall, leading the salmon people. Then the river spirit made human people."[87]

And the Yurok's relationship with the Klamath River had everything to do with the G-O Road case. The G-O Road complaint describes Blue Creek as having an "exceptional anadromous fish habitat": "Blue Creek, with its tributaries, is a primary fish producer for the Klamath River, which traverses the Hoopa Valley Indian Reservation. The Indians of the Reservation rely upon the fish of this river for their sustenance and cultural survival." The plaintiffs in the case are described through their relationship with the river. For example, plaintiff Jimmie James is presented thus: "Plaintiff James, who has lived most of his life along the Klamath River, possesses and exercises federally reserved fishing rights. He depends upon the fishery of the Klamath River and its tributaries to sustain himself and his family and for ceremonial use." The other individual plaintiffs are similarly presented. Yurok Associate Judge William Bowers says that Yurok people have been eating the salmon of the Klamath River for so long, they now share DNA with those fish. But most importantly, as Yurok scholar Kaitlin Reed argues, it is the continual struggle that the salmon and the Yurok share that unites their cause.[88]

Tribal Council attorney, Amy Cordalis, explains that the Yurok Tribal Council's resolution to extend rights to the Klamath River (quoted at the opening of this chapter) is a way to express the tribe's sovereignty and increase protection of the river through tribal law. Acknowledging the rights of nature means granting personhood rights for nature, and so the nature entity is treated like any person would be in a court of law, which gives it standing and the award of remedies. As we have seen, this has been done in Ecuador and Colombia, and recently in the United States the Ojibwe people recognized the rights of wild rice.[89] But this is still a new practice. Cordalis explains the centrality of the river to Yurok life:

> The Yurok people have lived along the Klamath River as well as the coastline in the north coast area since the beginning of time. We were never relocated, we have always been here, and the Klamath River is the lifeblood of our culture. Everything we do, in some way, relates to the river. We fish the river, we live along the river, we care for the river. In our core culture covenants, in our religious creation stories, it is basically set out that the Yurok people made an agreement with the creator, in which we had the great privilege of living on the river and benefitting from its immense bounty, but in exchange, we have the highest obligation and responsibility to protect it. And of course now, with all of the influences of climate change, there's lots of demands on water: poor water quality, dams, you name it, the river is in bad, bad shape. And so it is our duty, basically stemming from that original agreement we made with the Creator, to protect the river. There are really no words in the English language to describe the relation of the Yurok Tribe to the Klamath River.[90]

Granting the river rights means that the Yurok Tribal Court will have jurisdiction over anyone who harms the river. This resolution will authorize a cause of action in tribal court to protect the river and to recover a remedy to then address the harm inflicted by the offending entity. But apart from asserting tribal sovereignty through this resolution, there is also a real declaration here about the Yuroks' responsibility to protect the river as their kin. Cordalis compares this declaration to the acknowledgment of corporate personhood in US law:

> Law is a reflection of cultural values. In the U.S. we value economy, we value capitalism, and so the granting of corporation personhood is a reflection of that value. Here in Yurok, we value the river as our most sacred, our most important—and here we were struggling to find the right word, because it's not just an asset, it's not just a resource, it's more than that. And there isn't a word in the English language to describe that. But the gist is that we value it as one of the most important things here on the planet, and so it makes sense for us in our own tribal law to make sure that our modern tribal law reflects these cultural and religious values around the river.[91]

The resolution calls for creating a tribal ordinance, and so the Yurok are going through a legislative process now to create an infrastructure for these causes of action to proceed. This will take time, of course. And how the federal government, the State of California, and private corporations react to this resolution and to potential legal action remains to be seen.

In the meantime, we can think about what it means to declare this kinship. Wilson and Inkster remind us that "water conflicts are rooted in ontological differences between Indigenous and settler views of water"— water as a living being as opposed to water as a resource.[92] It is through the persistence of kinship relations with their environment, with their land and water, that Yurok people are resisting settler colonial invasion. Even as they extend rights to the Klamath River, what they talk about is their responsibility and obligation to care for it as part of their community. And in the name of this obligation, land can be all that it has been throughout this book: Yurok home and kin, sacred wilderness, and even property.

The Klamath Resolution shows us a way out of the mess created by federal litigation. The kinds of absurdities we saw in the G-O Road case are avoided when the Yurok declare that the Yurok Tribal Court will have jurisdiction over violations of the Klamath River's rights. If in federal courts Indigenous plaintiffs and their lawyers have to translate Indigenous concepts into English language and Western ideas in order to be legible to the court, here, supposedly, the other party to a potential case in tribal court would be accountable to Yurok values and language. Relatedly, and perhaps even more importantly, the Yurok avoid the acknowledgment of US sovereignty, or jurisdiction, over Yurok people and lands, implied by filing a lawsuit in federal court. This is where I see the biggest potential for Indigenous sovereignty to be exercised; actually, the resolution itself is an exercise of both sovereignty and religious freedom, if you will, and this is where I want the book to end. This is why rights are still crucial to my argument, even if I want to complicate this discourse. On the one hand, once we are in tribal court the procedures can be in line with Yurok law and values, which may be very different from federal legal procedures and center responsibility rather than rights. On the other hand, to take anyone to court, the Yurok still need to claim that the river's rights have been violated. While it is hard for me to imagine PacifiCorp showing up in Yurok Tribal Court any time soon, I do want to end the book envisioning what it would be like if that does happen.

Even though the resolution still remains in the realm of rights, I see it as declaring a kinship relationship between the Yurok and the river, thus asserting the Yurok responsibility for the river and its well-being. As I wrote earlier in this chapter, what I see the Yurok doing here is delineating the boundaries of their community so that it includes their nonhuman environment. As they do so, they adhere to Yurok law rather than to US law. If this book began by "looking for law in all the wrong places," what we find at the end is Indigenous law. And Indigenous law, especially in its manifestation through stories, as we saw in chapter 1, following Heidi Stark and others, is all about proper relationships. And "a core principle of proper relationships is recognition of these relationships' ongoing nature."[93]

These relationships are ongoing, even in the face of settler colonialism and genocide. The continuity that is so hard to find when it comes to religious practice, as we saw in chapter 3, can be found in the relationship between the Yurok and the Klamath River. Their responsibility to the river is asserted in the Klamath Resolution. It was much harder to assert their responsibility to the High Country in the G-O Road trial, though the witnesses did try. But while the federal judges had trouble understanding this and therefore translated everything the witnesses said into the language of free exercise, here it is Yurok law that governs the Yurok relationship with the river as kin. If we started this book's journey with the human right to use the land either as property or for religious purposes, we are ending it with the rights of the land itself, and so arguing for this land becomes, really, arguing for the land's rights and well-being.

In chapter 1, I argued, following Beth Piatote and others, that as the colonization and dispossession of Indigenous peoples were done through

an attack on the domestic sphere, resistance to colonization always begins in the home. My argument here is similar, acknowledging that it was
the disruption of kinship relations through which some of the most ter-
rifying, genocidal policies and strategies of the federal government were
manifested: kidnapping Indigenous children, sexual assault, regulating
and criminalizing marriage practices, and tearing Indigenous communities and individuals from their lands. "However, the continuation of strong
and dynamic kinship relations between Indigenous women, their families,
communities and their land has also been the source of growing forms of
resistance against cultural destruction."[94]

As literary scholar Mark Rifkin writes, "the coordinated assault on native social formations that has characterized U.S. policy since its inception,
conducted in the name of 'civilization,' [can] be understood as an organized
effort to make heterosexuality compulsory as a key part of breaking up
indigenous landholdings, 'detribalizing' native peoples, and/or translating
native territoriality and governance into the terms of U.S. liberalism and legal geography."[95] Therefore, resistance, or decolonization, has to come from
kinship as well. If "US-Indian policy . . . translates place-based indigeneity
into a matter of lineage,"[96] decolonial kinship reinforces the place-based
identity of Indigenous peoples: "A certain attachment results from knowing
that some of your relatives are the life-forms that share your place with you.
This belief influences one's sense of identity and thought/language."[97] If
the "representation of Indigenous peoples as if they were extended families,
and therefore necessarily something other than full polities"[98] is designed
to dismiss Indigenous sovereignty, then practices of kinship, as the one we
see in the Klamath Resolution, importantly insist on tribal sovereignty.

Cherokee scholar Daniel Heath Justice argues that "kinship is best
thought of as a verb, rather than a noun, because kinship, in most indigenous contexts, is something that's *done* more than something that simply
is"; similarly, "indigenous nationhood," or "*peoplehood*," can be understood as
based less on a logic of jurisdiction than "an understanding of common social interdependence within the community . . . that link[s] the People, the
land, and the cosmos together in an ongoing and dynamic system of mutually affecting relationships."[99] Religious studies scholar David Delgado
Shorter similarly asks for an ontological shift toward Indigenous intersub-
jectivity. He asks to replace the language of spirituality, a settler colonial
language that portrays Indigenous subjects as incapable of knowing themselves, with a notion of relationships.[100] And Indigenous studies scholars

Patricia Dudgeon (Bardi) and Abigail Bray connect this relationality with Indigenous law: "The law comes from the land, is the land. . . . For many Indigenous cultures, this law is a worldview, an ethics, which is governed by *responsibility* and *reciprocity* towards humans and more-than-human kin."[101]

Indigenous law is where I want to end this chapter. As Yurok Chief Judge Abby Abinanti wrote in her open letter to Justice O'Connor in response to *Lyng*, "The law is a reflection of the people. Yuroks will not give up, not now, not ever. Yuroks understand law, because we are a people governed by laws."[102] I end with Abinanti's words because I think her insistence on Yurok law as the path for healing the Yurok environment, its community, and its home is a triumph. Together with the Jump Dance and the White Deerskin Dance, the Yurok court—called "a justice center"—can fix the broken settler law; indeed, it is fixing the world that settler law has broken.

CONCLUSION

◆◆

LAND AS SOVEREIGN

In the book *A Basic Call to Consciousness*, journalist and scholar of Native American studies José Barreiro ties together "the meaning of sovereignty. The respect for Mother Earth. The search for integrity, the circle of life. Oppression, conquest, colonialism, exploitation. Genocide."[1] In other words, we can only understand sovereignty against the background of genocide and colonial dispossession. Sovereignty is, therefore, tightly related to land. If we think of sovereignty without reducing it to jurisdiction, then we can say that sovereignty does not mean the right to decide the fate of a territory; rather, sovereignty is a partnership with the land itself and a calling to respect the land as mother. And as we saw in the last chapter, rivers are especially helpful in challenging the binary notion of sovereignty—only nation-states can be sovereign—because they do not obey state borders. What does this notion of sovereignty have to do with Vine Deloria, Jr.'s assertion, with which I opened this book, that "the struggle by American Indians to protect their sacred sites and to have access to them for traditional ceremonies is a movement in which all peoples should become involved"?[2] This book asked to challenge the binary notion of land presented in Indigenous sacred sites cases, according to which land can be protected either as sacred or as property. Instead, it offered a multilayered understanding of land that transcends this binary.

In the G-O Road trial, the Indigenous witnesses talked about the High

154

Country as their home. This was a claim to sovereignty, because when I say a place is my home I also say I decide what life would look like in this place (think of a parent telling their rebellious teenage child, "as long as you live under my roof, you will obey my rules!"). As long as the Yurok, Karuk, and Tolowa plaintiffs' claim is about religious freedom, and as long as the discourse on religious freedom in US courts is a protestant discourse, to claim the High Country is their home is also to claim that this is the sphere in which they should be free to practice their religion as they wish, because in what law and religion scholar Winnifred Fallers Sullivan calls small-*p* protestantism, religion belongs in the private sphere. The government's response—which the Supreme Court ultimately accepts—is that the High Country is government property. As I argued in chapter 2, what the government is saying here is that even if the High Country is the Yurok, Karuk, and Tolowa home, they are no more than tenants, and the government is their landlord. In other words, the United States is the sovereign; the rights of the Indigenous residents are limited (Chief Justice John Marshall has called it "right of occupancy," and this right is always limited to what the real sovereign allows).

But when it comes to religious freedom, things get complicated. As government property, the High Country is really in the *public* sphere. If we understand religion in America as essentially protestant (read: private), then should practicing religion (Indigenous or otherwise) there even be allowed at all? Wouldn't protecting Yurok, Karuk, and Tolowa use of the High Country for religious purposes amount to the establishment of religion? Such an argument was rejected by the Ninth Circuit's Court of Appeals, and neither the Supreme Court nor the government pursued this route. Neither says that Indigenous religious practice is prohibited in the High Country. On the contrary, the court sees the construction of the G-O Road as constitutional because it *does not* prohibit the practice of religion in the High Country. This paradox is not addressed by scholarship on the *Lyng* case. In fact, if Justice William Brennan is serious about his recognition, in his dissenting opinion, of the High Country as sacred land, and of the Yurok, Karuk, and Tolowa peoples' right to practice their religion freely there, as we saw in chapter 3, doesn't this mean that Justice Sandra Day O'Connor is right in her evaluation, in the majority opinion, that this means de facto Indigenous ownership of the High Country? In other words, we can say that O'Connor is taking Indigenous religions more seriously than Brennan does when she refuses to allow it to be freely exercised on public land. She understands that arguing for religious freedom in this place also, essentially, means arguing for sovereignty over it.

As we saw in chapter 4, the High Country has been ultimately protected as wilderness. The government, in a sense, recognized the High Country as terra nullius; but this protection is unstable, as we can see in cases such as Bears Ears, which was recognized as a national monument in 2016 and reduced by 85 percent less than a year later. Essentially, this protection is unstable, because it further attaches the High Country to the US Government rather than to the Yurok, Karuk, and Tolowa peoples. It is with the Klamath Resolution that the Yurok Tribe declared sovereignty in its homeland. If the absurdities created by the game of recognition are revealed in the *Lyng* case—by asking the settler court to recognize Indigenous rights in the High Country, the Yurok, Karuk, and Tolowa inevitably recognized the sovereignty of the settler state—then in the Klamath Resolution, recognition is between the Yurok people and the Klamath River. If I suggested in the introduction that in federal Indian law, sovereignty has to do with the United States keeping the treaties it has signed with Indigenous peoples, here sovereignty has to do with the Yurok people keeping the treaty they have made with the Creator, as we saw in chapter 5. In this sense, the Klamath Resolution also means that the Yurok are exercising their religion freely in their homeland.

Remarkably, this is working. As I am writing this conclusion, work to remove four dams from the Klamath River— the largest river restoration project in US history—is beginning. In November 2022, US regulators approved a plan to demolish the dams and open up hundreds of miles of salmon habitat. "The Klamath salmon are coming home," said Yurok Chairman Joseph James. "The people have earned this victory and with it, we carry on our sacred duty to the fish that have sustained our people since the beginning of time."[3] In this short statement, land as home, as sacred, and as kin come together, and I would add that carrying this sacred duty to the salmon, as their kin, in their homeland, means living a sovereign life in Yurok, Karuk, and Tolowa country. Property rights are not a part of this story. Though mainstream media has referred to this project as restoring the river to its "wild" condition, the Yurok, Karuk, and Klamath tribes, who have fought for decades toward this dam removal, know better. PacifiCorp and the State of California will invest together more than five hundred million dollars in fish ladders, fish screens, and other conservation upgrades to help the salmon return to the Klamath River. Nothing about this process is natural or wild.

That this project is the result of collaboration between the Yurok, Karuk, and Klamath tribes, the States of Oregon and California, and US secretary of the interior Deb Haaland (Laguna Pueblo) brings to mind the ideas of concurrent sovereignty and overlapping jurisdiction advanced by political theorist Kevin Bruyneel and legal scholar Ayelet Shachar, which I discussed in chapter 2. Bruyneel writes that "the political history of Indigenous people's refusals of the false choice set out for them [they are either state-like entities or they are not sovereign] indicate a persistent effort both to self-determine what sovereignty means to them and to expose the uncertainty and even impossibility of U.S. sovereignty as a totalizing claim to supreme, legitimate authority."[4] The refusals of false choices are multiple in our case. The Yurok and Karuk witnesses in the G-O Road trial refused the limitations the religious freedom framework imposes even as they were asking the court to protect their religious freedom in the High Country. They did so by telling stories about the High Country as their home, thus refusing the private/public binary. Indeed, by claiming the High Country as their home, they turned the Indigenous home, which has been a central site of settler oppression, into a site of resistance.

Throughout the G-O Road case and its aftermath, they turned other sites of oppression—private property, religious ceremony, wilderness preservation, and kinship—into sites of resistance. Religious studies scholar Elisha Chi (Inupiat) explains such refusals as acts of sovereignty: "Refusal is a strong current resisting the structure of settler colonialism. It crashes, churns, and erodes the death-dealing dams of settler knowing. Its path turns away from the settler's gaze."[5] The Yurok Tribal Council's recognition of the Klamath River as a rights-bearing person, as kin, indeed turns away from the settler's gaze, but at the same time it allows the settler state to fulfill its trust responsibility to contribute to the project of releasing the river from its dams, to let it flow freely, as sovereign. In the spirit of refusing false binaries, it also transcends the rights discourse and moves toward a responsibility-centered discourse while granting rights to the river.

What does it all mean for ongoing struggles to protect Indigenous sacred sites, as in Oak Flat or on Mauna Kea? I want the movements to protect these sites to strive for the kind of protection that would recognize both Indigenous peoples' power to decide how to live with these sacred sites and the responsibility of the United States to promote the well-being of Indigenous communities, communities that include those lands, that respect the land as mother, as Barreiro tells us. Indigenous scholars such as Vine Deloria, Jr., (Lakota) and Winona LaDuke (Ojibwe) have also offered us ways to think about the sacred without subjecting it to Western ideas about religious freedom. They remind us that sacred lands are living beings and that those lands have witnessed genocide and colonial dispossession. Those lands should be protected as such—as sacred homes, as wild property, as sovereign kin.

NOTES

Introduction: The High Country

1. Vine Deloria, Jr., "Sacred Lands and Religious Freedom," in *For This Land: Writings on Religion in America* (London: Routledge, 1999), 212.

2. Deloria, Jr., "Sacred Lands and Religious Freedom," 213.

3. Anna V. Smith, "At Oak Flat, Courts and Politicians Fail Tribes," *High Country News*, July 26, 2022. https://www.hcn.org/articles/indigenous-affairs-justice-at-oak-flat-courts-and-politicians-fail-tribes.

4. *Apache Stronghold v. United States*, No. CV-21-0050, 2021 WL 535525, at *1 (D. Ariz. Feb. 12, 2021).

5. Kerry Mitchell, *Spirituality and the State: Managing Nature and Experience in America's National Parks* (New York: New York University Press, 2016).

6. Winnifred Fallers Sullivan, *The Impossibility of Religious Freedom* (Princeton, NJ: Princeton University Press, 2005).

7. 42 U.S.C. §1996 (1978).

8. Public Law 73–383 (1934).

9. Charlie Thom, "Oral History," in *Reinhabiting a Separate Country*, ed. Peter Berg (San Francisco: Planet Drum Foundation, 1978), 148.

10. Amy Bowers and Kristen A. Carpenter, "Challenging the Narrative of Conquest: The Story of *Lyng v. Northwest Indian Cemetery Protective Association*," in *Indian Law Stories*, ed. Carole Goldberg, Kevin K. Washburn, and Phillip P. Frickey (St. Paul, MN: Foundation Press, 2011), 497.

11. Abby Abinanti, "A Letter to Justice O'Connor," *Indigenous Peoples' Journal of Law, Culture, and Resistance* 1 (2004): 4–5.

12. Cutcha Risling Baldy, *We Are Dancing for You: Native Feminisms and the Revitalization of Women's Coming-of-Age Ceremonies* (Seattle: University of Washington Press, 2018).

13. Sara Neustadtl, *Moving Mountains: Coping with Change in Mountain Communities* (Boston: Appalachian Mountain Club, 1987), 181.

14. Neustadtl, *Moving Mountains*, 181.

15. Tony Platt writes extensively about this issue in *Grave Matters: Excavating California's Buried Past* (Berkeley, CA: Heyday, 2021).

16. Bowers and Carpenter, "Challenging the Narrative of Conquest," 505–506.

17. Theodoratus Cultural Research, *Cultural Resources of the Chimney Rock Section, Gasquet–Orleans Road, Six Rivers National Forest* (Fair Oaks, CA, 1979).

18. Theodoratus Report, 105.

19. 42 U.S.C. §§ 4321–4347.

20. 16 U.S.C. §§ 1131–1136.

21. 33 U.S.C. §§ 1251–1387.

22. 5 U.S.C. § 706.

23. 16 U.S.C. §§ 528–531.

24. U.S.C. § 1600.

25. Bowers and Carpenter, "Challenging the Narrative of Conquest," 510.

26. The witnesses were engineering geologists Eugene Kojan and Ralph Graham Scott, professor of environmental geology Robert Curry, fishery biologist Richard Wood, soil scientist Annette Parsons, resources consultant Larry Edwin Moss, consulting forester Greg Blomstrom, and forest policy analyst Kathleen Green.

27. The witnesses for the defendants were forest supervisor Joseph Harn, forest cultural resource specialist Kenneth Wilson, forest geologist Richard Farrington, director of building and planning Ernest Wesley Perry, forest engineer Robert Black, forest fishery biologist Jerry Barnes, forest hydrologist Christopher Knopp, and forest soil scientist Brent Roath.

28. Bowers and Carpenter, "Challenging the Narrative of Conquest."

29. Abinanti, "A Letter to Justice O'Connor."

30. Cutcha Risling Baldy, "Why We Gather: Traditional Gathering in Native Northwest California and the Future of Bio-Cultural Sovereignty," *Ecological Processes* 2 (2013).

31. See, for example, Donald Falk, "Note: *Lyng v. Northwest Indian Cemetery Protective Association*: Bulldozing First Amendment Protection of Indian Sacred Lands," *Ecology Law Quarterly* 16, no. 2 (March 1989): 515–570; Ellen Adair Page, "Note, The Scope of the Free Exercise Clause: *Lyng v. Northwest Indian Cemetery Protective Association*," *North Carolina Law Review* 68, no. 2 (1990): 410–422; J. Brett Pritchard, "Note, Conduct and Belief in the Free Exercise Clause: Developments and Deviations in *Lyng v. Northwest Indian Cemetery Protective Association*," *Cornell Law Review* 76 (1990): 268–296; S. Alan Ray, "Comment: *Lyng v. Northwest Indian Cemetery Protective Association*: Government Property Rights and the Free Exercise Clause," *Hastings Constitutional Law Quarterly* 16, no. 3 (Spring 1989): 483–511.

32. Walter R. Echo-Hawk, *In the Courts of the Conqueror: The 10 Worst Indian Law Cases Ever Decided* (Golden, CO: Fulcrum Publishing, 2010), 325–356.

33. Brian E. Brown, *Religion, Law, and the Land: Native Americans and the Judicial Interpretation of Sacred Land* (Westport, CT: Greenwood Press, 1999), 4.

34. Robert J. Miller, "Correcting Supreme Court 'Errors': American Indian Response to *Lyng v. Northwest Indian Cemetery Protective Association*," *Environmental Law* 20, no. 4 (1990): 1037–1062.

35. Allison M. Dussias, "Ghost Dance and Holy Ghost: The Echoes of

Nineteenth-Century Christianization Policy in Twentieth-Century Native American Free Exercise Cases," *Stanford Law Review* 49, no. 4 (1997): 759.

36. Abinanti, "A Letter to Justice O'Connor," 15.

37. Howard J. Vogel, "The Clash of Stories at Chimney Rock: A Narrative Approach to Cultural Conflict Over Native American Sacred Sites on Public Land," *Santa Clara Law Review* 41 (2001): 759.

38. Michael D. McNally, *Defend the Sacred: Native American Religious Freedom Beyond the First Amendment* (Princeton, NJ: Princeton University Press, 2020).

39. Vine Deloria, Jr., *God Is Red: A Native View of Religion* (Golden, CO: Fulcrum Publishing, 1973), 273.

40. Deloria, Jr., *God Is Red*, 273.

41. Deloria, 274.

42. Vine Deloria, Jr., "Trouble in High Places: Erosion of American Indian Rights to Religious Freedom in the United States," in *The State of Native America: Genocide, Colonization, and Resistance*, ed. M. Annette Jaimes (Boston: South End Press, 1992), 270–271.

43. Deloria, Jr., "Trouble in High Places," 277.

44. Deloria, 278.

45. Deloria, 286.

46. Miller, "Correcting Supreme Court Errors," 1055.

47. Miller, 1060–1061.

48. Marcia Yablon, "Property Rights and Sacred Sites: Federal Regulatory Responses to American Indian Religious Claims on Public Lands," *Yale Law Journal* 113, no. 7 (2004): 1632.

49. Yablon, "Property Rights and Sacred Sites," 1634.

50. Stephanie Hall Barclay and Michalyn Steele, "Rethinking Protections for Indigenous Sacred Sites," *Harvard Law Review* 134 (2021): 1301.

51. Barclay and Steele, "Rethinking Protections for Indigenous Sacred Sites," 1322.

52. Barclay and Steele, 1326.

53. Lori G. Beaman, "Aboriginal Spirituality and the Legal Construction of Freedom of Religion," *Journal of Church and State* 44, no. 1 (Winter 2002): 136.

54. Beaman, "Aboriginal Spirituality and the Legal Construction of Freedom of Religion," 142.

55. Robert S. Michaelsen, "Dirt in the Court Room: Indian Land Claims and American Property Rights," in *American Sacred Space*, ed. David Chidester and Edward T. Linenthal (Bloomington: Indiana University Press, 1995), 44.

56. McNally, *Defend the Sacred*, 70.

57. 476 U.S. 693 (1986).

58. 535 F.3d 1058 (9th Cir. 2008).

59. Barclay and Steele, "Rethinking Protections for Indigenous Sacred Sites," 1333.

60. Michael D. McNally, "Native American Religious Freedom as a Collective Right," *Brigham Young University Law Review* 2019, no. 1 (2019): 205–292.

61. Baldy, "Why We Gather," 5.

62. Baldy, 6.

63. Echo-Hawk, *In the Courts of the Conqueror*, 325.

64. Echo-Hawk, 326.

65. Echo-Hawk, 327.

66. 494 U.S. 872 (1990).

67. Patrick Wolfe, "Settler Colonialism and the Elimination of the Native," *Journal of Genocide Research* 8, no. 4 (2006): 387–409.

68. 592 U.S., _____ (2020).

69. 573 U.S. 682 (2014).

70. *Navajo Nation v. U.S. Forest Service*, 535 F.3d 1058 (9th Cir. 2008).

71. *Standing Rock Sioux Tribe v. Army Corps of Engineers*, 985 F.3d 1032 (D.C. Cir. 2021).

72. *In re Conservation District Use Application* HA-3568, 431 P.3d 752 (Hawai'i 2018).

73. *Apache Stronghold v. United States*, no. CV-21-0050, 2021 WL 535525, at *1, *8 (D. Ariz. February 12, 2021).

74. Kevin Bruyneel, *The Third Space of Sovereignty: The Postcolonial Politics of U.S.-Indigenous Relations* (Minneapolis: University of Minnesota Press, 2007).

Chapter 1. Land as Home in the G-O Road Trial

1. Chris Peters and Chisa Oros, "Voices from the Sacred: An Indigenous Worldview and Epistemology of Northwestern California," in *Ka'm-t'em: A Journey toward Healing*, ed. Kishan Lara-Cooper and Walter J. Lara, Sr. (Temecula, CA: Great Oak Press, 2019), 8–9.

2. Kevin Bruyneel, *The Third Space of Sovereignty: The Postcolonial Politics of U.S.-Indigenous Relations* (Minneapolis: University of Minnesota Press, 2007).

3. *Lyng v. Northwest Indian Cemetery Protective Association*, 485 U.S. 439, 441–442.

4. *Lyng*, 442.

5. Theodoratus Cultural Research, *Cultural Resources of the Chimney Rock Section, Gasquet–Orleans Road, Six Rivers National Forest* (Fair Oaks, CA, 1979). (Hereafter this source is cited as Theodoratus Report.)

6. Linda Tuhiwai Smith, *Decolonizing Methodologies: Research and Indigenous Peoples* (New York: Zed Books, 1999).

7. Cutcha Risling Baldy, *We Are Dancing for You: Native Feminisms and the Revitalization of Women's Coming-of-Age Ceremonies* (Seattle: University of Washington Press, 2018), 7. See also Mishuana Goeman, *Mark My Words: Native Women Mapping Our Nations* (Minneapolis: University of Minnesota Press, 2013).

8. Marianne Constable, Leti Volpp, and Bryan Wagner, eds., *Looking for Law in All the Wrong Places: Justice Beyond and Between* (New York: Fordham University Press, 2019).

9. Jack Norton, *Genocide in Northwestern California: When Our Worlds Cried* (San Francisco: Indian Historian Press, 1979), 27.

10. Heidi Kiiwetinepinesiik Stark, "Stories as Law: A Method to Live By," in *Sources and Methods in Indigenous Studies*, ed. Chris Andersen and Jean M. O'Brien (London: Routledge, 2017), 250.

11. Ronald Dworkin, "How Law Is Like Literature," in *A Matter of Principle* (Cambridge, MA: Harvard University Press, 1985), 146–166; Ronald Dworkin, *Law's Empire* (Cambridge, MA: Harvard University Press, 1986).

12. Philosopher Brian Burkhart (Cherokee) writes about the "delocality" of so-called Western philosophy and how the trickster Indigenous philosopher can expose it as local rather than universal. I argue that when Yurok, Karuk, and Tolowa law, religion, and geography of the High Country enters the settler court system, it similarly exposes US settler law as local rather than universal. Brian Burkhart, *Indigenizing Philosophy Through the Land: A Trickster Methodology for Decolonizing Environmental Ethics and Indigenous Futures* (East Lansing: Michigan State University Press, 2019).

13. Thomas King, *The Truth About Stories: A Native Narrative* (Minneapolis: University of Minnesota Press, 2003), 2.

14. "Transcript of Trial" (unpublished), at 84–85. (Hereafter, this source is cited as Reporter's Transcript.) Court decision published as *Northwest Indian Cemetery Protective Association v. Peterson*, 565 F. Supp. 586 (N.D. Calif. 1983).

15. King, *The Truth About Stories*, 10.

16. Reporter's Transcript, 227.

17. Arnold Pilling, "Yurok Aristocracy and 'Great Houses,'" *American Indian Quarterly* 13, no. 4 (1989): 422.

18. Reporter's Transcript, 228.

19. Chris Peters and Chisa Oros, "Protecting Our Sacred Sites: *Lyng v. Northwest Indian Cemetery Protective Association*," in *Ka'm-t'em: A Journey Toward Healing*, ed. Kishan Lara-Cooper and Walter J. Lara, Sr. (Temecula, CA: Great Oak Press, 2019), at 161.

20. I talk here about Indigenous or tribal law, as opposed to federal Indian law, which is an integral part of US law.

21. Winnifred Fallers Sullivan, "Afterword," in *Religion, Law, USA*, ed. Joshua Dubler and Isaac Weiner (New York: New York University Press, 2019), 284.

22. John Borrows, "The First Nations Quest for Justice in Canada," public address, Victoria, BC, April 26, 2013, YouTube Video, 35:05 (at 30:08), posted by Murdith McLean, May 4, 2021, https://www.youtube.com/watch?v=8PlAb2oOxzE, cited in Zoe Todd, "(An Answer)," *Anthrodendum* (blog), January 27, 2020, https://anthrodendum.org/2020/01/27/an-answer/.

23. Stark, "Stories as Law," 254.

24. Kathleen Birrell, *Indigeneity: Before and Beyond the Law* (New York: Routledge, 2016).

25. Cheryl Suzack, *Indigenous Women Writers and the Cultural Study of Law* (Toronto: University of Toronto Press, 2017), 6.

26. Suzack, *Indigenous Women Writers and the Cultural Study of Law*, 87.

27. Suzack, 100.

28. Stark, "Stories as Law," 250.

29. Stark, 255.

30. Michael Pfeffer, "CILS History: G-O Road Case," *CILS News* 10, Fall 2002.

31. Reporter's Transcript, 75–76.

32. Theodoratus Report, 12.

33. See, for example, Russel Lawrence Barsh, "The Illusion of Religious Freedom for Indigenous Americans," *Oregon Law Review* 65, no. 1 (1986): 363–412.

34. Theodoratus Report, 44.

35. Theodoratus Report, 10–11.

36. Reporter's Transcript, 70.

37. Inés Hernández-Ávila, "Relocations Upon Relocations: Home, Language and Native American Women's Writing," in *Reading Native American Women: Critical Creative Representation*, ed. Inés Hernández-Ávila (Lanham, MD: Altamira Press, 2005), 175.

38. Theodoratus Report, 45.

39. Reporter's Transcript, 112.

40. For more about Yurok cosmology, see Peters and Oros, "Voices from the Sacred."

41. Theodoratus Report, 45.

42. Theodoratus Report, 45. Infamous Berkeley anthropologist Alfred Kroeber, a student of Franz Boaz's, was the first to study Northern California Indigenous peoples, including the Yurok, and the Theodoratus Report greatly relied on his book *Yurok Myths* (Berkeley: University of California Press, 1976). But Kroeber has been harshly criticized by Indigenous scholars for his unethical ethnographic practices and for describing Indigenous cultures as "vanishing," mentioning neither their persecution nor their genocide. See, for example, Karl Kroeber and Clifton Kroeber, eds., *Ishi in Three Centuries* (Lincoln: University of Nebraska Press, 2003); Winona LaDuke, *Recovering the Sacred: The Power of Naming and Claiming* (Chicago: Haymarket Books, 2015), 67–86; and Baldy, *We Are Dancing for You*, 73–99.

43. Theodoratus Report, 70.

44. Audra Simpson, *Mohawk Interruptus: Political Life across the Borders of Settler States* (Durham, NC: Duke University Press, 2014), 105.

45. Thomas Buckley, *Standing Ground: Yurok Indian Spirituality, 1850–1990* (Berkeley: University of California Press, 2002), 170–201.

46. Buckley, *Standing Ground*, 180.

47. Baldy, *We Are Dancing for You*, 5.

48. Baldy, 5. For additional critique of the ethnographic study of Native communities, see, for example, Vine Deloria, Jr., "Anthropologists and Other Friends," in *Custer Died for Your Sins: An Indian Manifesto* (New York: Macmillan, 1969), 79–100; and Thomas Biolsi and Larry J. Zimmerman, eds., *Indians and Anthropologists: Vine Deloria, Jr., and the Critique of Anthropology* (Tucson: University of Arizona Press, 1997).

49. Theodoratus Report, 69. See also Reporter's Transcript, 120–121, 231–233.

50. Reporter's Transcript, 85.

51. Letter from Marilyn Miles to Judge Weigel, December 7, 1982, p. 1 (San Francisco National Archives).

52. Letter from Marilyn Miles to Judge Weigel, 2.

53. Miles to Judge Weigel, 2.

54. Reporter's Transcript, 57.

55. Reporter's Transcript, 77.

56. Marc O. DeGirolami, *The Tragedy of Religious Freedom* (Cambridge, MA: Harvard University Press, 2013), 170n16.

57. Reporter's Transcript, 64. Vine Deloria, Jr., writes that Indigenous sacred sites are places of revelation and therefore cannot be replaced or removed. See Vine Deloria, Jr., *God Is Red: A Native View of Religion* (Golden, CO: Fulcrum Publishing, 1973), 276–277.

58. Reporter's Transcript, 76.

59. Reporter's Transcript, 77.

60. Reporter's Transcript, 59.

61. Reporter's Transcript, 59–60.

62. Pfeffer, "CILS History."

63. Pfeffer, "CILS History."

64. Reporter's Transcript, 58.

65. Reporter's Transcript, 73–74.

66. Reporter's Transcript, 74.

67. Reporter's Transcript, 112.

68. Reporter's Transcript, 1201–1202.

69. Letter from U.S. Attorney Joseph Russoniello to Judge Weigel, December 7, 1982 (San Francisco National Archives).

70. Theodoratus Report, 75.

71. Sara Neustadtl, *Moving Mountains: Coping with Change in Mountain Communities* (Boston: Appalachian Mountain Club, 1987), 180.

72. Theodoratus Report, 96–106.

73. Theodoratus Report, 96.

74. Theodoratus Report, 96–97.

75. Theodoratus Report, 100.

76. *Wisconsin v. Yoder*, 406 U.S. 205 (1972).

77. Justice Brennan compares, in his dissent, the situation in *Lyng* with that in *Yoder*: "Here the threat posed by the desecration of sacred lands that are indisputably essential to respondents' religious practices is both more direct and more substantial than that raised by a compulsory school law that simply exposed Amish children to an alien value system. And of course respondents here do not even have the option, however unattractive it might be, of migrating to more hospitable locales; the site-specific nature of their belief system renders it nontransportable." See *Lyng*, 467–468 (Brennan, J., dissenting).

78. Reporter's Transcript, 64.

79. Reporter's Transcript, 80.

80. Reporter's Transcript, 81.

81. Reporter's Transcript, 90.

82. Reporter's Transcript, 91.

83. Reporter's Transcript, 91.

84. See, for example, Richard H. Pratt's 1892 speech, "Kill the Indian, Save the Man," reprinted in Richard H. Pratt, "The Advantages of Mingling Indians with Whites," in *Americanizing the American Indians: Writings by the "Friends of the Indian" 1880–1900*, ed. Francis Paul Prucha (Cambridge, MA: Harvard University Press, 1973), 260–271.

85. Beth H. Piatote, *Domestic Subjects: Gender, Citizenship, and Law in Native American Literature* (New Haven: Yale University Press, 2013), quoting *Cherokee Nation v. Georgia*, 30 U.S. (5 Peters) 1, 17 (1831).

86. *Cherokee Nation v. Georgia*, 30 U.S. (5 Peters) 1, 2 (1831).

87. Piatote, *Domestic Subjects*, 5.

88. Walter R. Echo-Hawk, *In the Courts of the Conqueror: The 10 Worst Indian Law Cases Ever Decided* (Golden, CO: Fulcrum Publishing, 2010), 350–351.

89. Piatote, *Domestic Subjects*, 4.

90. Susan Staiger Gooding, "At the Boundaries of Religious Identity: Native American Religions and American Legal Culture," *Numen* 43, no. 2 (1996): 160.

91. Gooding, "At the Boundaries of Religious Identity," 161.

92. A similar argument is made in Tisa Wenger, *We Have a Religion: The 1920s Pueblo Indian Dance Controversy and American Religious Freedom* (Chapel Hill: University of North Carolina Press, 2009). See also Lee Irwin, "Freedom, Law, and Prophecy: A Brief History of Native American Religious Resistance," *American Indian Quarterly* 21, no. 1 (1997): 35–55.

93. Amy Bowers and Kristen A. Carpenter, "Challenging the Narrative of Conquest: The Story of *Lyng v. Northwest Indian Cemetery Protective Association*," in *Indian Law Stories*, ed. Carole Goldberg, Kevin K. Washburn, and Phillip P. Frickey (St. Paul: Foundation Press, 2011), 501.

94. Reporter's Transcript, 329.

95. Nick Estes, "My Relatives Went to a Catholic School for Native Children: It Was a Place of Horror," *Guardian*, June 30, 2021, https://amp.theguardian.com/commentisfree/2021/jun/30/my-relatives-went-to-a-catholic-school-for-native-children-it-was-a-place-of-horrors.

96. Bowers and Carpenter, "Challenging the Narrative of Conquest," 502–503.

97. Bowers and Carpenter, 503.

98. Bowers and Carpenter, 503.

99. Reporter's Transcript, 83.

100. On colonialism as a structure, rather than as a discrete event, see Patrick Wolfe, "Settler Colonialism and the Elimination of the Native," *Journal of Genocide Research* 8, no. 4 (2006): 387–409.

101. Buckley, *Standing Ground*, 62. For a critique of salvage ethnography and its role in revitalizing Indigenous ceremonies, see Baldy, *We Are Dancing for You*, 73–99.

102. Reporter's Transcript, 230–231.

103. Reporter's Transcript, 233.

104. Pfeffer, "CILS History."

105. Ellen Alderman and Caroline Kennedy, *In Our Defense: The Bill of Rights in Action* (New York: HarperCollins, 1992), 67.

106. Pfeffer, "CILS History."

107. Neustadtl, *Moving Mountains*, 207.

108. Neustadtl, 207.

Chapter 2. Land as Property in the *Lyng* Decision

1. Carol M. Rose, "Property as Storytelling: Perspectives from Game Theory, Narrative Theory, Feminist Theory," *Yale Journal of Law and the Humanities* 2 (1990): 37–57.

2. John Locke, *Second Treatise of Government*, ed. C. B. Macpherson (Indianapolis, IN: Hackett Publishing, 1980); William Blackstone, *Commentaries on the Laws of England* (Oxford, UK: Clarendon Press, 1765–1769).

3. Rose, "Property as Storytelling," 38.

4. Nicholas Blomley, "Landscapes of Property," *Law and Society Review* 32 (1998): 568.

5. Chris Jocks, "Restoring Congruity: Indigenous Lives and Religious Freedom in the United States and Canada," in *Traditional, National, and International Law and Indigenous Communities*, ed. Marianne O. Nielsen and Karen Jarratt-Snider (Tucson: University of Arizona Press, 2020), 88.

6. *Lyng*, 465 (Brennan, J., dissenting), emphasis added.

7. *Lyng*, 472 (Brennan, J., dissenting).

8. 21 U.S. (8 Wheat.) 543 (1823).

9. 374 U.S. 398 (1963).

10. 406 U.S. 205 (1972).

11. 476 U.S. 693 (1986).

12. Brian Edward Brown, *Religion, Law, and the Land: Native Americans and the Judicial Interpretation of Sacred Land* (Westport, CT: Greenwood Press, 1999), 7.

13. The dissenting opinion was filed by Justice William Brennan, who was joined by Justices Thurgood Marshall and Harry Blackmun. Justice Anthony Kennedy, who was appointed to the Supreme Court after the hearing of *Lyng*, took no part in the consideration or decision of the case.

14. *Lyng*, 447.

15. *Roy*, 699–700.

16. *Lyng*, 449.

17. *Lyng*, 449 (citing Brief for Indian Respondents, 33–34).

18. *Lyng*, 449.

19. Later in her opinion, O'Connor responds to Brennan's dissent, elaborating

further on this issue: "The dissent proposes a legal test under which it would decide which public lands are 'central' or 'indispensable' to which religions, and by implication which are 'dispensable' or 'peripheral,' and would then decide which government programs are 'compelling' enough to justify 'infringement of those practices.' We would accordingly be required to weigh the value of every religious belief and practice that is said to be threatened by any government program. Unless a 'showing of centrality' is nothing but an assertion of centrality, the dissent thus offers us the prospect of this Court holding that some sincerely held religious beliefs and practices are not 'central' to certain religions, despite protestations to the contrary from the religious objectors who brought the lawsuit. In other words, the dissent's approach would require us to rule that some religious adherents misunderstand their own religious beliefs" (*Lyng,* 457). It seems that both the majority approach to the G-O Road case and the dissent's approach lead to absurd results, which may suggest religious freedom is the wrong lens through which to look at this case altogether. I discuss this further in the next chapter.

20. *Lyng,* 450.

21. Similarly, Adell Sherbert argues that she is not allowed to work on Saturdays rather than arguing that if she worked on Saturday something bad would happen to her (*Sherbert v. Verner,* 374 U.S. 398 [1963]); the Yoders argue that it is against their belief to send their teenage kids to public schools rather than saying that something bad would happen to them if sent to school (*Wisconsin v. Yoder,* 406 U.S. 205 (1972)).

22. *Lyng,* 450–451.

23. Walter R. Echo-Hawk, *In the Courts of the Conqueror: The 10 Worst Indian Law Cases Ever Decided* (Golden, CO: Fulcrum Publishing, 2010), 327.

24. *Lyng,* 451.

25. *Lyng,* 451.

26. *Lyng,* 451.

27. *Lyng,* 451.

28. *Lyng,* 451.

29. *Lyng,* 451.

30. *Lyng,* 452.

31. *Lyng,* 452–453.

32. Vine Deloria, Jr., *For This Land: Writings on Religion in America* (London: Routledge, 1999), 204.

33. *Lyng,* 452.

34. *Lyng,* 453 (emphasis added).

35. *Lyng,* 453–454.

36. *Lyng,* 454.

37. *Lyng,* 455.

38. *Lyng,* 455.

39. *Lyng,* 442.

40. Cutcha Risling Baldy and Kayla Begay, "Xo'ch Na:nahsde'tl'-te Survivance, Resilience and Unbroken Traditions in Northwest California," in *Ka'm-t'em: A Journey*

Toward Healing, ed. Kishan Lara-Cooper and Walter J. Lara, Sr. (Temecula, CA: Great Oak Press, 2019), 50.

41. Edward W. Soja, *Postmodern Geographies: The Reassertion of Space in Critical Social Theory* (New York: Verso, 1990), 14. Cited in Blomley, "Landscapes of Property," 569.

42. *Lyng*, 442.

43. Lynn Huntsinger and Sarah McCaffrey, "A Forest for the Trees: Forest Management and the Yurok Environment, 1850 to 1994," *American Indian Culture and Research Journal* 19, no. 4 (1995): 167.

44. Huntsinger and McCaffrey, "A Forest for the Trees," 167.

45. Huntsinger and McCaffrey, 169.

46. Huntsinger and McCaffrey, 170.

47. Huntsinger and McCaffrey, 171.

48. Kari Marie Norgaard and William Tripp, *Karuk Climate Adaptation Plan*, Karuk Tribe Department of Natural Resources, March 2019, 51, https://karuktribeclimatechangeprojects.files.wordpress.com/2019/10/reduced-size_final-karuk-climate-adaptation-plan.pdf.

49. Huntsinger and McCaffrey, "A Forest for the Trees," 173.

50. Norgaard and Tripp, *Karuk Climate Adaptation Plan*, 45–47.

51. Netta Cohen, "Between Ecology and Ideology: Climate Change and Forestation Sciences in Mandatory Palestine/Israel," *Political Theology Network*, May 28, 2020, https://politicaltheology.com/between-ecology-and-ideology-climate-change-and-forestation-sciences-in-mandatory-palestine-israel/.

52. Robert Nichols, *Theft Is Property! Dispossession and Critical Theory* (Durham, NC: Duke University Press, 2020), 6.

53. Blomley, "Landscapes of Property," 568.

54. Beth Rose Middleton Manning and Kaitlin Reed, "Returning the Yurok Forest to the Yurok Tribe: California's First Tribal Carbon Credit Project," *Stanford Environmental Law Journal* 39, no. 1 (2019): 86–87.

55. Kathleen Sands, "Territory, Wilderness, Property, and Reservation: Land and Religion in Native American Supreme Court Cases," *American Indian Law Review* 36, no. 2 (2012): 265.

56. Joseph W. Singer, "The Continuing Conquest: American Indian Nations, Property Law, and Gunsmoke," in *Reconstruction*, vol. 1 (1991): 97–103, 102 (cited in Cheryl I. Harris, "Whiteness as Property," *Harvard Law Review* 106 (1993): 1710–1791, 1716n17).

57. Harris, "Whiteness as Property," 1723–1724.

58. Harris, 1714.

59. Aileen Moreton-Robinson, *The White Possessive: Property, Power, and Indigenous Sovereignty* (Minneapolis: University of Minnesota Press, 2015).

60. Eve Tuck and K. Wayne Yang, "Decolonization Is Not a Metaphor," *Decolonization: Indigeneity, Education & Society* 1 (2012): 5.

61. Richard Truscott, "Property Rights Are the Key to Indian Prosperity," Taxpayer.

com, July 29, 2002. Cited in Val Napoleon and Emily Snyder, "Housing on Reserve: Developing a Critical Indigenous Feminist Property Theory," in *Creating Indigenous Property: Power, Rights, and Relationships*, ed. Angela Cameron, Sari Graben, and Val Napoleon (Toronto: University of Toronto Press, 2020), 42.

62. Kenneth H. Bobroff, "Retelling Allotment: Indian Property Rights and the Myth of Common Ownership," *Vanderbilt Law Review* 54 (2001): 1561.

63. Bobroff, "Retelling Allotment," 1562.

64. Napoleon and Snyder, "Housing on Reserve," 42.

65. Kim TallBear, "Caretaking Relations, Not American Dreaming," *Kalfou* 6, no. 1 (Spring 2019): 32.

66. Allan Greer, *Property and Dispossession: Natives, Empires and Land in Early Modern North America* (Cambridge, UK: Cambridge University Press, 2018), 2.

67. Bobroff, "Retelling Allotment," 1563.

68. Bobroff, "Retelling Allotment," 1589.

69. Theodoratus Cultural Research, *Cultural Resources of the Chimney Rock Section, Gasquet–Orleans Road, Six Rivers National Forest* (Fair Oaks, CA, 1979), 39.

70. Lucy Thompson, *To the American Indian: Reminiscences of a Yurok Woman* (Berkeley: Heyday Books, 1991), 80–81.

71. Jack Norton, *Genocide in Northwestern California: When Our Worlds Cried* (San Francisco: Indian Historian Press, 1979), 6–7.

72. Thomas Buckley, *Standing Ground: Yurok Indian Spirituality, 1850–1990* (Berkeley: University of California Press, 2002), 184.

73. Echo-Hawk, *In the Courts of the Conqueror*, 58–59.

74. Karena Shaw, *Indigeneity and Political Theory: Sovereignty and the Limits of the Political* (London: Routledge, 2008), 8–9.

75. Jennifer Hamilton, *Indigeneity in the Courtroom: Law, Culture, and the Production of Difference in North American Courts* (London: Routledge, 2009), 3.

76. Hamilton, *Indigeneity in the Courtroom*, 2.

77. Hamilton, 8.

78. Hamilton, 8.

79. Kevin Bruyneel, *The Third Space of Sovereignty: The Postcolonial Politics of U.S.-Indigenous Relations* (Minneapolis: University of Minnesota Press, 2007), xi.

80. Legal scholar Ayelet Shachar, albeit asking a different question, suggests a similar solution, which she calls "overlapping jurisdictions." See Ayelet Shachar, *Multicultural Jurisdictions: Cultural Differences and Women's Rights* (Cambridge, UK: Cambridge University Press, 2001).

81. On the theological dimension, see, for example, George E. Tinker, *Spirit and Resistance: Political Theology and American Indian Liberation* (Minneapolis, MN: Fortress Press, 2004); and Steven T. Newcomb, *Pagans in the Promised Land: Decoding the Doctrine of Christian Discovery* (Golden, CO: Fulcrum Publishing, 2008). On the legal dimension, see, for example, Robert A. Williams, *Like a Loaded Weapon: The*

Rehnquist Court, Indian Rights, and the Legal History of Racism in America (Minneapolis: University of Minnesota Press, 2005); and Lisa Ford, *Settler Sovereignty: Jurisdiction and Indigenous People in America and Australia, 1788–1836* (Cambridge, MA: Harvard University Press, 2011).

82. Ford, *Settler Sovereignty*, 2; Mark Rifkin, "Indigenizing Agamben: Rethinking Sovereignty in Light of the 'Peculiar' Status of Native Peoples," *Cultural Critique* 73 (2009): 89.

83. Religious studies scholar Tisa Wenger argues that Christianity is still very much present in *Johnson* but concealed in later cases that rely on it, applying its logic without mentioning the doctrine of discovery. According to this reading, Marshall lays the groundwork for secularizing sovereignty in *Johnson*, and it is actually in later cases that it is secularized. Tisa Wenger, "Sovereignty," in *Religion, Law, USA*, ed. Joshua Dubler and Isaac Weiner (New York: New York University Press, 2019), 113–114.

84. Patrick Wolfe, *Traces of History: Elementary Structures of Race* (New York: Verso, 2016), 173.

85. See, for example, Williams, *Like a Loaded Weapon*.

86. Jodi A. Byrd, *The Transit of Empire: Indigenous Critiques of Colonialism* (Minneapolis: University of Minnesota Press, 2011), xxiii. There is another issue that Byrd does not mention but relates to property: the focus of mainstream media on the profits recognized tribes make from casinos takes part in masking the territorial issue at hand. And the focus on those profits is not unrelated to the racialization of Native Americans. See Renée Ann Cramer, *Cash, Color, and Colonialism: The Politics of Tribal Acknowledgement* (Norman: University of Oklahoma Press, 2005), xvi.

87. Choctaw anthropologist Circe Dawn Sturm reminds us that racial blending leads to what might be the most acute "danger [that] is posed to Native-American sovereignty and even continuity if the federal government continues to identify Native Americans on a racial instead of a cultural or more explicitly political basis." See Circe Dawn Sturm, *Blood Politics: Race, Culture and Identity in the Cherokee Nation of Oklahoma* (Berkeley: University of California Press, 2002), 3. Native American culture is treated as something that is either dying or belongs in the past, and therefore it is repressed in favor of blood quantum or documentation, as the two main criteria for determining Indigenous identity. For an important critique of blood quantum and DNA, see Kim TallBear, *Native American DNA: Tribal Belonging and the False Promise of Genetic Science* (Minneapolis: University of Minnesota Press, 2013).

88. Patrick Wolfe, "Settler Colonialism and the Elimination of the Native," *Journal of Genocide Research* 8, no. 4 (2006): 388.

89. Rifkin, "Indigenizing Agamben," 91.

90. Joanne Barker, "Confluence: Water as an Analytic of Indigenous Feminisms," *American Indian Culture and Research Journal* 43 no. 3 (2019): 11.

91. Barker, "Confluence," 13.

92. Joanne Barker, *Native Acts: Law, Recognition, and Cultural Authenticity* (Durham,

NC: Duke University Press, 2011), 40. What is ignored here, I argue, is Native peoples' right to sovereignty both according to the Western conception of sovereignty and the Native conception of it.

93. Tinker, *Spirit and Resistance*, 7.

94. Eva Marie Garroutte, *Real Indians: Identity and the Survival of Native America* (Berkeley: University of California Press, 2003); Kathleen Birrell, *Indigeneity: Before and Beyond the Law* (London: Routledge, 2016); Hamilton, *Indigeneity in the Courtroom*; Wenger, *We Have a Religion*.

95. Linda Tuhiwai Smith, *Decolonizing Methodologies: Research and Indigenous Peoples* (London: Zed Books, 1999), 24.

96. Barker, *Native Acts*, 35.

97. Shachar, *Multicultural Jurisdictions*, 11.

98. An example for the conflict that may be the result of accommodation can be found in Wenger, *We Have a Religion*.

99. James Clifford, *Returns: Becoming Indigenous in the Twenty-First Century* (Cambridge, MA: Harvard University Press, 2013), 17.

100. Hamilton, *Indigeneity in the Courtroom*, 4.

101. Birrell, *Indigeneity*, 4.

102. George D. Pappas, *The Literary and Legal Genealogy of Native American Dispossession: The Marshall Trilogy Cases* (London: Routledge, 2017).

103. Pappas, *Literary and Legal Genealogy of Native American Dispossession*, 14.

104. Jean Bethke Elshtain, *Sovereignty: God, State, and Self* (New York: Basic Books, 2012), xiv.

105. Elshtain, *Sovereignty*, 2.

106. Elshtain, 95.

107. Elshtain, ixi.

108. Cutcha Risling Baldy, "Why We Gather: Traditional Gathering in Native Northwest California and the future of Bio-Cultural Sovereignty," *Ecological Processes* 2 (2013): 1–10.

109. Julian Lang, "Being of the Same Mind," in *Ka'm-t'em: A Journey toward Healing*, ed. Kishan Lara-Cooper and Walter J. Lara, Sr. (Temecula, CA: Great Oak Press, 2019), 252–256.

110. Sovereign freedom, Cocks writes, is "quintessentially modern, along with the idea of the sovereign individual, ethnonational sovereignty, popular sovereignty, and the dream that the human race might rule the earth and eventually even the universe." Joan Cocks, *On Sovereignty and Other Political Delusions* (New York: Bloomsbury, 2014), 4.

111. Cocks, *On Sovereignty and Other Political Delusions*, 9.

112. Cocks, 24.

113. Taiaiake Alfred, "Sovereignty," in *Sovereignty Matters: Locations of Contestation and Possibility in Indigenous Struggles for Self-Determination*, ed. Joanne Barker (Lincoln: University of Nebraska Press, 2005), 38.

114. Bruyneel, *The Third Space of Sovereignty*, 217.

115. Literary scholar Cheryl Suzack (Batchewana First Nation) adds that the sovereignty of an Indigenous group would not mean much if it would not protect the dignity of the minorities (specifically women) within the group. Cheryl Suzack, *Indigenous Women's Writing and the Cultural Study of Law* (Toronto: University of Toronto Press, 2017).

116. Bruyneel, *The Third Space of Sovereignty*, 218.

117. Bernadette Atuahene, *We Want What's Ours: Learning from South Africa's Land Restitution Program* (Oxford: Oxford University Press, 2014), 45. An application of Atuahene's conception of dignity to the case of Hopi religion is found in Justin B. Richland, "Dignity as (Self-)Determination: Hopi Sovereignty in the Face of U.S. Dispossessions," *Law and Social Inquiry* 41, no. 4 (2016).

118. Atuahene, *We Want What's Ours*, 21.

119. *Johnson*, 574.

120. *Johnson*, 577–588.

121. Carol M. Rose, "Property and Expropriation: Themes and Variations in American Law," *Utah Law Review* 2000, no. 1 (2000): 30.

122. Jeremy Waldron, "Why Is Indigeneity Important?" in *Reparations: Interdisciplinary Inquiries*, ed. Jon Miller and Rahul Kumar (Oxford: Oxford University Press, 2007), 23–42.

Chapter 3. Land as Sacred in Justice Brennan's Dissent

1. *Sherbert v. Verner*, 374 U.S. 398 (1963).

2. *Lyng v. Northwest Indian Cemetery Protective Association*, 485 U.S. 439, 459 (Brennan, J., dissenting).

3. Theodoratus Cultural Research, *Cultural Resources of the Chimney Rock Section, Gasquet–Orleans Road, Six Rivers National Forest* (Fair Oaks, CA, 1979) (hereafter "Theodoratus Report"), 44.

4. Vine Deloria, Jr., *For This Land: Writings on Religion in America* (London: Routledge, 1999), 228.

5. Chris Jocks, "Restoring Congruity: Indigenous Lives and Religious Freedom in the United States and Canada," in *Traditional, National, and International Law and Indigenous Communities*, ed. Marianne O. Nielsen and Karen Jarratt-Snider (Tucson: University of Arizona Press, 2020), 85.

6. A. L. Kroeber, *Handbook of the Indians of California* (Berkeley: California Book Company, 1953), 830; Thomas Buckley, *Standing Ground: Yurok Indian Spirituality, 1850–1990* (Berkeley: University of California Press, 2002), 11.

7. Buckley, *Standing Ground*, 13.

8. Michael D. McNally, "From Substantial Burden on Religion to Diminished Spiritual Fulfillment: The San Francisco Peaks Case and the Misunderstanding of Native American Religion," *Journal of Law and Religion* 30 (2015): 36–64.

9. Michael Pfeffer, "CILS History: G-O Road Case," *CILS News* 10, Fall 2002.

10. Jace Weaver, "Losing My Religion: Native American Religious Traditions and American Religious Freedom," in *Native American Religious Identity*, ed. Jace Weaver (New York: Orbis Books, 1998), 219.

11. *Lyng*, 459 (Brennan, J., dissenting).

12. *Lyng*, 459 (Brennan, J., dissenting).

13. *Lyng*, 459 (Brennan, J., dissenting).

14. Stephanie Hall Barclay and Michalyn Steele, "Rethinking Protections for Indigenous Sacred Sites," *Harvard Law Review* 134 (2021): 1303.

15. Kristen A. Carpenter, "Living the Sacred: Indigenous Peoples and Religious Freedom," *Harvard Law Review* 134 (2021): 2021.

16. Barclay and Steele, "Rethinking Protections for Indigenous Sacred Sites," 1304.

17. *Lyng*, 459 (Brennan, J., dissenting).

18. Tisa Wenger, *We Have a Religion: The 1920s Pueblo Indian Dance Controversy and American Religious History* (Chapel Hill: University of North Carolina Press, 2009), 7.

19. Michael D. McNally, *Defend the Sacred: Native American Religious Freedom Beyond the First Amendment* (Princeton, NJ: Princeton University Press, 2020).

20. Jocks, "Restoring Congruity," 98–99.

21. Jocks, 84.

22. *Lyng*, 460 (Brennan, J., dissenting).

23. *Lyng*, 460–461 (Brennan, J., dissenting).

24. 404 U.S. 205 (1972).

25. *Lyng*, 467–468 (Brennan, J., dissenting).

26. *Lyng*, 467 (Brennan, J., dissenting); *Yoder*, 211.

27. *Lyng*, 473. This contrast that Brennan creates between property and the sacred should also be doubted. Native Americans have been portrayed, in popular culture and in federal Indian law alike, as incapable of possessing property, a portrayal that helped to justify their dispossession, as I discuss in chapter 2.

28. *Lyng*, 473 (Brennan, J., dissenting).

29. *Lyng*, 475 (Brennan, J., dissenting).

30. Reporter's Transcript, 230; Theodoratus Report, 45, 50.

31. Greg Johnson, "Ritual, Advocacy, and Authority: The Challenge of Being an Irreverent Witness," in *Irreverence and the Sacred: Critical Studies in the History of Religions*, ed. Hugh B. Urban and Greg Johnson (New York: Oxford University Press, 2017), 140.

32. *Lyng*, 476 (Brennan, J., dissenting).

33. Reporter's Transcript, 57.

34. Reporter's Transcript, 82–83.

35. Ronald Niezen, *Spirit Wars: Native North American Religions in the Age of Nation Building* (Berkeley: University of California Press, 2000), 1.

36. Reporter's Transcript, 82–83.

37. Reporter's Transcript, 78.

38. Johnson, "Ritual, Advocacy, and Authority," 141.

39. 620 F.2d 1159 (6th Cir. 1980).

40. 476 U.S. 693 (1986).

41. Méadhbh McIvor, *Representing God: Christian Legal Activism in Contemporary England* (Princeton, NJ: Princeton University Press, 2020), 6.

42. Benjamin L. Berger, *Law's Religion: Religious Difference and the Claims of Constitutionalism* (Toronto: University of Toronto Press, 2015).

43. Winnifred Fallers Sullivan, *The Impossibility of Religious Freedom* (Princeton, NJ: Princeton University Press, 2005).

44. Eduardo Peñalver, "Note: The Concept of Religion," *Yale Law Journal* 107, no. 3 (December 1997): 791–822.

45. Sullivan, *The Impossibility of Religious Freedom*.

46. Durkheim defines religion as "a unified system of beliefs and practices relative to sacred things, that is to say, things set apart and forbidden—beliefs and practices which unite into one single moral community called a Church, all those who adhere to them." Émile Durkheim, *The Elementary Forms of Religious Life*, trans. Karen E. Fields (New York: Free Press, 1995), 44.

47. According to Geertz, religion is "(1) a system of symbols which acts to (2) establish powerful, pervasive, and long-lasting moods and motivations in men by (3) formulating conceptions of a general order of existence and (4) clothing these conceptions with such an aura of factuality that (5) the moods and motivations seem uniquely realistic." Clifford Geertz, "Religion as a Cultural System," in *The Interpretation of Cultures: Selected Essays* (New York: Basic Books, 1993), 90.

48. Paul Tillich defined faith as anything of "ultimate concern" in *Dynamics of Faith* (New York: Harper, 1958), 1–2.

49. John Sexton, "Note, Toward a Constitutional Definition of Religion," *Harvard Law Review* 91, no. 5 (March 1978): 1056–1089.

50. Kent Greenavalt, "Religion as a Concept in Constitutional Law," *California Law Review* 72, no. 5 (September 1984): 753–816.

51. Peñalver, "Note," 814–821.

52. Berger, *Law's Religion*, 36.

53. Paul Kahn, *Putting Liberalism in Its Place* (Princeton, NJ: Princeton University Press, 2005).

54. Bette Novit Evans, *Interpreting the Free Exercise of Religion: The Constitution and American Pluralism* (Chapel Hill: University of North Carolina Press, 1997).

55. Sullivan, *The Impossibility of Religious Freedom*, 2.

56. Elizabeth Shakman Hurd, *Beyond Religious Freedom: The New Global Politics of Religion* (Princeton, NJ: Princeton University Press, 2015), 6.

57. Hurd, *Beyond Religious Freedom*, 6.

58. 98 U.S. 145 (1878). Legal historian Sarah Baringer Gordon critiques the court as making, rather than interpreting, history in the *Reynolds* decision. See Sarah Barringer Gordon, *The Mormon Question: Polygamy and Constitutional Conflict in Nineteenth-Century America* (Chapel Hill: University of North Carolina Press, 2002),

119–146. Philosopher Martha Nussbaum presents a similar critique of the *Reynolds* decision, arguing that it does not offer equal protection to the minority, as it does to the majority. See Martha Nussbaum, *Liberty of Conscience: In Defense of America's Traditions of Religious Equality* (New York: Basic Books, 2008).

59. *Reynolds*, 166–167.

60. John Locke argues in his "Letter Concerning Toleration" that while belief should be tolerated, certain acts can (and must) be outlawed. See John Locke, *A Letter Concerning Toleration and Other Writings* (Indianapolis, IN: Liberty Fund, 2010).

61. See J. Brett Pritchard, "Conduct and Belief in the Free Exercise Clause: Developments and Deviations in *Lyng v. Northwest Indian Cemetery Protective Association*," *Cornell Law Review* 76, no. 1 (November 1990): 268–296.

62. 310 U.S. 296 (1940).

63. *Cantwell*, 303.

64. *Cantwell*, 303.

65. *Cantwell*, 304.

66. *Cantwell*, 305.

67. Donald Falk, "Note: *Lyng v. Northwest Indian Cemetery Protective Association*: Bulldozing First Amendment Protection of Indian Sacred Lands," *Ecology Law Quarterly* 16, no. 2 (March 1989): 532; *Cantwell*, 305–307.

68. 310 U.S. 586 (1940). *Gobitis* was decided two weeks after *Cantwell* and was overruled by *West Virginia State Board of Education v. Barnette*, 319 U.S. 624 (1943).

69. *Gobitis*, 594.

70. Sarah Barringer Gordon, *The Spirit of the Law: Religious Voices and the Constitution in Modern America* (Cambridge, MA: Harvard University Press, 2010), 29.

71. Gordon, *The Spirit of the Law*, 30.

72. *Barnette* was decided three years after *Gobitis* and was based on identical facts. Falk explains the Justices' change of heart by the appointment of Justice Jackson, who joined the Supreme Court after the *Gobitis* decision, by the wide criticism the Supreme Court faced after *Gobitis*, as well as by Congress's endorsement of a voluntary flag salute in 1942; see Falk, "Bulldozing First Amendment Protection," 533n164.

73. *Barnette*, 639.

74. Falk, "Bulldozing First Amendment Protection," 533; *Barnette*, 638–640.

75. 367 U.S. 488 (1961).

76. *Torcaso*, 495n11.

77. 366 U.S. 599 (1961).

78. *Sherbert*, 404.

79. *Sherbert*, 403.

80. *Sherbert*, 407.

81. 450 U.S. 707 (1981).

82. 475 U.S. 503 (1986).

83. *Goldman*, 510.

84. *Roy*, 696.

85. *Roy*, 699. The court also found that the Roys failed to prove that the government's requirement infringed upon their free exercise rights, which means that the case could have been decided using traditional free exercise analysis, without invoking the "internal procedure" test.

86. *Roy*, 704, 708.

87. *Roy*, 707–708.

88. *Roy*, 727.

89. *Roy*, 732.

90. 480 U.S. 136 (1987).

91. *Hobbie*, 141.

92. Law and religion scholar Brian Edward Brown dedicated a book to these cases. See Brian Edward Brown, *Religion, Law, and the Land: Native Americans and the Judicial Interpretation of Sacred Land* (Westport: Greenwood Press, 1999).

93. 620 F.2d 1159 (6th Cir. 1980).

94. *Sequoyah*, 1160.

95. *Sequoyah*, 1164–1165.

96. 638 F.2d 172 (10th Cir. 1980).

97. 708 F.2d 735 (D.C. Cir. 1983).

98. *Wilson*, 744.

99. *Wilson*, 743–744.

100. *Northwest Indian Cemetery Protective Association v. Peterson*, 565 F. Supp. 586 (N.D. Cal. 1983).

101. *Northwest Indian Cemetery Protective Association v. Peterson*, 795 F.2d 688, 692 (9th Cir. 1986).

102. Amy Bowers and Kristen A. Carpenter, "Challenging the Narrative of Conquest: The Story of *Lyng v. Northwest Indian Cemetery Protective Association*," in *Indian Law Stories*, ed. Carole Goldberg, Kevin K. Washburn, and Phillip P. Frickey (St. Paul: Foundation Press, 2011), 492.

103. Jennifer Hamilton, *Indigeneity in the Courtroom: Law, Culture, and the Production of Difference in North American Courts* (London: Routledge, 2009), 4.

104. Robert J. Miller, "Correcting Supreme Court 'Errors': American Indian Response to *Lyng v. Northwest Indian Cemetery Protective Association*," *Environmental Law* 20, no. 4 (1990): 1062.

105. Peñalver, "Note," 793.

106. *Lyng*, 475 (Brennan, J., dissenting).

107. Jennifer Graber, *The Gods of Indian Country: Religion and the Struggle for the American West* (New York: Oxford University Press, 2018), 11.

108. Pamela E. Klassen, "Spiritual Jurisdictions: Treaty People and the Queen of Canada," in Paul Christopher Johnson, Pamela E. Klassen, and Winnifred Fallers Sullivan, *Ekklesia: Three Inquiries in Church and State* (Chicago: University of Chicago Press, 2018), 110.

109. Annual Report of Secretary Teller, 1883: ser. 2190, xi, cited in Justin B. Richland,

Arguing with Tradition: The Language of Law in Hopi Tribal Court (Chicago: University of Chicago Press, 2008), 9.

110. Susan Staiger Gooding, "At the Boundaries of Religious Identity: Native American Religions and American Legal Culture," *Numen* 43, no. 2 (May 1996): 161.

111. Richland, *Arguing with Tradition*, 11.

112. Theodoratus Report, 173.

113. Theodoratus Report, 174.

114. Theodoratus Report, 175.

115. Theodoratus Report, 177.

116. Norton, *Genocide in Northwestern California*, 112.

117. Theodoratus Report, appendix C.

118. Theodoratus Report, 178. According to Thomas Buckley, the Jump Dance was revitalized in 1984, forty-five years after its last performance, in 1939 (Buckley, *Standing Ground*, 4).

119. Theodoratus Report, 1.

120. Reporter's Transcript, 82–83.

121. 42 U.S.C. §1996 (1978).

122. Suzan Shown Harjo, "American Indian Religious Freedom Act After 25 Years," *Wicazo Sa Review* 19, no. 2 (2004): 130.

123. Theodore Catton, *American Indians and National Forests* (Tucson: University of Arizona Press, 2017), 4.

124. Catton, *American Indians and National Forests*, 141.

125. US Senate, Select Committee on Indian Affairs, *Improvement of the American Indian Religious Freedom Act*, 23–24; cited in Catton, *American Indians and National Forests*, 142.

126. 42 U.S.C. § 2000bb–42 U.S.C. § 2000bb-4.

127. 494 U.S. 872 (1990).

128. 535 F.3d 1058 (9th Cir. 2008).

129. *Standing Rock Sioux Tribe v. Army Corps of Engineers*, 985 F.3d 1032 (D.C. Cir. 2021).

130. In re Conservation District Use Application HA-3568, 431 P.3d 752 (Hawai'i 2018).

131. *Apache Stronghold v. United States*, 519 F. Supp. 3d 591 (D. Ariz. 2021).

132. *Apache Stronghold v. United States*, 9.

133. Carpenter, "Living the Sacred," 2106.

134. Carpenter, 2110.

135. Kristen A. Carpenter, Sonia K. Katyal, and Angela R. Riley, "In Defense of Property," *Yale Law Journal* 118 (2009): 1022–1125, 1051–1052.

136. Jack Norton, "The Past Is Our Future: Thoughts on Identity, Tradition and Change," in *Ka'm-t'em: A Journey Toward Healing*, ed. Kishan Lara-Cooper and Walter J. Lara, Sr. (Temecula, CA: Great Oak Press, 2019), 130.

Chapter 4. Land as Wild in the California Wilderness Act

1. Public Law 98-425 (1984).

2. Public Law 101-612 (1990).

3. *Northwest Indian Cemetery Protective Association v. Peterson*, 565 F. Supp. 586 (N.D. Cal. 1983), Complaint, 1.

4. Complaint, 1.

5. *Northwest Indian Cemetery Protective Association v. Peterson*, "Transcript of Trial" (unpublished), 1010 (hereafter this source is cited as Reporter's Transcript).

6. Reporter's Transcript, 1014.

7. 42 U.S.C. § 4321 et seq.

8. Reporter's Transcript, 1018.

9. The Wilderness Act itself designated nine million acres of Forest Service land as wilderness areas. The act also directed the secretaries of agriculture and the interior to review whether additional federal lands should be added to the wilderness system. That process yielded two studies during the 1970s, denominated RARE I and RARE II, which identified seventy-one million acres of national forest lands that could qualify as wilderness, but Congress continues to debate many of those recommendations. There are also ongoing disputes about the status of "wilderness study areas" that may possess the characteristics of wilderness but that Congress has not designated as wilderness areas (see John Copeland Nagle, "The Spiritual Values of Wilderness," *Environmental Law* 35 [2005]: 961–962).

10. Reporter's Transcript, 1028.

11. Reporter's Transcript, 1029.

12. Reporter's Transcript, 1030.

13. Reporter's Transcript, 1031.

14. Reporter's Transcript, 1031–1032.

15. Reporter's Transcript, 1032.

16. Reporter's Transcript, 1035.

17. Reporter's Transcript, 1048.

18. Reporter's Transcript, 267.

19. Reporter's Transcript, 267.

20. Reporter's Transcript, 268.

21. Reporter's Transcript, 268.

22. Cutcha Risling Baldy, *We Are Dancing for You: Native Feminisms and the Revitalization of Women's Coming-of-Age Ceremonies* (Seattle: University of Washington Press, 2018), 73–99.

23. Walt Lara, Sr., and Kishan Lara-Cooper, "Across the Lagoon: The Inspiration behind the Northwest Indian Cemetery Protection Association (NICPA)," in *Ka'm-t'em: A Journey Toward Healing*, ed. Kishan Lara-Cooper and Walter J. Lara, Sr. (Temecula, CA: Great Oak Press, 2019), 158.

24. Chris Peters and Chisa Oros, "Protecting Our Sacred Sites: *Lyng v. Northwest Indian Cemetery Protective Association*," in *Ka'm-t'em: A Journey Toward Healing*, ed. Kishan Lara-Cooper and Walter J. Lara, Sr. (Temecula, CA: Great Oak Press, 2019), 177–178.

25. Peters and Oros, "Protecting Our Sacred Sites," 184.

26. H.R. REP. No. 40, 98th Cong., 1st Sess. 32 (1983); S.REP. No. 582, 98th Cong., 2d Sess. 28–29 (1984). Cited in Robert J. Miller, "Correcting Supreme Court 'Errors': American Indian Response to *Lyng v. Northwest Indian Cemetery Protective Association*," *Environmental Law* 20, no. 4 (1990): 1051.

27. The House Committee on Interior and Insular Affairs declared, "The Committee does not adopt any position with respect to the so-called 'G-O' (Gasquet-Orleans) road project" (H.R. REP. No. 40, 98th Cong., 1st Sess. 32 [1983]). According to Miller, in leaving this twelve-hundred-foot corridor, Congress did take a stand with regards to the road. Miller, "Correcting Supreme Court 'Errors,'" 1051.

28. Cutcha Risling Baldy, "Why We Gather: Traditional Gathering in Native Northwest California and the Future of Bio-Cultural Sovereignty," *Ecological Processes* 2 (2013): 3.

29. Wilderness Act (1964), Public Law 88-577 (16 U.S.C. 1131–1136), 2(c).

30. Nagle, "The Spiritual Values of Wilderness," 981–986.

31. Linda H. Graber, *Wilderness as Sacred Space* (Washington, DC: Association of American Geographers, 1974), x.

32. Theodoratus Cultural Research, *Cultural Resources of the Chimney Rock Section, Gasquet–Orleans Road, Six Rivers National Forest* (Fair Oaks, CA, 1979), 75.

33. Hi'ilei Julia Hobart, "At Home on the Mauna: Ecological Violence and Fantasies of Terra Nullius on Maunakea's Summit," *Native American and Indigenous Studies* 6 (2019): 30.

34. Hobart, "At Home on the Mauna," 31.

35. Hobart, 30.

36. *Tsilhqot'in Nation v. British Columbia* [2014] 2 SCR 256.

37. John Borrows, *Law's Indigenous Ethics* (Toronto: University of Toronto Press, 2019), 98.

38. Theodoratus Report, 46.

39. Theodoratus Report, 46.

40. Reporter's Transcript, 237–238.

41. Theodoratus Report, 47, 70; Reporter's Transcript, 237.

42. Theodoratus Report, 48–49.

43. Chris Peters and Chisa Oros, "Voices from the Sacred: An Indigenous Worldview and Epistemology of Northwestern California," in *Ka'm-t'em: A Journey toward Healing*, ed. Kishan Lara-Cooper and Walter J. Lara, Sr. (Temecula, CA: Great Oak Press, 2019), 8.

44. Peters and Oros, "Voices from the Sacred," 8.

45. Peters and Oros, 11.

46. M. Kat Anderson, *Tending the Wild: Native American Knowledge and the Management of California's Natural Resources* (Berkeley: University of California Press, 2005), 125–126.

47. Kari Marie Norgaard, *Salmon and Acorns Feed Our People: Colonialism, Nature, and Social Action* (New Brunswick, NJ: Rutgers University Press, 2020), 2–3.

48. Anderson, *Tending the Wild*, 1.

49. Beth Rose Middleton Manning and Kaitlin Reed, "Returning the Yurok Forest to the Yurok Tribe: California's First Tribal Carbon Credit Project," *Stanford Environmental Law Journal* 39 (2019): 87–88.

50. Amy Bowers and Kristen A. Carpenter, "Challenging the Narrative of Conquest: The Story of *Lyng v. Northwest Indian Cemetery Protective Association*," in *Indian Law Stories*, ed. Carole Goldberg, Kevin K. Washburn, and Phillip P. Frickey (St. Paul: Foundation Press, 2011), 493.

51. Vine Deloria, Jr., *God Is Red: A Native View on Religion* (Golden, CO: Fulcrum Publishing, 2013), 271–286. Religious studies scholar Kathleen Sands writes that "because the entire world is sacred, tribal religions find the spiritual realm on earth, rather than in a metaphysically separate sphere. At a more intense level, the sacred is encountered at the specific places—mountains, plains, lakes, and woods—where different tribal ancestors historically lived. Native American religions are thus local rather than portable, and collective rather than individualistic. They are the holistic life-ways of particular tribes, in certain geographical settings, rather than purely personal beliefs about metaphysical matters. Christianity, on the other hand, has conceived itself as a universal religion, not bound to any one group or any one place. It is eminently portable and, in contrast to tribal religions, decidedly otherworldly. But in historical practice, Christianity, like other universalistic religions, has not settled for being 'nowhere;' instead it has striven to be everywhere and to encompass everyone." See Kathleen Sands, "Territory, Wilderness, Property, and Reservation: Land and Religion in Native American Supreme Court Cases," *American Indian Law Review* 36, no. 2 (2012): 258.

52. Nicolas Howe, *Landscapes of the Secular: Law, Religion, and American Sacred Space* (Chicago: University of Chicago Press, 2016), 117.

53. John Brinckerhoff Jackson, *A Sense of Place, A Sense of Time* (New Haven, CT: Yale University Press, 1996), 76.

54. Jackson, *A Sense of Place, A Sense of Time*, 87.

55. Jackson, 87.

56. Howe, *Landscapes of the Secular*, 120.

57. Graber, *Wilderness as Sacred Space*, 8.

58. Cited in Nagle, "The Spiritual Values of Wilderness," 958.

59. John Muir, *Letters from Alaska*, ed. Robert Engberg and Bruce Merrell (Madison: University of Wisconsin Press, 1993), 30.

60. Roderick Frazier Nash, *Wilderness in the American Mind* (New Haven, CT: Yale University Press, 2001), 280.

61. Henry David Thoreau, "Walking," *Atlantic Monthly* 9 (1862): 665.

62. Baldy, "Why We Gather," 7. Linda Graber reminds us that wilderness designation does not even promise real preservation: "In practice, however, certain human modifications are permitted in legally defined Wilderness Areas.... In the National Park wildernesses, trees cannot be logged by private industry, but they can be removed to build recreational amenities such as trails. Wild animals cannot be hunted, but the equally wild fish can be taken without a fishing license" (Graber, *Wilderness as Sacred Space*, 10).

63. Abby Abinanti, "A Letter to Justice O'Connor," *Indigenous Peoples' Journal of Law, Culture, and Resistance* 1 (2004): 2.

64. Frieda Knobloch, *The Culture of Wilderness: Agriculture as Colonization in the American West* (Chapel Hill: University of North Carolina Press, 1996), 2.

65. Mark David Spence, *Dispossessing the Wilderness: Indian Removal and the Making of the National Parks* (New York: Oxford University Press, 2000), 3.

66. William Cronon, "The Trouble with Wilderness; Or, Getting Back to the Wrong Nature," in *Uncommon Ground: Rethinking the Human Place in Nature*, ed. William Cronon (New York: W. W. Norton, 1995), 69–90.

67. Scholars have demonstrated how both development and preservation have worked as tools of dispossession in Palestine/Israel as well. See Netta Cohen, "Between Ecology and Ideology: Climate Change and Forestation Sciences in Mandatory Palestine/Israel," *Political Theology Network*, May 28, 2020, https://politicaltheology.com/between-ecology-and-ideology-climate-change-and-forestation-sciences-in-mandatory-palestine-israel/; Edna Gorney, "(Un)Natural Selection: The Drainage of the Hula Wetlands, an Ecofeminist Reading," *International Feminist Journal of Politics* 9, no. 4 (2007): 465–474.

68. Vine Deloria, Jr., "Trouble in High Places: Erosion of American Indian Rights to Religious Freedom in the United States," in *The State of Native America: Genocide, Colonization, and Resistance*, ed. M. Annette Jaimes (Boston: South End Press: 1992), 281.

69. Ramachandra Guha, "Radical American Environmentalism and Wilderness Preservation: A Third World Critique," *Environmental Ethics* 11, no.1 (Spring 1989): 72.

70. Guha, "Radical American Environmentalism and Wilderness Preservation," 73.

71. Guha, 79. Mark David Spence writes that preservationist efforts only succeed when outdoor enthusiasts view wilderness as "an uninhabited Eden that should be set aside for the benefit and pleasure of vacationing Americans." Native peoples who continued to hunt and light purposeful fires in such places were understood as unable to appreciate natural beauty. "To guard against these 'violations,' the establishment of the first national parks necessarily entailed the exclusion or removal of native peoples" (Spence, *Dispossessing the Wilderness*, 4).

72. David Truer, "Return the National Parks to the Tribes," *Atlantic*, April 12, 2021, https://www.theatlantic.com/magazine/archive/2021/05/return-the-national-parks-to-the-tribes/618395/.

73. *Johnson v. M'Intosh*, 21 U.S. (8 Wheat.) 543 (1823), 590.

74. Dina Gilio-Whitaker, *As Long as Grass Grows: The Indigenous Fight for Environmental Justice, from Colonization to Standing Rock* (Boston: Beacon Press, 2019), 39.

75. Gilio-Whitaker, *As Long as Grass Grows*, 97n11.

76. Patrick Wolfe, "Settler Colonialism and the Elimination of the Native," *Journal of Genocide Research* 8, no. 4 (2006): 387–409; Philip Deloria, *Playing Indian* (New Haven, CT: Yale University Press, 1999).

Chapter 5. Land as Kin in the Klamath River Resolution

1. Yurok Tribal Council, "Resolution 19-40: Resolution Establishing the Rights of the Klamath River," May 9, 2019, http://files.harmonywithnatureun.org/uploads /upload833.pdf.

2. Robert Alexander Innes, *Elder Brother and the Law of the People: Contemporary Kinship and Cowessess First Nation* (Winnipeg: University of Manitoba Press, 2013), 6.

3. Aileen Moreton-Robinson, "Relationality: A Key Presupposition of an Indigenous Social Research Paradigm," in *Sources and Methods in Indigenous Studies*, ed. Chris Anderson and Jean M. O'Brien (London: Routledge, 2017), 71.

4. Kyle Powys Whyte, "Time as Kinship," in *Cambridge Companion to Environmental Humanities*, ed. Jeffrey Jerome Cohen and Stephanie Foote (Cambridge, UK: Cambridge University Press, 2021), 42.

5. Native American studies scholar Cutcha Risling Baldy (Hupa, Yurok, Karuk) writes that what the Wilderness Act protects is not really wilderness, because it allows for several recreational activities, such as camping, hiking, hunting, and fishing. The one thing the act does not mention as allowed is Native management of the area. Cutcha Risling Baldy, "Why We Gather: Traditional Gathering in Native Northwest California and the Future of Bio-Cultural Sovereignty," *Ecological Processes* 2 (2013): 7.

6. República del Ecuador Constitucion de 2008, http://therightsofnature.org/wp-content/uploads/pdfs/Rights-for-Nature-Articles-in-Ecuadors-Constitution.pdf.

7. Ley de Derechos de la Madre Tierra, Law 071, December 2010 (Bol.) translated in http://f.cl.ly/items/2Z2n2D0g2x2E0X1B272Y/law_of_mother_earth_translation .pdf (designating Mother Earth to be the titleholder of certain rights ensuring protection for her and her life-systems).

8. Te Urewera Act 2014 (N.Z.), http://www.legislation.govt.nz/act/public/2014 /0051/latest/DLM6183601.html; *Mohd Salim v. State of Uttarakhand & others*, WP-PIL 126/2014 (High Court of Uttarakhand), 2017.

9. Court judgment (Supreme Court of Bangladesh), *Human Rights and Peace for Bangladesh and others v. Secretary of the Ministry of Shipping and others*, Writ Petition No. 13989 of 2016.

10. The bill was declared unconstitutional by a federal judge in 2020. *Drewes Farms P'Ship v. City of Toledo*, No. 3:19 CV 434, 2020 WL 966628 (N.D. Ohio, 2020).

11. "For the First Time, a River is Granted Official Rights and Legal Personhood in Canada," *PR Newswire*, February 23, 2021, available at https://www.prnewswire

.com/news-releases/for-the-first-time-a-river-is-granted-official-rights-and-legal
-personhood-in-canada-301233731.

12. Legal scholar Erin L. O'Donnell explains, "In the Ganges and Yamuna case, this
moral duty to protect nature was extended by the Court's assessment of the status of the
rivers as 'sacred and revered . . . central to the existence of half the Indian population.'
Whilst the Court was clear that not all Indians regard the rivers as sacred, this link to
the Hindu population is possibly controversial. Some commentators have argued that
this ruling elevates the Hindu beliefs and undermines religious tolerance in India. In
fact, rivers are explicitly considered as not sacred to many people in India, which could
make this a shaky foundation for the creation of legal rights for the rivers themselves."
Erin L. O'Donnell, "At the Intersection of the Sacred and the Legal: Rights for Nature
in Uttarakhand, India," *Journal of Environmental Law* 30, no. 1 (2018): 140.

13. Dian Million, "Indigenous Relations of Well-Being vs. Humanitarian Health
Economies," in *Routledge Handbook of Critical Indigenous Studies*, ed. Brendan Hokow-
hitu, Aileen Moreton-Robinson, Linda Tuhiwai-Smith, Chris Andersen, and Steve
Larkin (London: Routledge, 2021), 395.

14. See Kevin Bruyneel, *The Third Space of Sovereignty: The Postcolonial Politics of
U.S.-Indigenous Relations* (Minneapolis: University of Minnesota Press, 2017).

15. Charles Sepulveda, "Our Sacred Waters: Theorizing *Kuuyam* as a Decolonial
Possibility," in *Decolonization: Indigeneity, Education & Society* 7, no. 1 (2018): 48.

16. Ashish Kothari and Shrishtee Bajpai, "Rivers and Human Rights: We
Are the River, the River Is Us?" *Vikalp Sangam* November 3, 2017, https://
vikalpsangam.org/article/rivers-and-human-rights-we-are-the-river-the-river-is-us/.

17. Christopher Stone, *Should Trees Have Standing? Law, Morality, and the Environment* (New York: Oxford University Press, 2010).

18. Kothari and Bajpai, "Rivers and Human Rights."

19. Nicole J. Wilson and Jody Inkster, "Respecting Water: Indigenous Water Governance, Ontologies, and the Politics of Kinship on the Ground," *Environment and
Planning E: Nature and Space* 1 (2018): 531–532.

20. Daniel Wildcat, "Indigenizing Politics and Ethics," in Vine Deloria, Jr., and
Daniel Wildcat, *Power and Place: Indian Education in America* (Golden, CO: Fulcrum
Publishing, 2001), 93.

21. Suzanne Crawford O'Brien and Inés Talamantez, *Religion and Culture in Native
America* (Lanham, MD: Rowman and Littlefield, 2020), 24.

22. Kim TallBear, "Caretaking Relations, Not American Dreaming," *Kalfou* 6, no. 1
(Spring 2019): 25.

23. Vine Deloria, Jr., "Knowing and Understanding," in Vine Deloria, Jr., and Daniel
Wildcat, *Power and Place: Indian Education in America* (Golden, CO: Fulcrum Publishing, 2001), 44.

24. Lawrence Tribe, "Ways Not to Think About Plastic Trees: New Foundations
for Environmental Law," *Yale Law Journal* 83 (1974): 1345.

25. Tribe, "Ways Not to Think About Plastic Trees," 1346.

26. Joanne Barker, "Confluence: Water as an Analytic of Indigenous Feminisms," *American Indian Culture and Research Journal* 43 (2019): 18.

27. Miranda Johnson, "The River Is Not a Person: Indigeneity and the Sacred in Aotearoa New Zealand," *Immanent Frame*, June 14, 2017, https://tif.ssrc.org/2017/06/14/the-river-is-not-a-person/.

28. O'Brien and Talamantez, *Religion and Culture in Native America*, 83.

29. Melanie K. Yazzie and Cutcha Risling Baldy, "Introduction: Indigenous Peoples and the Politics of Water," *Decolonization: Indigeneity, Education, & Society* 7, no. 1 (2018): 2.

30. Michelle Bryan, "Valuing Sacred Tribal Waters Within Prior Appropriation," *Natural Resources Journal* 57, no. 1 (2017): 141n10.

31. Natalie Avalos, "Indigenous Stewardship: Religious Praxis and 'Unsettling' Settler Ecologies," *Political Theology* (forthcoming, 2023).

32. Nick Estes, *Our History Is the Future: Standing Rock versus the Dakota Access Pipeline, and the Long Tradition of Indigenous Resistance* (New York: Verso, 2019), 21.

33. Yazzie and Risling Baldy, "Introduction," 1. See also Cutcha Risling Baldy, "Water Is Life: The Flower Dance Ceremony," *News from Native California* 30, no. 3 (2017).

34. Bryan, "Valuing Sacred Tribal Waters Within Prior Appropriation," 144n26.

35. Quoted in Michael McNally, *Defend the Sacred: Native American Religious Freedom beyond the First Amendment* (Princeton, NJ: Princeton University Press, 2020), 21.

36. 207 U.S. 564 (1908).

37. Lloyd Burton, *American Indian Water Rights and the Limits of Law* (Lawrence: University Press of Kansas, 1991), 6.

38. Burton, *American Indian Water Rights and the Limits of Law*, 6.

39. Burton, 7.

40. Burton, 19–20.

41. The stated purpose for the reservations, according to *Winters*, was to assimilate Native Americans into a "pastoral and civilized people." Since "the lands were arid, and, without irrigation, were practically valueless," there was an implied right to water in order to grow crops and for other purposes necessary to effectuate the reservation's purposes (*Winters*, 576).

42. According to Robert T. Anderson, land and water were plentiful at that time, and therefore there was no explicit reference to water rights in the treaties creating these reservations. See Robert T. Anderson, "Indigenous Rights to Water and Environmental Protection," *Harvard Civil Rights-Civil Liberties Law Review* 53 (2018): 340–341.

43. *Arizona v. California*, 373 U.S. 546 (1963); See Judith Royster, "A Primer on Indian Water Rights," *Tulsa Law Review* 30, no. 1 (1994): 67.

44. Royster, "A Primer on Indian Water Rights," 337.

45. As we saw in chapter 2, land (or water) that is the subject of property rights is understood as a commodity, which, ultimately, enables its taking.

46. Royster, "A Primer on Indian Water Rights," 350–351.

47. 723 F.2d 1394 (9th Cir. 1983), 1409.

48. Native American Rights Fund, "Klamath Tribes' Water Rights," accessed December 18, 2022: https://www.narf.org/cases/klamath-tribes-water-rights/.

49. *Adair*, 1414. Note that this is exactly the type of cases that the court loves, where tribes can show continuity and stasis.

50. Bryan, "Valuing Sacred Tribal Waters Within Prior Appropriation," 150.

51. Bryan, 151.

52. Bryan explains that diversion is a foundational principle in western water law. Because sacred tribal waters tend to be valued in situ, they run counter to this traditional requirement of diversion. Bryan, "Valuing Sacred Tribal Waters Within Prior Appropriation," 152.

53. Bryan, 151–152.

54. Dean B. Suagee and Peter Bungart, "Taking Care of Native American Cultural Landscapes," *National Resources and Environment* 27, no. 4 (2013): 24 (quoted in Bryan, "Valuing sacred Tribal Waters Within Prior Appropriation," 154).

55. 42 U.S.C. § 1996.

56. 16 U.S.C. ch. 1A, subch. II § 470 et seq.

57. 16 U.S.C. 470aa–470mm.

58. 25 U.S.C. ch. 32 § 3001 et seq.

59. 42 U.S.C. § 4321 et seq.

60. Bryan, "Valuing Sacred Tribal Waters Within Prior Appropriation," 154–157.

61. 33 U.S.C.A. § 1377(e).

62. Bryan, "Valuing Sacred Tribal Waters Within Prior Appropriation," 159.

63. Bryan, 176.

64. *Bear Lodge Multiple Use Assoc. v. Babbitt*, 2 F. Supp. 2d 1448 (D. Wyo. 1998). A review and analysis of this case can be found in Lloyd Burton, *Worship and Wilderness: Culture, Religion, and Law in Public Lands Management* (Madison: University of Wisconsin Press, 2002).

65. Bryan, "Valuing Sacred Tribal Waters Within Prior Appropriation," 176.

66. Barker, "Confluence," 18.

67. *Mattz v. Arnett*, 412 U.S. 481 (1973).

68. Gillian Flaccus, "Plan to Remove Four Dams on Lower Klamath River Clears Regulatory Hurdle," *Register Guard*, June 17, 2021, https://www.register guard.com/story/news/2021/06/17/klamath-river-dams-removal-clear-regula tory-hurdle/7740765002/.

69. Public Law 73-383 (1934).

70. Michael W. Orcutt, "Tribal Water Rights: Klamath-Trinity River," in *Ka'm-t'em: A Journey Toward Healing*, ed. Kishan Lara-Cooper and Walter J. Lara, Sr. (Temecula: Great Oak Press, 2019), 203.

71. https://yurok.tribal.codes/Constitution/Preamble.

72. Walter J. Lara, Sr., and Kishan Lara-Cooper, "Fish Wars on the Klamath River," in *Ka'm-t'em: A Journey Toward Healing*, ed. Kishan Lara-Cooper and Walter J. Lara, Sr. (Temecula, CA: Great Oak Press, 2019), 214.

73. Wilson and Inkster, "Respecting Water," 525.

74. On the close ties between protest and ceremony in Native traditions, see, for example, Lee Irwin, *Coming Down from Above: Prophecy, Resistance, and Renewal in Native American Religions* (Norman: University of Oklahoma Press, 2008); Dennis Kelley, *Tradition, Performance, and Religion in Native America* (London: Routledge, 2014); and Avalos, "Indigenous Stewardship."

75. Glen Sean Coulthard, *Red Skin, White Masks: Rejecting the Colonial Politics of Recognition* (Minneapolis: University of Minnesota Press, 2014), 61.

76. Lara, Sr., and Lara-Cooper, "Fish Wars on the Klamath River," 217.

77. Amy Bowers and Kristen A. Carpenter, "Challenging the Narrative of Conquest: The Story of *Lyng v. Northwest Indian Cemetery Protective Association*," in *Indian Law Stories*, ed. Carole Goldberg, Kevin K. Washburn, and Phillip P. Frickey (St. Paul: Foundation Press, 2011), 504.

78. Lara and Lara-Cooper, "The Fish Wars," 219.

79. Lara and Lara-Cooper, 220.

80. Theodoratus Cultural Research, *Cultural Resources of the Chimney Rock Section, Gasquet–Orleans Road, Six Rivers National Forest* (Fair Oaks, CA, 1979), 8.

81. Lara and Lara-Cooper, "The Fish Wars," 224.

82. Public Law 100-580 (1988).

83. Lara and Lara-Cooper, "The Fish Wars," 222.

84. Orcutt, "Tribal Water Rights," 201.

85. Winona LaDuke, *Recovering the Sacred: The Power of Naming and Claiming* (Chicago: Haymarket Books, 2005), 48.

86. Lucy Thompson, *To the American Indian: Reminiscences of a Yurok Woman* (Berkeley: Heyday Books, 1991), 196.

87. Stephen Most, *Rivers of Renewal: Myth and History in the Klamath Basin* (Seattle: University of Washington Press, 2016), 69.

88. Kaitlin Reed, "We Are Salmon People: Constructing Yurok Sovereignty in the Klamath Basin," Senior Thesis, Vassar College, 2014, 16.

89. See *Minnesota Department of Natural Resources v. White Earth Band of Ojibwe*, No. 21-cv-1869, 2021 WL 4034582, at *1 n. 1 (District of Minnesota Sept. 3, 2021), denying an injunction to prohibit the case from proceeding in tribal court. For a draft copy of the tribal court complaint, see Complaint for Declaratory and Injunctive Relief, *Manoomin v. Minnesota Department of Natural Resources* (White Earth Nation of Ojibwe Tribal Court Aug. 4, 2021), available at https://turtletalk.files.wordpress.com /2021/08/manoomin-et-al-v-dnr-complaint-w-exhibits-8-4-21.pdf.

90. Jefferson Exchange Team, "Yuroks Grant Rights to the Klamath River," May 29, 2019, https://www.ijpr.org/show/the-jefferson-exchange/2019-05-29/yuroks-grant -rights-to-the-klamath-river#stream/0.

91. Jefferson Exchange Team, "Yuroks Grant Rights to the Klamath River."

92. Wilson and Inkster, "Respecting Water," 517.

93. Heidi Kiiwetinepinesiik Stark, "Stories as Law: A Method to Live By," in *Sources*

and Methods in Indigenous Studies, ed. Chris Andersen and Jean M. O'Brien (London: Routledge, 2017), 254.

94. Patricia Dudgeon and Abigail Bray, "Indigenous Relationality: Women, Kinship and the Law," *Genealogy* 3, no. 2 (2019): 24.

95. Mark Rifkin, *When Did Indians Become Straight? Kinship, the History of Sexuality, and Native Sovereignty* (New York: Oxford University Press, 2011), 5–6.

96. Mark Rifkin, "Around 1978: Family, Culture, and Race in the Federal Production of Indianness," in *Critically Sovereign: Indigenous Gender, Sexuality, and Feminist Studies*, ed. Joanne Barker (Durham, NC: Duke University Press, 2017), 172.

97. Enrique Salmón, "Kincentric Ecology: Indigenous Perceptions of the Human-Nature Relationship," *Ecological Applications* 10 (2000): 1329.

98. Rifkin, "Around 1978," 172.

99. Daniel Heath Justice, "'Go Away Water!': Kinship Criticism and the Decolonization Imperative," in *Reasoning Together: The Native Critics Collection* (Norman: University of Oklahoma Press, 2008), 147–168, 151–152.

100. David Delgado Shorter, "Spirituality," in *The Oxford Handbook of American Indian History*, ed. Frederick E. Hoxie (New York: Oxford University Press, 2016), 433–452.

101. Dudgeon and Bray, "Indigenous Relationality," 23.

102. Abby Abinanti, "A Letter to Justice O'Connor," *Indigenous Peoples' Journal of Law, Culture, and Resistance* 1 (2004): 18.

Conclusion: Land as Sovereign

1. José Barreiro, "Geneva, 1977: A Report on the Hemispheric Movement of Indigenous Peoples," in *A Basic Call to Consciousness*, ed. Akwesasne Notes (Summertown, TN: Native Voices, 1978), 77.

2. Vine Deloria, Jr., "Sacred Lands and Religious Freedom," in *For This Land: Writings on Religion in America* (London: Routledge, 1999), 212.

3. Associated Press, "The Largest Dam Demolition in History Is Approved for a Western River," November 17, 2022, https://www.npr.org/2022/11/17/1137442481/dam-demolition-klamath-river-california-federal-regulators-salmon.

4. Kevin Bruyneel, *The Third Space of Sovereignty: The Postcolonial Politics of U.S.-Indigenous Relations* (Minneapolis: University of Minnesota Press, 2007), 221.

5. Elisha Chi, "Refusal," *Political Theology Network*, November 15, 2022, https://politicaltheology.com/refusal/.

BIBLIOGRAPHY

Case Law

Apache Stronghold v. United States, 519 F. Supp. 3d 591 (D. Ariz. 2021).

Badoni v. Higginson, 638 F.2d 172 (10th Cir. 1980).

Bear Lodge Multiple Use Assoc. v. Babbitt, 2 F. Supp. 2d 1448 (D. Wyo. 1998).

Bowen v. Roy, 476 U.S. 693 (1986).

Braunfeld v. Brown, 366 U.S. 599 (1961).

Brendale v. Confederated Tribes and Bands of the Yakima Indian Nation, 492 U.S. 408 (1998).

Cantwell v. Connecticut, 310 U.S. 296 (1940).

Cherokee Nation v. Georgia, 30 U.S. (5 Peters) 1 (1831).

Drewes Farms P'Ship v. City of Toledo, No. 3:19 CV 434, 2020 WL 966628 (N.D. Ohio, 2020).

Employment Division, Department of Human Resources of Oregon v. Smith, 494 U.S. 872 (1990).

Goldman v. Weinberger, 475 U.S. 503 (1986).

Hobbie v. Unemployment Appeals Commission of Florida, 480 U.S. 136 (1987).

In re Conservation District Use Application HA-3568, 431 P.3d 752 (Hawai'i 2018).

Johnson v. M'Intosh, 21 U.S. (8 Wheat.) 543 (1823).

Lyng v. Northwest Indian Cemetery Protective Association, 485 U.S. 439 (1988).

Manoomin v. Minnesota Department of Natural Resources (White Earth Nation of Ojibwe Tribal Court Aug. 4, 2021).

Mattz v. Arnett, 412 U.S. 481 (1973).

Minersville School District v. Gobitis, 310 U.S. 586 (1940).

Minnesota Department of Natural Resources v. White Earth Band of Ojibwe, No. 21-cv-1869, 2021 WL 4034582, at *1 n. 1 (District of Minnesota, September 3, 2021).

Montana v. U.S., 450 U.S. 544 (1981).

Navajo Nation v. U.S. Forest Service, 535 F.3d 1058 (9th Cir. 2008).

Northwest Indian Cemetery Protective Association v. Peterson, 795 F.2d 688, 692 (9th Cir. 1986).

Northwest Indian Cemetery Protective Association v. Peterson, 565 F. Supp. 586 (N.D. Cal. 1983).

Reynolds v. U.S., 98 U.S. 145 (1878).

Roman Catholic Diocese of Brooklyn, NY v. Cuomo, 592 U.S. _____ (2020).
Sequoyah v. Tennessee Valley Authority, 620 F.2d 1159 (6th Cir. 1980).
Sherbert v. Verner, 374 U.S. 398 (1963).
Standing Rock Sioux Tribe v. Army Corps of Engineers, 985 F.3d 1032 (D.C. Cir. 2021).
Thomas v. Review Board of the Indiana Employment Security Division, 450 U.S. 707 (1981).
Torcaso v. Watkins, 367 U.S. 488 (1961).
Tsilhqot'in Nation v. British Columbia [2014] 2 SCR 256.
United States v. Adair, 723 F.2d 1394 (9th Cir. 1983), 1409.
West Virginia State Board of Education v. Barnette, 319 U.S. 624 (1943).
Wilson v. Block, 708 F.2d 735 (D.C. Cir. 1983).
Winters v. United States, 207 U.S. 564 (1908).
Wisconsin v. Yoder, 406 U.S. 205 (1972).

Legislation

Administrative Procedure Act, 5 U.S.C. § 706 (1946).
American Indian Religious Freedom Act, 42 U.S.C. § 1996 (1978).
California Wilderness Act, Public Law 98–425 (1984).
Federal Water Pollution Control Act, 33 U.S.C. §§ 1251–1387 (1948).
Hoopa-Yurok Settlement Act, Public Law 100–580 (1988).
Indian Reorganization Act, Public Law 73–383 (1934).
Ley de Derechos de la Madre Tierra ((2010) Law 071 (Bolivia)o.
Multiple-Use Sustained-Yield Act, 16 U.S.C. §§ 528–531 (1960).
National Environmental Policy Act, 42 U.S.C. §§ 4321–4347 (1969).
National Forest Management Act, U.S.C. § 1600 (1976).
Religious Freedom Restoration Act, Public Law 103–141 (1993).
Smith River National Recreation Area Act, Public Law 101–612 (1990).
Te Urewera Act (2014) No. 51 (New Zealand).
Wilderness Act, 16 U.S.C. 1131–1136 (1964).

Books and Articles

Abinanti, Abby. "A Letter to Justice O'Connor." *Indigenous Peoples' Journal of Law, Culture, and Resistance* 1 (2004): 1–22.
Alderman, Ellen, and Caroline Kennedy. *In Our Defense: The Bill of Rights in Action.* New York: HarperCollins, 1992.
Alfred, Taiaiake. "Sovereignty." In *Sovereignty Matters: Locations of Contestation and Possibility in Indigenous Struggles for Self-Determination*, ed. Joanne Barker, 33–50. Lincoln: University of Nebraska Press, 2005.
Anderson, M. Kat. *Tending the Wild: Native American Knowledge and the Management of California's Natural Resources.* Berkeley: University of California Press, 2005.
Anderson, Robert T. "Indigenous Rights to Water and Environmental Protection." *Harvard Civil Rights-Civil Liberties Law Review* 53 (2018): 337–379.

Atuahene, Bernadette. *We Want What's Ours: Learning from South Africa's Land Restitution Program.* Oxford: Oxford University Press, 2014.

Avalos, Natalie. "Indigenous Stewardship: Religious Praxis and 'Unsettling' Settler Ecologies." *Political Theology* (forthcoming, 2023).

Baldy, Cutcha Risling. "Water Is Life: The Flower Dance Ceremony." *News from Native California* 30, no. 3 (2017): 13–15.

———. *We Are Dancing for You: Native Feminisms and the Revitalization of Women's Coming-of-Age Ceremonies.* Seattle: University of Washington Press, 2018.

———. "Why We Gather: Traditional Gathering in Native Northwest California and the Future of Bio-Cultural Sovereignty." *Ecological Processes* 2 (2013): 1–10.

Barclay, Stephanie Hall, and Michalyn Steele. "Rethinking Protections for Indigenous Sacred Sites." *Harvard Law Review* 134 (2021): 1294–1359.

Barker, Joanne. "Confluence: Water as an Analytic of Indigenous Feminisms." *American Indian Culture and Research Journal* 43, no. 3 (2019): 1–40.

———. *Native Acts: Law, Recognition, and Cultural Authenticity.* Durham, NC: Duke University Press, 2011.

Barreiro, José. "Geneva, 1977: A Report on the Hemispheric Movement of Indigenous Peoples." In *A Basic Call to Consciousness,* ed. Akwesasne Notes, 55–79. Summertown, TN: Native Voices, 1978.

Barsh, Russel Lawrence. "The Illusion of Religious Freedom for Indigenous Americans." *Oregon Law Review* 65, no. 1 (1986): 363–412.

Beaman, Lori G. "Aboriginal Spirituality and the Legal Construction of Freedom of Religion." *Journal of Church and State* 44, no. 1 (Winter 2002): 135–149.

Berger, Benjamin L. *Law's Religion: Religious Difference and the Claims of Constitutionalism* (Toronto: University of Toronto Press, 2015).

Biolsi, Thomas, and Larry J. Zimmerman, eds. *Indians and Anthropologists: Vine Deloria, Jr., and the Critique of Anthropology.* Tucson: University of Arizona Press, 1997.

Birrell, Kathleen. *Indigeneity: Before and Beyond the Law.* London: Routledge, 2016.

Blackstone, William. *Commentaries on the Laws of England.* Oxford, UK: Clarendon Press, 1765–1769.

Blomley, Nicholas. "Landscapes of Property." *Law and Society Review* 32 (1998): 567–612.

Bobroff, Kenneth H. "Retelling Allotment: Indian Property Rights and the Myth of Common Ownership." *Vanderbilt Law Review* 54 (2001): 1559–1623.

Borrows, John. "The First Nations Quest for Justice in Canada," public address, Victoria, BC, April 26, 2013. YouTube Video, 35:05 (at 30:08), posted by Murdith McLean, May 4, 2021.

———. *Law's Indigenous Ethics.* Toronto: University of Toronto Press, 2019.

Bowers, Amy, and Kristen A. Carpenter. "Challenging the Narrative of Conquest: The Story of *Lyng v. Northwest Indian Cemetery Protective Association.*" In *Indian Law Stories,* ed. Carole Goldberg, Kevin K. Washburn, and Phillip P. Frickey, 489–533. St. Paul, MN: Foundation Press, 2011.

Brown, Brian Edward. *Religion, Law, and the Land: Native Americans and the Judicial Interpretation of Sacred Land*. Westport, CT: Greenwood Press, 1999.

Bruyneel, Kevin. *The Third Space of Sovereignty: The Postcolonial Politics of U.S.–Indigenous Relations*. Minneapolis: University of Minnesota Press, 2007.

Bryan, Michelle. "Valuing Sacred Tribal Waters Within Prior Appropriation." *Natural Resources Journal* 57, no. 1 (2017): 139–181.

Buckley, Thomas. *Standing Ground: Yurok Indian Spirituality, 1850–1990*. Berkeley: University of California Press, 2002.

Burkhart, Brian. *Indigenizing Philosophy Through the Land: A Trickster Methodology for Decolonizing Environmental Ethics and Indigenous Futures*. East Lansing: Michigan State University Press, 2019.

Burton, Lloyd. *American Indian Water Rights and the Limits of Law*. Lawrence: University Press of Kansas, 1991.

———. *Worship and Wilderness: Culture, Religion, and Law in Public Lands Management*. Madison: University of Wisconsin Press, 2002.

Byrd, Jodi A. *The Transit of Empire: Indigenous Critiques of Colonialism*. Minneapolis: University of Minnesota Press, 2011.

Carpenter, Kristen A. "Living the Sacred: Indigenous Peoples and Religious Freedom." *Harvard Law Review* 134 (2021): 2103–2156.

Carpenter, Kristen A., Sonia K. Katyal, and Angela R. Riley. "In Defense of Property." *Yale Law Journal* 118 (2009): 1022–1125.

Catton, Theodore. *American Indians and National Forests*. Tucson: University of Arizona Press, 2017.

Chi, Elisha. "Refusal." *Political Theology Network*, November 15, 2022, https://politicaltheology.com/refusal/.

Clifford, James. *Returns: Becoming Indigenous in the Twenty-First Century*. Cambridge, MA: Harvard University Press, 2013.

Cocks, Joan. *On Sovereignty and Other Political Delusions*. New York: Bloomsbury, 2014.

Cohen, Netta. "Between Ecology and Ideology: Climate Change and Forestation Sciences in Mandatory Palestine/Israel." *Political Theology Network*, May 28, 2020, https://politicaltheology.com/between-ecology-and-ideology-climate-change-and-forestation-sciences-in-mandatory-palestine-israel/.

Constable, Marianne, Leti Volpp, and Bryan Wagner, eds. *Looking for Law in All the Wrong Places: Justice Beyond and Between*. New York: Fordham University Press, 2019.

Coulthard, Glen Sean. *Red Skin, White Masks: Rejecting the Colonial Politics of Recognition*. Minneapolis: University of Minnesota Press, 2014.

Cramer, Renée Ann. *Cash, Color, and Colonialism: The Politics of Tribal Acknowledgement*. Norman: University of Oklahoma Press, 2005.

Cronon, William. "The Trouble with Wilderness; Or, Getting Back to the Wrong Nature." In *Uncommon Ground: Toward Reinventing Nature*, ed. William Cronon, 69–90. New York: W. W. Norton, 1995.

DeGirolami, Marc O. *The Tragedy of Religious Freedom*. Cambridge, MA: Harvard University Press, 2013.

Deloria, Jr., Vine. *Custer Died for Your Sins: An Indian Manifesto*. New York: Macmillan, 1969.

———. *God Is Red: A Native View of Religion*. Golden, CO: Fulcrum Publishing, 1973.

———. "Knowing and Understanding." In *Power and Place: Indian Education in America*, Vine Deloria, Jr., and Daniel Wildcat, 41–46. Golden, CO: Fulcrum Publishing, 2001.

———. "Sacred Lands and Religious Freedom." In *For This Land: Writings on Religion in America*, 203–213. London: Routledge, 1999.

———. "Trouble in High Places: Erosion of American Indian Rights to Religious Freedom in the United States." In *The State of Native America: Genocide, Colonization, and Resistance*, ed. M. Annette Jaimes, 267–290. Boston: South End Press, 1992.

Deloria, Philip J. *Playing Indian*. New Haven, CT: Yale University Press, 1999.

Dudgeon, Patricia, and Abigail Bray. "Indigenous Relationality: Women, Kinship and the Law." *Genealogy* 3, no. 2 (2019): 23–34.

Durkheim, Émile. *The Elementary Forms of Religious Life*. Trans. Karen E. Fields. New York: Free Press, 1995.

Dussias, Allison M. "Ghost Dance and Holy Ghost: The Echoes of Nineteenth-Century Christianization Policy in Twentieth-Century Native American Free Exercise Cases." *Stanford Law Review* 49, no. 4 (1997): 773–852.

Dworkin, Ronald. "How Law Is Like Literature." In *A Matter of Principle*, 146–166. Cambridge, MA: Harvard University Press, 1985.

———. *Law's Empire*. Cambridge, MA: Harvard University Press, 1986.

Echo-Hawk, Walter R. *In the Courts of the Conqueror: The 10 Worst Indian Law Cases Ever Decided*. Golden, CO: Fulcrum Publishing, 2010.

Elshtain, Jean Bethke. *Sovereignty: God, State, and Self*. New York: Basic Books, 2012.

Estes, Nick. "My Relatives Went to a Catholic School for Native Children: It Was a Place of Horror." *Guardian*, June 30, 2021. https://amp.theguardian.com/commentisfree/2021/jun/30/my-relatives-went-to-a-catholic-school-for-native-children-it-was-a-place-of-horrors.

———. *Our History Is the Future: Standing Rock versus the Dakota Access Pipeline, and the Long Tradition of Indigenous Resistance*. New York: Verso, 2019.

Evans, Bette Novit. *Interpreting the Free Exercise of Religion: The Constitution and American Pluralism*. Chapel Hill: University of North Carolina Press, 1997.

Falk, Donald. "Note: *Lyng v. Northwest Indian Cemetery Protective Association*: Bulldozing First Amendment Protection of Indian Sacred Lands." *Ecology Law Quarterly* 16, no. 2 (March 1989): 515–570.

Flaccus, Gillian. "Plan to Remove Four Dams on Lower Klamath River Clears Regulatory Hurdle." *Register Guard*, June 17, 2021. https://www.registerguard.com/story/news/2021/06/17/klamath-river-dams-removal-clear-regulatory-hurdle/7740765002/.

Ford, Lisa. *Settler Sovereignty: Jurisdiction and Indigenous People in America and Australia, 1788–1836*. Cambridge, MA: Harvard University Press, 2011.

Garroutte, Eva Marie. *Real Indians: Identity and the Survival of Native America*. Berkeley: University of California Press, 2003.

Geertz, Clifford. "Religion as a Cultural System." In *The Interpretation of Cultures: Selected Essays*, 87–125. New York: Basic Books, 1993.

Gilio-Whitaker, Dina. *As Long as Grass Grows: The Indigenous Fight for Environmental Justice, from Colonization to Standing Rock*. Boston: Beacon Press, 2019.

Goeman, Mishuana. *Mark My Words: Native Women Mapping Our Nations*. Minneapolis: University of Minnesota Press, 2013.

Gooding, Susan Staiger. "At the Boundaries of Religious Identity: Native American Religions and American Legal Culture." *Numen* 43, no. 2 (1996): 157–183.

Gordon, Sarah Barringer. *The Mormon Question: Polygamy and Constitutional Conflict in Nineteenth-Century America*. Chapel Hill: University of North Carolina Press, 2002.

———. *The Spirit of the Law: Religious Voices and the Constitution in Modern America*. Cambridge, MA: Harvard University Press, 2010.

Gorney, Edna. "(Un)Natural Selection: The Drainage of the Hula Wetlands, an Ecofeminist Reading." *International Feminist Journal of Politics* 9, no. 4 (2007): 465–474.

Graber, Jennifer. *The Gods of Indian Country: Religion and the Struggle for the American West*. New York: Oxford University Press, 2018.

Graber, Linda H. *Wilderness as Sacred Space*. Washington, DC: Association of American Geographers, 1974.

Greenavalt, Kent. "Religion as a Concept in Constitutional Law." *California Law Review* 72, no. 5 (September 1984): 753–816.

Greer, Allan. *Property and Dispossession: Natives, Empires and Land in Early Modern North America*. Cambridge, UK: Cambridge University Press, 2018.

Guha, Ramachandra. "Radical American Environmentalism and Wilderness Preservation: A Third World Critique." *Environmental Ethics* 11, no. 1 (Spring 1989): 71–83.

Hamilton, Jennifer. *Indigeneity in the Courtroom: Law, Culture, and the Production of Difference in North American Courts*. London: Routledge, 2009.

Harjo, Suzan Shown. "American Indian Religious Freedom Act After 25 Years." *Wicazo Sa Review* 19, no. 2 (2004): 129–136.

Harris, Cheryl I. "Whiteness as Property." *Harvard Law Review* 106 (1993): 1710–1791.

Hernández-Ávila, Inés. "Relocations Upon Relocations: Home, Language and Native American Women's Writing." In *Reading Native American Women: Critical Creative Representation*, ed. Inés Hernández-Avila, 171–188. Lanham, MD: Altamira Press, 2005.

Hobart, Hi'ilei Julia. "At Home on the Mauna: Ecological Violence and Fantasies of Terra Nullius on Maunakea's Summit." *Native American and Indigenous Studies* 6 (2019): 30–50.

Howe, Nicolas. *Landscapes of the Secular: Law, Religion, and American Sacred Space.* Chicago: University of Chicago Press, 2016.

Huntsinger, Lynn, and Sarah McCaffrey. "A Forest for the Trees: Forest Management and the Yurok Environment, 1850 to 1994." *American Indian Culture and Research Journal* 19, no. 4 (1995): 155–192.

Hurd, Elizabeth Shakman. *Beyond Religious Freedom: The New Global Politics of Religion.* Princeton, NJ: Princeton University Press, 2015.

Innes, Robert Alexander. *Elder Brother and the Law of the People: Contemporary Kinship and Cowessess First Nation.* Winnipeg: University of Manitoba Press, 2013.

Irwin, Lee. *Coming Down from Above: Prophecy, Resistance, and Renewal in Native American Religions.* Norman: University of Oklahoma Press, 2008.

———. "Freedom, Law, and Prophecy: A Brief History of Native American Religious Resistance." *American Indian Quarterly* 21, no. 1 (1997): 35–55.

Jackson, John Brinckerhoff. *A Sense of Place, A Sense of Time.* New Haven, CT: Yale University Press, 1996.

Jefferson Exchange Team. "Yuroks Grant Rights to the Klamath River," May 29, 2019, https://www.ijpr.org/show/the-jefferson-exchange/2019-05-29/yuroks-grant-rights-to-the-klamath-river#stream/0.

Jocks, Chris. "Restoring Congruity: Indigenous Lives and Religious Freedom in the United States and Canada." In *Traditional, National, and International Law and Indigenous Communities,* ed. Marianne O. Nielsen and Karen Jarratt-Snider, 81–103. Tucson: University of Arizona Press, 2020.

Johnson, Greg. "Ritual, Advocacy, and Authority: The Challenge of Being an Irreverent Witness." In *Irreverence and the Sacred: Critical Studies in the History of Religions,* ed. Hugh B. Urban and Greg Johnson, 131–155. New York: Oxford University Press, 2017.

Johnson, Miranda. "The River Is Not a Person: Indigeneity and the Sacred in Aotearoa New Zealand." *Immanent Frame,* June 14, 2017. https://tif.ssrc.org/2017/06/14/the-river-is-not-a-person/.

Justice, Daniel Heath. "'Go Away Water!': Kinship Criticism and the Decolonization Imperative." In *Reasoning Together: The Native Critics Collection,* ed. Craig S. Womack, Daniel Heath Justice, and Christopher B. Teuton, 147–168. Norman: University of Oklahoma Press, 2008.

Kahn, Paul. *Putting Liberalism in Its Place.* Princeton, NJ: Princeton University Press, 2005.

Kelley, Dennis. *Tradition, Performance, and Religion in Native America.* London: Routledge, 2014.

King, Thomas. *The Truth About Stories: A Native Narrative.* Minneapolis: University of Minnesota Press, 2003.

Klassen, Pamela E. "Spiritual Jurisdictions: Treaty People and the Queen of Canada." In *Ekklesia: Three Inquiries in Church and State,* Paul Christopher Johnson, Pamela

E. Klassen, and Winnifred Fallers Sullivan, 107–173. Chicago: University of Chicago Press, 2018.

Knobloch, Frieda. *The Culture of Wilderness: Agriculture as Colonization in the American West.* Chapel Hill: University of North Carolina Press, 1996.

Kothari, Ashish, and Shrishtee Bajpai. "Rivers and Human Rights: We are the River, the River is Us?" *Vikalp Sangam,* November 3, 2017. https://vikalpsangam.org/article/rivers-and-human-rights-we-are-the-river-the-river-is-us/.

Kroeber, A. L. *Handbook of the Indians of California.* Berkeley: California Book Company, 1953.

———. *Yurok Myths.* Berkeley: University of California Press, 1976.

Kroeber, Karl, and Clifton Kroeber, eds. *Ishi in Three Centuries.* Lincoln: University of Nebraska Press, 2003.

LaDuke, Winona. *Recovering the Sacred: The Power of Naming and Claiming.* Chicago: Haymarket Books, 2015.

Lang, Julian, "Being of the Same Mind." In *Ka'm-t'em: A Journey toward Healing,* ed. Kishan Lara-Cooper and Walter J. Lara, Sr., 252–256. Temecula, CA: Great Oak Press, 2019.

Lara, Sr., Walt, and Kishan Lara-Cooper. "Across the Lagoon: The Inspiration behind the Northwest Indian Cemetery Protection Association (NICPA)." In *Ka'm-t'em: A Journey Toward Healing,* ed. Kishan Lara-Cooper and Walter J. Lara, Sr., 151–160. Temecula, CA: Great Oak Press, 2019.

———. "Fish Wars on the Klamath River." In *Ka'm-t'em: A Journey Toward Healing,* ed. Kishan Lara-Cooper and Walter J. Lara Sr., 213–227. Temecula, CA: Great Oak Press, 2019.

Locke, John. *Second Treatise of Government,* ed. C. B. Macpherson. Indianapolis, IN: Hackett Publishing, 1980.

———. *A Letter Concerning Toleration and Other Writings.* Indianapolis, IN: Liberty Fund, 2010.

Manning, Beth Rose Middleton, and Kaitlin Reed. "Returning the Yurok Forest to the Yurok Tribe: California's First Tribal Carbon Credit Project." *Stanford Environmental Law Journal* 39, no. 1 (2019): 71–124.

McIvor, Méadhbh. *Representing God: Christian Legal Activism in Contemporary England.* Princeton, NJ: Princeton University Press, 2020.

McNally, Michael D. *Defend the Sacred: Native American Religious Freedom Beyond the First Amendment.* Princeton, NJ: Princeton University Press, 2020.

———. "From Substantial Burden on Religion to Diminished Spiritual Fulfillment: The San Francisco Peaks Case and the Misunderstanding of Native American Religion." *Journal of Law and Religion* 30 (2015): 36–64.

———. "Native American Religious Freedom as a Collective Right." *Brigham Young University Law Review* 2019, no. 1 (2019): 205–292.

Michaelsen, Robert S. "Dirt in the Court Room: Indian Land Claims and American Property Rights." In *American Sacred Space,* ed. David Chidester and Edward T. Linenthal, 43–96. Bloomington: Indiana University Press, 1995.

Miller, Robert J. "Correcting Supreme Court 'Errors': American Indian Response to *Lyng v. Northwest Indian Cemetery Protective Association.*" *Environmental Law* 20, no. 4 (1990): 1037–1062.

Million, Dian. "Indigenous Relations of Well-Being vs. Humanitarian Health Economies." In *Routledge Handbook of Critical Indigenous Studies*, ed. Brendan Hokowhitu, Aileen Moreton-Robinson, Linda Tuhiwai-Smith, Chris Andersen, and Steve Larkin, 392–404. London: Routledge, 2021.

Mitchell, Kerry. *Spirituality and the State: Managing Nature and Experience in America's National Parks.* New York: New York University Press, 2016.

Moreton-Robinson, Aileen. *The White Possessive: Property, Power, and Indigenous Sovereignty.* Minneapolis: University of Minnesota Press, 2015.

———. "Relationality: A Key Presupposition of an Indigenous Social Research Paradigm." In *Sources and Methods in Indigenous Studies*, ed. Chris Andersen and Jean M. O'Brien, 69–77. London and New York: Routledge, 2017.

Most, Stephen. *Rivers of Renewal: Myth and History in the Klamath Basin.* Seattle: University of Washington Press, 2016.

Muir, John. *Letters from Alaska*, ed. Robert Engberg and Bruce Merrell. Madison: University of Wisconsin Press, 1993.

Nagle, John Copeland. "The Spiritual Values of Wilderness." *Environmental Law* 35 (2005): 955–1003.

Napoleon, Val, and Emily Snyder. "Housing on Reserve: Developing a Critical Indigenous Feminist Property Theory." In *Creating Indigenous Property: Power, Rights, and Relationships*, ed. Angela Cameron, Sari Graben, and Val Napoleon, 41–93. Toronto: University of Toronto Press, 2020.

Nash, Roderick Frazier. *Wilderness in the American Mind.* New Haven, CT: Yale University Press, 2001.

Native American Rights Fund. "Klamath Tribes' Water Rights." *Native American Rights Fund*, February 24, 2021. https://www.narf.org/cases/klamath-tribes-water-rights/.

Neustadtl, Sara. *Moving Mountains: Coping with Change in Mountain Communities.* Boston: Appalachian Mountain Club, 1987.

Newcomb, Steven T. *Pagans in the Promised Land: Decoding the Doctrine of Christian Discovery.* Golden, CO: Fulcrum Publishing, 2008.

Nichols, Robert. *Theft Is Property! Dispossession and Critical Theory.* Durham, NC: Duke University Press, 2020.

Niezen, Ronald. *Spirit Wars: Native North American Religions in the Age of Nation Building.* Berkeley: University of California Press, 2000.

Norgaard, Kari Marie. *Salmon and Acorns Feed Our People: Colonialism, Nature, and Social Action.* New Brunswick, NJ: Rutgers University Press, 2020.

Norton, Jack. *Genocide in Northwestern California: When Our Worlds Cried.* San Francisco: Indian Historian Press, 1979.

———. "The Past Is Our Future: Thoughts on Identity, Tradition and Change." In

Ka'm-t'em: A Journey Toward Healing, ed. Kishan Lara-Cooper and Walter J. Lara, Sr., 115–133. Temecula, CA: Great Oak Press, 2019.

Nussbaum, Martha. *Liberty of Conscience: In Defense of America's Traditions of Religious Equality*. New York: Basic Books, 2008.

O'Brien, Suzanne Crawford, and Inés Talamantez. *Religion and Culture in Native America*. Lanham, MD: Rowman and Littlefield, 2020.

O'Donnell, Erin L. "At the Intersection of the Sacred and the Legal: Rights for Nature in Uttarakhand, India." *Journal of Environmental Law* 30, no. 1 (2018): 135–144.

Orcutt, Michael W. "Tribal Water Rights: Klamath-Trinity River." In *Ka'm-t'em: A Journey Toward Healing*, ed. Kishan Lara-Cooper and Walter J. Lara, Sr., 201–212. Temecula, CA: Great Oak Press, 2019.

Page, Ellen Adair. "Note: The Scope of the Free Exercise Clause: *Lyng v. Northwest Indian Cemetery Protective Association*." *North Carolina Law Review* 68, no. 2 (1990): 410–422.

Pappas, George D. *The Literary and Legal Genealogy of Native American Dispossession: The Marshall Trilogy Cases*. London: Routledge, 2017.

Peñalver, Eduardo. "Note: The Concept of Religion." *Yale Law Journal* 107, no. 3 (December 1997): 791–822.

Peters, Chris, and Chisa Oros. "Protecting Our Sacred Sites: *Lyng v. Northwest Indian Cemetery Protective Association*." In *Ka'm-t'em: A Journey Toward Healing*, ed. Kishan Lara-Cooper and Walter J. Lara, Sr., 161–186. Temecula, CA: Great Oak Press, 2019.

———. "Voices from the Sacred: An Indigenous Worldview and Epistemology of Northwestern California." In *Ka'm-t'em: A Journey toward Healing*, ed. Kishan Lara-Cooper and Walter J. Lara, Sr., 3–14. Temecula, CA: Great Oak Press, 2019.

Pfeffer, Michael. "CILS History: G-O Road Case." *CILS News* 10, Fall 2002.

Piatote, Beth H. *Domestic Subjects: Gender, Citizenship, and Law in Native American Literature*. New Haven, CT: Yale University Press, 2013.

Pilling, Arnold. "Yurok Aristocracy and 'Great Houses.'" *American Indian Quarterly* 13, no. 4 (1989): 421–436.

Platt, Tony. *Grave Matters: Excavating California's Buried Past*. Berkeley, CA: Heyday, 2021.

Pratt, Richard H. "The Advantages of Mingling Indians with Whites." In *Americanizing the American Indians: Writings by the "Friends of the Indian" 1880–1900*, ed. Francis Paul Prucha, 260–271. Cambridge, MA: Harvard University Press, 1973.

Pritchard, J. Brett. "Conduct and Belief in the Free Exercise Clause: Developments and Deviations in *Lyng v. Northwest Indian Cemetery Protective Association*." *Cornell Law Review* 76, no. 1 (November 1990): 268–296.

Ray, S. Alan. "Comment: *Lyng v. Northwest Indian Cemetery Protective Association*: Government Property Rights and the Free Exercise Clause." *Hastings Constitutional Law Quarterly* 16, no. 3 (Spring 1989): 483–511.

Reed, Kaitlin. "We Are Salmon People: Constructing Yurok Sovereignty in the Klamath Basin." Senior thesis, Vassar College, 2014.

Richland, Justin B. *Arguing with Tradition: The Language of Law in Hopi Tribal Court.* Chicago: University of Chicago Press, 2008.

———. "Dignity as (Self-)Determination: Hopi Sovereignty in the Face of U.S. Dispossessions." *Law and Social Inquiry* 41, no. 4 (2016): 917–938.

Rifkin, Mark. "Around 1978: Family, Culture, and Race in the Federal Production of Indianness." In *Critically Sovereign: Indigenous Gender, Sexuality, and Feminist Studies*, ed. Joanne Barker, 169–206. Durham, NC: Duke University Press, 2017.

———. "Indigenizing Agamben: Rethinking Sovereignty in Light of the 'Peculiar' Status of Native Peoples." *Cultural Critique* 73 (2009): 88–124.

———. *When Did Indians Become Straight? Kinship, the History of Sexuality, and Native Sovereignty.* New York: Oxford University Press, 2011.

Rose, Carol M. "Property and Expropriation: Themes and Variations in American Law." *Utah Law Review* 2000, no. 1 (2000): 1–38.

———. "Property as Storytelling: Perspectives from Game Theory, Narrative Theory, Feminist Theory." *Yale Journal of Law and the Humanities* 2 (1990): 37–57.

Royster, Judith. "A Primer on Indian Water Rights." *Tulsa Law Review* 30 (1994): 61–104.

Salmón, Enrique. "Kincentric Ecology: Indigenous Perceptions of the Human-Nature Relationship," *Ecological Applications* 10, no. 5 (2000): 1327–1332.

Sands, Kathleen. "Territory, Wilderness, Property, and Reservation: Land and Religion in Native American Supreme Court Cases." *American Indian Law Review* 36, no. 2 (2012): 253–320.

Sepulveda, Charles. "Our Sacred Waters: Theorizing *Kuuyam* as a Decolonial Possibility." *Decolonization: Indigeneity, Education & Society* 7 (2018): 40–58.

Sexton, John. "Note: Toward a Constitutional Definition of Religion." *Harvard Law Review* 91, no. 5 (March 1978): 1056–1089.

Shachar, Ayelet. *Multicultural Jurisdictions: Cultural Differences and Women's Rights.* Cambridge, UK: Cambridge University Press, 2001.

Shaw, Karena. *Indigeneity and Political Theory: Sovereignty and the Limits of the Political.* London: Routledge, 2008.

Shorter, David Delgado. "Spirituality." In *The Oxford Handbook of American Indian History*, ed. Frederick E. Hoxie, 433–452. New York: Oxford University Press, 2016.

Simpson, Audra. *Mohawk Interruptus: Political Life across the Borders of Settler States.* Durham, NC: Duke University Press, 2014.

Singer, Joseph W. "The Continuing Conquest: American Indian Nations, Property Law, and Gunsmoke." *Reconstruction* 1 (1991): 97–103.

Smith, Anna V. "At Oak Flat, Courts and Politicians Fail Tribes." *High Country News*, July 26, 2022. https://www.hcn.org/articles/indigenous-affairs-justice-at-oak-flat-courts-and-politicians-fail-tribes.

Smith, Linda Tuhiwai. *Decolonizing Methodologies: Research and Indigenous Peoples.* New York: Zed Books, 1999.

Soja, Edward W. *Postmodern Geographies: The Reassertion of Space in Critical Social Theory.* New York: Verso, 1990.

Spence, Mark David. *Dispossessing the Wilderness: Indian Removal and the Making of the National Parks*. New York: Oxford University Press, 2000.

Stark, Heidi Kiiwetinepinesiik. "Stories as Law: A Method to Live By." In *Sources and Methods in Indigenous Studies*, ed. Chris Andersen and Jean M. O'Brien, 249–256. London: Routledge, 2017.

Stone, Christopher. *Should Trees Have Standing? Law, Morality, and the Environment*. New York: Oxford University Press, 2010.

Sturm, Circe Dawn. *Blood Politics: Race, Culture and Identity in the Cherokee Nation of Oklahoma*. Berkeley: University of California Press, 2002.

Suagee, Dean B., and Peter Bungart. "Taking Care of Native American Cultural Landscapes." *National Resources and Environment* 27 (2013): 1–5.

Sullivan, Winnifred Fallers. *The Impossibility of Religious Freedom*. Princeton, NJ: Princeton University Press, 2005.

———. "Afterword." In *Religion, Law, USA*, ed. Isaac Weiner and Joshua Dubler, 283–288. New York: New York University Press, 2019.

Suzack, Cheryl. *Indigenous Women Writers and the Cultural Study of Law*. Toronto: University of Toronto Press, 2017.

TallBear, Kim. *Native American DNA: Tribal Belonging and the False Promise of Genetic Science*. Minneapolis: University of Minnesota Press, 2013.

———. "Caretaking Relations, Not American Dreaming." *Kalfou* 6, no. 1 (Spring 2019): 24–41.

Theodoratus Cultural Research. *Cultural Resources of the Chimney Rock Section, Gasquet–Orleans Road, Six Rivers National Forest*. Fair Oaks, CA, 1979.

Thom, Charlie. "Oral History." In *Reinhabiting a Separate Country*, ed. Peter Berg, 148–151. San Francisco: Planet Drum Foundation, 1978.

Thompson, Lucy. *To the American Indian: Reminiscences of a Yurok Woman*. Berkeley: Heyday Books, 1991.

Thoreau, Henry David. "Walking." *Atlantic Monthly* 9 (1862): 657–674.

Tillich, Paul. *Dynamics of Faith*. New York: Harper, 1958.

Tinker, George E. *Spirit and Resistance: Political Theology and American Indian Liberation*. Minneapolis, MN: Fortress Press, 2004.

Tribe, Lawrence. "Ways Not to Think About Plastic Trees: New Foundations for Environmental Law." *Yale Law Journal* 83 (1974): 1315–1346.

Tuck, Eve, and K. Wayne Yang. "Decolonization Is Not a Metaphor." *Decolonization: Indigeneity, Education & Society* 1 (2012): 1–40.

Truer, David. "Return the National Parks to the Tribes." *Atlantic*, April 12, 2021, https://www.theatlantic.com/magazine/archive/2021/05/return-the-national-parks-to-the-tribes/618395/.

Truscott, Richard. "Property Rights Are the Key to Indian Prosperity." *Taxpayer.com*, July 29, 2002.

Vogel, Howard J. "The Clash of Stories at Chimney Rock: A Narrative Approach to

Cultural Conflict Over Native American Sacred Sites on Public Land." *Santa Clara Law Review* 41 (2001): 757–806.

Waldron, Jeremy. "Why Is Indigeneity Important?" In *Reparations: Interdisciplinary Inquiries*, ed. Jon Miller and Rahul Kumar, 23–42. New York: Oxford University Press, 2007.

Weaver, Jace. "Losing My Religion: Native American Religious Traditions and American Religious Freedom." In *Native American Religious Identity*, ed. Jace Weaver, 217–229. New York: Orbis Books, 1998.

Wenger, Tisa. "Sovereignty." In *Religion, Law, USA*, ed. Isaac Weiner and Joshua Dubler, 108–128. New York: New York University Press, 2019.

———. *We Have a Religion: The 1920s Pueblo Indian Dance Controversy and American Religious Freedom*. Chapel Hill: University of North Carolina Press, 2009.

Whyte, Kyle Powys. "Time as Kinship." In *Cambridge Companion to Environmental Humanities*, ed. Jeffrey Jerome Cohen and Stephanie Foote, 39–55. Cambridge, UK: Cambridge University Press, 2021.

Wildcat, Daniel. "Indigenizing Politics and Ethics." In Vine Deloria, Jr., and Daniel Wildcat, *Power and Place: Indian Education in America*, 87–100. Golden, CO: Fulcrum Publishing, 2001.

Williams, Robert A. *Like a Loaded Weapon: The Rehnquist Court, Indian Rights, and the Legal History of Racism in America*. Minneapolis: University of Minnesota Press, 2005.

Wilson, Nicole J., and Jody Inkster. "Respecting Water: Indigenous Water Governance, Ontologies, and the Politics of Kinship on the Ground." *Environment and Planning E: Nature and Space* 1 (2018): 516–538.

Wolfe, Patrick. "Settler Colonialism and the Elimination of the Native." *Journal of Genocide Research* 8, no. 4 (2006): 387–409.

———. *Traces of History: Elementary Structures of Race*. New York: Verso, 2016.

Yablon, Marcia. "Property Rights and Sacred Sites: Federal Regulatory Responses to American Indian Religious Claims on Public Lands." *Yale Law Journal* 113, no. 7 (2004): 1623–1662.

Yazzie, Melannie K., and Cutcha Risling Baldy. "Introduction: Indigenous Peoples and the Politics of Water." *Decolonization: Indigeneity, Education & Society* 7, no. 1 (2018): 1–18.

Yurok Tribal Council. "Resolution 19–40: Resolution Establishing the Rights of the Klamath River," May 9, 2019. http://files.harmonywithnatureun.org/uploads/upload833.pdf.

INDEX